In Shackleton's Footsteps

In Shackleton's Footsteps

A Return to the Heart of the Antarctic

Henry Worsley

2 4 6 8 10 9 7 5 3

Published in 2011 by Virgin Books, an imprint of Ebury Publishing
A Random House Group Company

The Random House Group Limited Reg. No. 954009

Addresses for companies within the Random House Group can be found at:
www.randomhouse.co.uk

A CIP catalogue record for this book
is available from the British Library

The Random House Group Limited supports The Forest Stewardship Council
[FSC], the leading international forest certification organisation. All our titles
that are printed on Greenpeace-approved FSC-certified paper carry the FSC
logo. Our paper procurement policy can be found at
www.rbooks.co.uk/environment

Mixed Sources
Product group from well-managed
forests and other controlled sources
www.fsc.org Cert no. TT-COC-2139
© 1996 Forest Stewardship Council

Printed in the UK by CPI Mackays, Chatham, ME5 8TD

ISBN 9781905264933

To buy books by your favourite authors and register for offers visit
www.rbooks.co.uk

Illustration, second page: A watercolour of Ernest Shackleton in front of Nimrod,
by F. Haenen.

Endpapers: Author's map of the expedition, plotting daily progress.

To Joanna, Max and Alicia

Contents

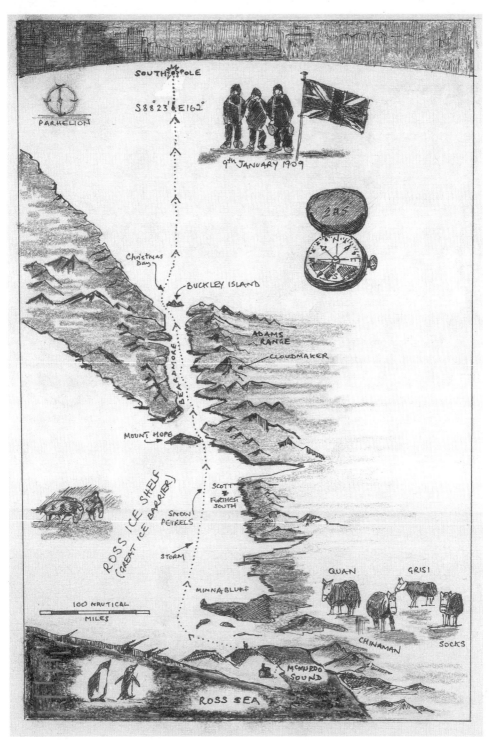

Author's sketch of the expedition route.

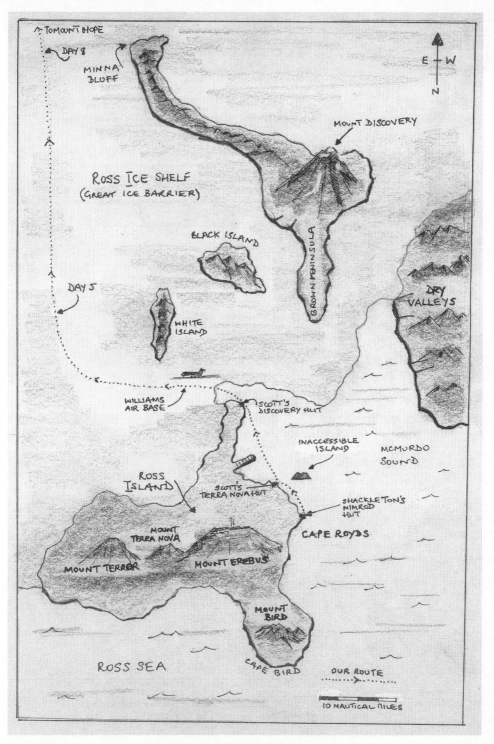

Ross Island and McMurdo Sound.

Cast List

Nimrod Expedition: 29 October 1908–3 March 1909

Ernest Shackleton, 34
Former Merchant Marine officer, turned Antarctic explorer, born in Kilkea, County Kildare, Ireland, leader of the *Nimrod* expedition.

Frank Wild, 35
Former Royal Navy officer from Skelton, North Yorkshire, and the only man to take part in all of Shackleton's Antarctic expeditions.

Eric Marshall, 29
Ship's surgeon and cartographer, responsible for mapping detail on the inland expedition. Like Shackleton, suffered badly from dysentery on the return journey, their weakened state slowing their return to the coast before the agreed date by which Nimrod was due to depart.

Jameson Boyd Adams, 27
Youngest of the four men, from Rippingale, Lincolnshire, serving as a lieutenant in the Royal Naval Reserve, before joining the *Nimrod* expedition as meteorologist. He turned 28 just before the team's 'Furthest South' achievement.

*

Matrix Shackleton Centenary Expedition:
14 November 2008–19 January 2009

Ice team:

Henry Worsley, 48
Army officer from Hereford, and a descendant of Shackleton's *Endurance* skipper, Frank Worsley.

Will Gow, 35
A City worker from Ashford, Kent, Shackleton's great-nephew by marriage and the one who first thought of the centenary expedition.

Henry Adams, 34
A shipping lawyer from Snape, near Woodbridge, Suffolk, and a great-grandson of Jameson Boyd Adams, Shackleton's number two on the unsuccessful expedition.

*

97-Mile Team (Team members who flew to the 97-mile point on 9 January 2009 to complete the final stage of the journey):

Dave Cornell, 38
From Andover, Hampshire, a City fund manager and another great-grandson of Jameson Boyd Adams.

Tim Fright, 25
Policy analyst from Billingshurst, West Sussex, and a great-great-nephew of Frank Wild.

Andrew Ledger, 23
A policy researcher from Dronfield, near Sheffield, who won his place on the expedition as part of a national competition.

Ronnie Gray, 38
Ex-Army officer who generously joined the 97-Mile team late in the centenary expedition's planning.

Matty McNair, 58
The leading female polar guide of her generation.

Author's Note

Distance, temperature and weight on the Nimrod expedition were recorded by Ernest Shackleton in *The Heart of the Antarctic* in nautical miles, degrees 'of frost' in Fahrenheit and pounds of weight. During the modern expedition, we measured the distance travelled in nautical miles, our sledge weight in kilograms and the temperature in degrees Celsius. In Appendix II, which records the daily details of our journey, also illustrates the difference in mean air temperature and the effect of the wind which creates a 'wind chill' factor. The lowest temperature we encountered was -52°C of wind chill. Only two measurements in statute miles are mentioned in this book: Shackleton's journey to the point he stopped and turned around was in the region of 820 statute miles and our journey covered 920 statute miles (799 nautical miles).

The cigarette cards at the end of each chapter are from a collection issued to mark the success of the *Nimrod* expedition.

Prologue

'Men go out into the void spaces of the world for various reasons. Some are actuated simply by a love of adventure, some have the keen thirst for scientific knowledge, and others are drawn away from the trodden paths by the "lure of little voices", the mysterious fascination of the unknown.'

EHS, The Heart of the Antarctic, 1909

November 2003

I turned inland from the water's edge and walked the slight slope over the tussock grass towards the white picket fence. I opened the gate and headed to the back of the enclosure, where I stopped. Turning around I sat down on my rucksack and stared out across the bay, the water rippling in the weakening light. The feeling of excitement on doing something that had seemed beyond all possibility, yet was now actually about to happen, wrapped itself around me. I unpacked my sleeping bag, wriggled inside it and, settling down into the gathering warmth, turned to face the upright block of granite at arm's length from my face. The metal lettering

1

hammered into the rough face of the stone was just visible. Reaching out to touch it I considered for a moment just how significant a moment in my life this was; all my life I'd hoped one day to be here. I was about to spend the night in the whaler's cemetery in Grytviken on the island of South Georgia beside the grave of my hero since childhood – Sir Ernest Shackleton.

My interest in the daring exploits of Shackleton and Captain Scott began when as a boy I came across accounts of their expeditions in the travel and exploration section of the school library. Ignoring reminders from the librarian that my books were long overdue, I saw the *Discovery*, *Nimrod*, *Terra Nova* and *Endurance* expeditions come vividly alive through the brilliant camera work of the expedition photographers, Frank Hurley and Herbert Ponting. There was also delicate and skilful artwork produced by Edward Wilson and George Marston, which added colour to the panoramas and wildlife that the monochrome photographs were unable to capture. But it was the story of Shackleton's *Endurance* expedition in 1914, captured by Hurley, that first transported me back to a time that I longed to have been part of – the Edwardian heroic age of polar exploration.

Hurley's images of the *Endurance* trapped and crushed in the ice of the Weddell Sea, the campsites set up on the treacherous floating ice when the expedition's crew had to abandon the ship to her fate, the entire party of twenty-eight men escaping in the ship's lifeboats to Elephant Island where they survived on a diet of seabirds, seals and seaweed and then the unimaginable rescue after Shackleton and five others had sailed the open boat *James Caird*, more than eight hundred nautical miles across the Southern Ocean to South Georgia to seek help. This extraordinary story of courage, fortitude and outstanding leadership depicted an age where hope and optimism would unquestionably prevail over adversity and disaster. There can be no better example of that optimism and willingness for duty and sacrifice than the following text from a crew member of the

Endurance writing to his father in August 1914: 'Dear old Dad. Just a line before we sail. We've had a very good time so far and I think we shall do well. I hope to be home again within 19 months and go straight to the Front. What a glorious age we live in.'

In the archives of polar exploration, Shackleton's 1914–1916 *Endurance* expedition is probably the most well known because despite disaster and adversity, extraordinary triumph prevailed. The South Pole had been conquered by the Norwegian Roald Amundsen in December 1911, with Britain's Captain Robert Falcon Scott arriving three weeks later, only to perish tragically with the other members of his *Terra Nova* team on the return journey. With the South Pole claimed, only one further crown remained – a crossing of the entire Antarctic Continent. This was the prize which Shackleton sought for Britain on his 1914 *Endurance* expedition. His plan was to sail from South Georgia into the Weddell Sea, making a landing on the shores of the Antarctic. From there he would lead a sledging party more than seven hundred miles to the South Pole and then continue onwards to the other side of the continent, to the coast of the Ross Sea. A second group, having set sail from New Zealand, would lay food depots over the second half of the journey to supply the transcontinental team once they had reached the Pole.

But disaster struck in the very early stages when the *Endurance* became trapped in the unrelenting ice of the Weddell Sea. Once the ship finally succumbed to the intense pressure of the thickening sea ice and sank, the expedition became a race for survival. Under Shackleton's leadership, the crew dragged the three lifeboats across the sea ice then rowed to the desolate, rocky outcrop which is Elephant Island. The subsequent journey of the *James Caird* to South Georgia rightly has its place in maritime history as the greatest of its kind ever attempted. It took four months before Shackleton was able to return with a rescue ship to Elephant Island but he achieved it and eventually all of his comrades returned to England – not a man had been lost.

3

I became mesmerised by the extraordinary levels of hardship these men were prepared to endure in order to achieve those early polar explorations. The relentless struggle of man having to operate at the utmost limit of his capability against the deadly forces of nature appealed to me. The diaries that the Edwardian explorers so assiduously wrote, even when death stalked them to the very last page, provided the added detail of those hopeful, but also dreadful, journeys.

By the time I joined the British Army in 1980, Shackleton had become more than a hero to me; I looked upon him as a mentor. I was going into the business of leading men and as a nineteen-year-old, new to his trade, I believed that there was no better example to follow than his. Leading, particularly through times of setback and crisis, requires someone who can make his men do things that often go against their natural judgement. Therefore, in order for the team to follow, they must trust their leader. There is no better way to build up that trust than by demonstrating to them that their welfare, and their lives, matter most of all. With this guiding principle uppermost in his mind, it is not surprising that no one died under Shackleton's command.

Shackleton's Antarctic baptism had occurred some twelve years before the 1914 *Endurance* epic when, as a young officer in the Merchant Navy, he volunteered to join the British National Antarctic Expedition under the leadership of Commander Scott. On Christmas Eve 1901, final letters having been written by the crew to their wives and sweethearts, the expedition ship *Discovery* set sail for the Southern Ocean from New Zealand. Although he was unaware of its significance at the time, this expedition would change Shackleton's life for ever. Like everyone else on board he was soon to witness the Antarctic for the first time and the 'stark polar land had gripped his heart'. But it was not a happy time for Shackleton. Although he had been chosen by Scott to travel with him and naturalist and doctor Edward Wilson on the journey to the Pole in

1902, the entire expedition did not go to plan. The polar team members suffered from the onset of scurvy and returned to the *Discovery* hut ninety-four days later having penetrated only about two hundred and fifty miles across the Great Ice Barrier. But it was a record-breaking 'Furthest South' journey. However, Shackleton was singled out by Scott and invalided back to England on grounds of ill health. It was a huge blow, but ignited within him a desire to return again – on his own terms.

As I faced challenging situations in my army career, Shackleton's example was always there to add a steady hand on the tiller if I required it. When facing a demanding challenge I might ask myself, 'How would Shacks get out of this, then?' One particular incident in Bosnia during 2001 springs to mind. During a highly charged riot in which a civilian had been beaten to death, I became separated from my group of soldiers and forced to take refuge in a small café. Stones began raining down on to the building, smashing all the windows in an attempt to flush me out. Rather like the *Endurance* disaster, I couldn't stand and wait in the hope that the situation would improve; I had to be decisive and make a move, as Shackleton had done. I made a dash for it and somehow avoided the rocks and bottles that filled the air as I ran for further cover. Of course it is a much more simplistic example than the decisions which had to be taken in the Antarctic, but I remember fleetingly recalling Shackleton's unwavering boldness, and this almost subconsciously helped me to act quickly. But Shackleton also knew how important it was to maintain morale during difficult times when patience is tested and boredom threatens. Again, this could often apply to life in the army on operations and I found Shackleton's style of leadership helpful if I ever needed to be reminded of how to get it right.

As the years passed I absorbed all that had been written about him. I had read the books he had written after the *Nimrod* and *Endurance* expeditions and many of the biographies by others.

There were also accounts and diaries written by those who had been part of his expeditions which provided a rounded perspective on the man, and what was so clear to me was the faith that his crew had in him, well described by Frank Hurley, who said, 'I always found him rising to his best and inspiring confidence when things were at their blackest'. A few found him a hard taskmaster but the rest adored him, trusting him with their lives.

Collecting 'Shackletonia' slowly became an obsession for me. Many hours – and many hundreds of pounds – were spent ferreting through antique shops and auction houses in search of anything associated with his exploits or, better still, items that he had owned or bore his signature. I found old magazines containing accounts of his expeditions, first-edition books, photographs, cigarette cards and, given to me by my wife Joanna, my most treasured possession of all, the copy of *South* that Shackleton gave his parents inscribed, 'To Mother and Father, For Christmas, With Love from Ernest, Xmas 1919.'

My fascination with Shackleton had a further, personal link: I was connected to that heroic age through a distant relative called Frank Worsley. Worsley was the captain of the *Endurance* and is revered in polar lore for his navigation of the *James Caird* on the journey from Elephant Island to South Georgia in 1916. I am not a close descendent of his, but we each have a traceable line to the Worsleys of Yorkshire. As an American fellow polar buff once said to me as I played down the connection, 'Damn it, man – you must have the same genes.'

On return from the *Discovery* expedition, Shackleton's mood changed from disappointment at being sent home early to restlessness with having to earn a living in a series of desk-bound jobs. He had married his sweetheart Emily Dorman but found professional work tiresome; he wanted only one thing and that was to return south and be the first to the Pole. Using his abundant charm, he raised enough money to announce in February 1907 that he was to lead an expedition to do just that. He purchased the *Nimrod*, equipped her and on New Year's Day 1908, waved off by a crowd of thousands, he departed New Zealand bound for the Southern Ocean. Four weeks later the heavily laden ship reached the Antarctic and in the shelter of Cape Royds the team built a hut as the base for the journey to the Pole the following summer. When the sun finally rose three months later, heralding the end of the constant darkness of the Antarctic winter, Shackleton's plan was ready. He had chosen Frank Wild, Jameson Adams and Eric Marshall to form the southern party. On 29 October 1908 the team of four, each leading a pony and sledge, set off across the frozen sea into the unknown.

After a month, Shackleton had passed the 'Furthest South' point reached with Scott in 1903. But then disaster struck. Snow-blind, off their food and weakening fast, three of the four ponies had to be destroyed. Nevertheless, the optimistic Shackleton persevered and on climbing some high ground, discovered a mighty glacier that led the team, now man-hauling their sledges, through the Transantarctic mountains and on to the polar plateau. On joining the glacier the last remaining pony plummeted down a crevasse to an icy death, nearly taking Frank Wild with him. Through extraordinary leadership Shackleton held the team together and, on half-rations and pulling two sledges, continued the arduous journey across the polar plateau. Then on 9 January 1909, just ninety-seven miles from their goal, Shackleton made what must be the most selfless and astonishing decision ever in the history of polar exploration. Having covered eight hundred and twenty miles, he stopped in his tracks and ordered the Union Flag which Queen Alexandra had given the expedition to be planted. Shackleton could see that if they were to go on, the chances of surviving were virtually non-existent. He would take no further risks. Despite the glistening prize of the South Pole staring him in the face, the lives of his men were too important.

The journey home became a fight for survival. Travelling downhill, the crevassed glacier again came close to claiming more lives. Crippled by dysentery from eating pony meat, the four stumbled feebly on to the waiting *Nimrod*, which picked them up, ironically, from Scott's *Discovery* hut, where they had taken refuge. Shackleton's decision and judgement were evidence of his extraordinary leadership. Despite staggering hardship and a display of unbreakable mental strength, he had pioneered a route right to the heart of the Antarctic and returned to Britain to be knighted a hero.

In November 1992, a comparable, ground-breaking polar expedition caught my eye and confirmed to me just how much I wanted to take part in something similar; in an immature way I felt jealous because someone else was living out their dream. Sir Ranulph Fiennes and Dr Mike Stroud had set off from the Filchner-Ronne Ice Shelf where it joins the Weddell Sea, aiming to complete the first unsupported crossing of the Antarctic continent. Ninety-seven days later their journey ended on the Ross Ice Shelf, just three hundred miles short of the Ross Sea which marked their goal. Despite not quite making it, their journey was an astonishing feat of endurance. They had laid an unbroken trail of more than thirteen hundred miles across the Antarctic and blazed their way into the record books.

For months on end I dreamed about taking part in a similar venture but, to be honest, I lacked the boldness to even consider undertaking such a project. I was afraid of the unknown – the planning, the training, the fund-raising and, not least, the risk of failure. I had no idea where to start and it all seemed to be too overwhelming to even give it a go. But I knew I had the passion, and I believed I was developing the mental toughness to succeed.

Deep within me, I had an eagerness and ambition to one day get to the polar regions. I didn't know when it would be but I was beginning to learn in life that if your heart lifts at the thought of fulfilling a dream then all that stands in your way is to take the first step and enter the arena. As long as my passion for Shackleton and the Antarctic burned with a bright flame, I did truly believe that one day I would get there. I would walk in Shackleton's footsteps.

CHAPTER 1

A Family Affair

'The difficulty that confronts most men who wish to undertake exploration work is that of finance, and in this respect I was rather more than ordinarily handicapped. The equipment and despatch of an Antarctic expedition means the expenditure of very many thousands of pounds, without the prospect of any speedy return, and with reasonable probability of no return at all.'

EHS, The Heart of the Antarctic, 1909

2004

'You must meet my cousin, Will Gow,' said Alexandra Shackleton. 'Like you, he admires my grandfather very much and for a few years now has had an idea for an expedition in 2008 to celebrate the centenary of the *Nimrod* journey. I will arrange for you both to meet.'

Ernest and Emily Shackleton had three children: Raymond, Cecily and Edward. Edward, later Lord Shackleton and himself an explorer and geographer, was Alexandra Shackleton's father. I had met Alexandra first at the annual polar sale at Christie's auction house in London, where I had bid successfully on a portrait photograph signed by her grandfather. Later our paths were to cross at lectures at the Royal Geographical Society, polar society receptions – in fact, wherever and whenever there was an event with a polar theme. Will Gow, the man she wanted me to meet, was Shackleton's great-nephew by marriage; Will's great-aunt was Emily Dorman, Shackleton's wife.

In conversation with Alexandra Shackleton over the years, I had made it obvious that I aspired to visit the Antarctic and, if I was lucky, preferably somewhere linked to her grandfather's expeditions. I'd already told her about sleeping beside his grave on South Georgia so I doubted she needed any further evidence of my deep interest and ambition. Alexandra had explained that Will's plan was not simply to celebrate the *Nimrod* expedition centenary, but to do so with descendants of Shackleton, Wild, Adams and Marshall, if he could find some who were eager, committed and capable of taking part. It was a bold and original idea and sounded very interesting. This was the opportunity that I had been longing for.

I arrived last at the Fox and Hounds pub in Battersea, south London early one March evening in 2004, and headed towards the table where Alexandra and Will were already sitting.

'Henry, meet Will.' A stocky, powerfully built, dark-haired man rose from his chair and we shook hands.

'I thought that you two should meet,' said Alexandra. 'I have told you about Will's idea and I know how interested you are in my grandfather – perhaps you could be involved in Will's plans. And please, call me Zaz.' Although this first meeting was hardly a formal selection interview, I was keen to get across to Will that I was more than eager to be part of his expedition. Aside from my interest in Shackleton and the longing to travel across the Antarctic, I explained that I was a serving soldier, had been in the army for twenty-four years and was working in the Ministry of Defence. I was pretty confident that the army would give me time off to take part. But I also thought I should be frank with Will about my family claim – if he was looking for a descendent of the original *Nimrod* party, then I was not qualified, as my link to Shackleton was through Frank Worsley, who had been on the later *Endurance* expedition. As we relaxed and talked further, it became clear that Will and I would get on well. His optimism and drive were obvious from the start. I learned that he had first thought of the centenary expedition idea after leading a group of children to Nordkapp in north Norway in 2002 as a volunteer staff member of the British Schools Exploring Society. He also had some experience of organising fund-raising events, having helped to raise more than £100,000 for multiple sclerosis charities, the disease which had recently been responsible for his mother's death. Will, who worked for a financial services company, clearly loved the outdoor life and saw the *Nimrod* centenary as too exciting an opportunity to ignore.

'How are you getting on finding descendants?' I asked.

'Not too bad,' he replied. 'Zaz has a son, Patrick. So between him and me we have the Shackleton link. I have recently met Dave Cornell, a great-grandson of Jameson Adams and we know of some great-great-nephews of Frank Wild – hopefully one of them will be up for it. But no news yet of a Marshall.'

By extraordinary coincidence I knew Dave Cornell quite well. Now working in the City, he had spent a few years in the army, commissioned into the Royal Green Jackets, which was also my regiment. An interesting feature of this project was already beginning to emerge: the final team would be made up not of close mates with friendships forged over time, but of strangers drawn together only by a line of descent to four Edwardian polar explorers. With nearly five years to go until the expedition's start, there would be time for team spirit to grow but I wondered also whether our disparities may prove to be the source of future difficulties. There was an obvious parallel with army life here. Soldiers come together from all backgrounds to form teams of many sizes, but it is the shared experiences of training together and learning to trust each other, ultimately with their lives, that glues them together as a team. But it takes time for the glue to harden and for everyone in the team to respect and trust one another. In order to give ourselves the best chance of building a strong unit for this venture, we would have to optimise the time available before the expedition began.

'How did you get on?' asked my wife Joanna, half an hour after I had left the pub and returned home to our army flat in Putney. I explained what we had talked about, how much I had liked Will and highlighted our similar interests.

'Yes, but are you going?'

'I don't know, darling. I wasn't expecting to be told this evening but I couldn't have been more enthusiastic and interested. I explained what I could offer – based in London, time available to train and fund-raise, etc. We have arranged to meet up soon to talk things through in more detail, which is a positive sign. He has two others in the frame already – funnily enough, one of whom I know from the army, Dave Cornell. But it is early days yet, so I musn't get too excited.'

I tried to play down the meeting and looking back now, probably came across as rather dismissive to Joanna's enthusiastic questions, which was foolish. For if I was going to be part of this five-year project then she would be the person whose support I would need most. If she was excluded from my selfish dream, then I would be a damn fool. Joanna had been unbelievably understanding over the twelve years that we had been married, never once complaining as I flew off on an army deployment for yet another six months, leaving her alone with our two children, Max and Alicia. Utterly selfless, she strongly believes that partners in a marriage should not feel that they must cast aside things they are passionate about. And she knew I was passionate about achieving my lifetime's dream.

L–R: Shackleton, Scott and Wilson at 'Furthest South', 30 December 1902.

1902

The genesis of Shackleton's dream to venture to the then-unknown centre of the Antarctic started on the *Discovery* expedition with Commander Scott in 1902. 'Like three polar knights they were away with banners flying in the wind, a small party but full of grit and determination' was how Louis Bernacchi, the physicist on Scott's expedition, remembered Scott, Shackleton and Wilson departing from Hut Point, heading for the Great Ice Barrier on 2 November 1902. The journey got off to a worrying start. Deep snow, heavy loads and disobedient dogs caused progress to be sluggish and, once the support party had left them, the three men faced a daunting array of tasks on their own. The weather mocked them as they battled against a merciless headwind and driving spindrift – their skis, too difficult to use in this weather, had long since been stowed away. The allocated sledging rations soon proved inadequate as the weather slowed their progress, forcing them on to a reduced intake of food. And so it continued, day on day. The weaker dogs began to tire and, overcome by the cold, fatigue and poor nourishment, some curled up at the end of the day, never to wake again; others had to be shot. This placed an even greater burden on Scott, Wilson and Shackleton who were now forced to relay their sledges, taking one load forward together then returning for the next, through the still-deep snow, often covering fifteen miles but, as Shackleton noted, making only 'five miles to the good. But there is satisfaction that every foot of ground is new'. Yet by mid-December 1902 they had crossed the symbolic 80°S line of latitude and were heading to the centre of the golden circle that marked the ten remaining degrees to the Pole.

Despite the hardships, Christmas Day 1902 was celebrated in style. Breakfast, wrote Shackleton, consisted of 'a pannikin of seal's liver with bacon mixed with biscuit, each topped up with a spoonful of blackberry jam . . .'. Having made ten miles that day they camped and Shackleton took over the cooking to ensure he could produce a morale-raising surprise at the end of supper; '. . . the other two chaps did not know about the plum pudding. It only weighed 6oz and I had it stowed away in my socks (clean ones) in my sleeping bag, with a little piece of holly which I got from the ship. It was a glorious surprise for them – that plum-pudding – when I produced it.' But away from the celebrations, unseen forces were at work, as Shackleton recorded in his diary that Christmas night. 'Now we are doing the pulling, the dogs being practically useless', and 'We have definitely settled our furthest south to be on the 28th, as examination shows that the Captain and I have slight scurvy signs. It will not be safe to go further.'

Stumbling along due to snow-blindness and growing exhaustion the gallant men pushed south until the end of the year. On 30 December 1902, leaving Shackleton to rest for a few hours, Wilson and Scott made a final push to claim the furthest point reached by man, S82° 17'. Pausing briefly to consider the significance of their achievement, they looked ahead through bloodshot eyes and silently pondered what might lie ahead. To the west, Commander Scott spied a break in the face of the mountain range which he named

Shackleton Inlet. The two most prominent peaks that rose above the distant skyline he named after his loyal supporters, Mounts Longstaff and Markham – Sir Clements Markham being awarded the highest peak perhaps with the hope of securing his support for a future expedition. Back with the sledge, Shackleton rested awkwardly on the frozen fabric of the tent and reindeer-skin sleeping bags, awaiting their return. Staring first towards the same spine of mountains and then ahead to the horizon that separated the white and blue, I imagine that he must have spent time considering the precarious state they were in and their prospects of a safe return journey. But I also believe that, alone with his thoughts, he promised himself that one day he would return on his own terms to venture past this point and not stop until he had reached 90°S.

The return journey, like many in extreme expeditions of that time, became a race against death. Dwindling food supplies, snow-blindness, increasing fatigue, irrational judgement and merciless weather conditions came close to claiming their lives. The remaining dogs were killed and eaten as the weakening trio staggered from one food depot to the other. On windy days they created a makeshift sail for the sledge but they lacked the energy to keep up with it. Bleeding, spongy gums, loose teeth and anaemia were signs in all of them that scurvy was fast taking hold. Then in the distance the flattened cone shape of Mount Erebus and the outlines of Black Island and White Island sharpened with every mile as they moved painfully towards the sanctuary of the *Discovery*.

On 3 February 1903, after ninety-four days away from their winter quarters, the torment came to an end. As they drew closer and saw the familiar outline of Hut Point and the three masts of the *Discovery*, they noticed that the relief ship, the *Morning* had also arrived from New Zealand and was at anchor in the open water of the bay. 'It was a great homecoming, and as we turned past Cape Armitage we saw the ship decorated from top to toe with flags and

The Morning *cutting through ice returning to New Zealand.*

all the ship's company up the rigging round the gangway ready to cheer us, which they did most lustily as we came on aboard', wrote Wilson in his diary that night.

A few days later, having rested and recovered, Scott called Shackleton to his cabin and informed him that he had decided to invalid him home on grounds of poor health. The following day, from the stern of the *Morning*, a devastated Shackleton fixed his stare on the broken sea ice, cracked open and parting as the ship headed north, away from the frozen continent. Behind her she created a dark highway through the pancake ice that led back to Hut Point and the faint outline of the distant peaks. The longing to return South was burning inside him. Shackleton turned to face the other way for he was not a man to look backwards and into the past – he was interested only in the future. Over the following three weeks he paced the deck of the *Morning*, deep in thought, his head awash with ideas and dreams. But in the quiet of his cabin his mind focussed on home and his beloved Emily and what the future had in store for them.

Prior to leaving England, Shackleton had made clear to Emily's father that on his return he intended to ask for her hand in marriage. That moment was now only a few months away, and despite the obvious love that he had for her, expressed so tenderly in his letters, Emily was shortly to learn that she would have to share him with a captivating mistress – the virgin-pure wasteland of the Antarctic.

2004

Over the months that followed that first meeting with Will, I re-read accounts of that *Discovery* expedition to fully understand the beginnings of Shackleton's obsession and his longing to return south. But it was the detail in *The Heart of the Antarctic* – Shackleton's personal account of his 1907/09 expedition, the one we were to retrace, that I needed to understand completely. Although I was familiar with what he achieved, my knowledge of the route and daily detail of the struggle were sketchy. All the information we needed was in the pages of his book. I read it many times and each time it was alarming. There was the sheer scale to comprehend – a nine hundred-mile journey, a climb to over ten thousand feet and the immense and extremely dangerous crevasses of the Beardmore Glacier to contend with. On top of all this, there was the merciless southerly wind and sub-zero temperatures that certainly I had never experienced before. But I kept reassuring myself that we had plenty of time to prepare.

I met with Will in his London flat on a fairly regular basis to hear and develop his concept for the five years of preparation that he had sensibly set aside before the centenary expedition. Dave Cornell joined us when he could, a tall, thinly built man, like a long-distance runner, who came across as very determined, sharp and articulate. And so, too, did Patrick, Shackleton's great-grandson. Patrick was very amusing and extremely bright but from the first did not strike me as a chip off his great-grandfather's block. Far from being the outdoors type, Patrick quickly confessed that he never took regular exercise and despite admiring his adventurous forebear greatly, the explorer had not been a major influence in Patrick's life. Although Patrick was clearly going to be great company, the more I absorbed the harrowing detail of the everyday hardships faced in *The Heart of the Antarctic*, I begun to doubt he was really going to be up for the whole journey. But long ago I learned to be wary of first impressions, and also realised that a lot can happen over five years.

As the summer of 2004 passed by, a clearer plan began to emerge. Although it had never been specifically said by Will, I felt very much as if I was a definite member of the team now. We talked at length about the training required and the timescale we had allowed ourselves to prepare, but because we were all new to this polar adventuring, we were going to have to master the basics pretty quickly. Will was one-up here – he had recently invested three weeks' holiday on Baffin Island in northern Canada on a polar course run by the renowned Matty McNair, the leading female polar guide in the world at that time. Matty had set foot on both poles on more than one occasion, she snow-kited wherever there was wind and handled sledge-dogs with ease. She was totally in tune with the polar way of life and Will was adamant that she should be our teacher over the next few years and that we should all start by attending her course in Canada.

As daylight shortened and winter approached, my mind wandered away from the training schedule and into an aspect of the project that worried me far more. Will's idea had allowed us plenty of time to train for the expedition, and I was confident that we would be well trained in time. However, where was the money going to come from? I had never sought sponsorship for anything before and I kept asking myself why anyone would want to pay for us to go to the South Pole? Perhaps I was being overly gloomy but I was not familiar with the financial world. But I kept reminding myself that expeditions on the same scale as ours had been funded in the past, so there was no reason why ours should not. I just needed an injection of Shackleton's optimism.

My main concern was that I sensed the others were also unsure of where to start. We talked about drawing up lists of potential sponsors, organising fund-raising events, running marathons, doing car boot sales and pestering relations and friends for help. There were lots of good ideas but it all seemed rather amateurish to me. Based on research of recent expeditions, I reckoned we would have to raise at least £200,000, probably much more, and I began to understand that no company would commit money upfront, so far away from the start of an event.

Towards the turn of the year, still with no money in the bank, Will suggested that the four of us should take part in a demanding endurance event held annually each February across the wilderness of the Canadian Yukon. Called the Yukon Arctic Ultra, it is a race over three hundred miles to be completed in eight days on foot, bike or skis. All survival equipment is pulled behind in a small sledge and if you fail to meet certain checkpoints on time then you are disqualified. Even with four years to go, it was a good idea to put ourselves through such a test at this time, as the race was a perfect test for us. It was a third of our expedition journey, to be completed in just over a week and we would probably experience temperatures around -25°C. But beyond coping with the physical demands, I wanted to see if I had the mental strength to complete such a task. Simple mathematics told me that we would have to do up to forty miles every twenty-four hours, which meant a minimum of around fifteen hours' travelling through day and night. And it would be an individual effort, so there would be no encouragement from others. For me, there was no option but to dig into my own money and holiday allocation and join Will; unfortunately, neither Dave nor Patrick were able to escape from work to compete. So in February 2005, Will and I set off for the frozen wilds of the Yukon in western Canada.

The Yukon race turned out to be a significantly valuable experience, for it placed exceptional physical and mental demands on us both. It was a relentless battle to stay within the time frame allowed, but I was spurred on by the sight of other racers who had given up. I was nervous that I might contemplate doing the same, for any sign of quitting on this short event would spell disaster for the future challenge and, if I did give up on the Yukon event, I would have to seriously consider my place in the expedition team. For me, the real value of the experience was being forced to dig deep into my mental reserves. As the days wore on I became increasingly exhausted. I had no one to encourage me onwards – just the silence of the forestry blocks, frozen lakes, monochrome wilderness and the night-time spectacle of the Northern Lights for company. At my lowest, and hallucinating because of intense fatigue, I had to find ways to motivate myself through each hour. Resorting to drastic measures, I forced myself to imagine that in my sledge I was pulling my dangerously sick daughter to a doctor who lived in the town where we would finish the race. It worked. Both Will – never one to quit, as I would discover – and I completed the race and returned to England with aching limbs and very swollen feet. But, most important, we had shared an intensely brutal adventure which I was quite sure would benefit us enormously later on, as it had shown us what we were able to achieve when running on empty.

The remaining months of 2005 passed swiftly. The four of us continued to meet every few weeks but too often I came away from each meeting thinking we were making little headway; there was no overall leadership, no one really pushing to get things moving. We did, though, at least have a training plan sketched out for the next three years, which was centred around an overseas event each year. We agreed that first, in spring 2006, we should all go off to Baffin Island to attend Matty McNair's course.

1903

There was no flag-waving crowd to meet the downhearted Shackleton when he returned to England in June 1903, as he had travelled the final stage of the journey on a nondescript mail ship. But his beloved Emily was waiting patiently on the quayside to welcome him home. She had been longing for this moment for eighteen months. They had much to talk about, including their future together. But Emily's plans were to be short-lived, for Shackleton was in huge demand and she was forced to step back into the shadows. Both the Admiralty Board and Sir Clements Markham, president of the Royal Geographical Society, were furious with Scott for wintering again in the Antarctic, as expedition funds had dried up. Allowing the *Discovery* to be trapped in the pack ice for another season appeared careless, a standard not expected from a Royal Navy officer. Shackleton's account of the expedition, the 'Furthest South' journey and the decision by Scott to stay on provided an invaluable update and enough information for the organisers to decide to mount a rescue. Despite the use of the *Morning* as a relief ship, the Admiralty agreed to send a second ship to assist in the recovery. The *Terra Nova*, a whaler built in Dundee and capable of withstanding the mighty Southern Ocean was purchased and provisioned, with advice from Shackleton, who was now regarded as an experienced polar explorer.

But Shackleton had to turn his attention, in the short term at least, to a life on land. Emily's father had died leaving her financially cushioned for the rest of her life but Shackleton still needed, and wanted, to work. An attempt to creep in through the back door of the Admiralty selection board for a Royal Navy commission was unsuccessful for the former merchant navy officer, as was a hopeful foray into the world of journalism. So when an application to be the secretary of the Royal Scottish Geographical Society (RSGS) was successfully approved, Shackleton felt that, for the time being, his financial future was assured. With his move to Edinburgh he could now support Emily, whom he married in London on 9 April 1904.

But it wasn't long before he became frustrated. Despite swelling the membership of the RSGS and broadening its image he found the work too easy and the society resistant to change. But one member of the society's council, Sir William Beardmore, a wealthy Scottish industrialist, was impressed by Shackleton and became a supporter of significant influence and an ally who was later to prove invaluable. On the outside, Shackleton was charming and impressed everyone he met, but inside he was restless; he yearned to be stretched. After only one year in the job he resigned from the RSGS in order to prepare for the 1906 election, in which he stood as Liberal Unionist candidate for the Dundee seat. His bid for a career in politics was short-lived, as he failed to win the seat. He needed a new challenge.

Scott, now promoted from Commander to Captain, had returned to England and published his account of the expedition in *The Voyage of the Discovery*. Shackleton was reminded of the sledging journey in which it was suggested he was the weakest member. To the reader it was clear that Shackleton's sickness and exhaustion had been the contributing cause of their disappointing progress across the Great Ice Barrier. He felt wounded by Scott's version of what happened. Elsewhere, other polar events were making the headlines. In August 1905, in the Arctic north, Roald Amundsen had become the first man to sail through the north-west passage. Shackleton read of other audacious plans to reach the North Pole using dogs and even airships. It was all too much for him – he needed to be in the vanguard of similar endeavours. It was time to stop dreaming and to act.

2005

The year was speeding by at an alarming rate. Our monthly meetings continued and we drew up endless lists of likely sponsors to target, what we could offer them and held long debates over the design of a website. One task I particularly enjoyed was to research which companies that had supplied food and equipment for the original expedition were still in existence. The plan was to ask them to match their donation one hundred years on, but uplifting it for inflation. We were, however, keen to avoid offerings such as the 300 lbs of tea kindly donated by Lipton's in 1908 – a financial sponsorship from Cadbury's, Burberry or Jaeger would be much more useful.

No further overseas trips were planned for 2005, but the four of us headed off for a spring weekend in Wales to be taught basic rope work under the eye of an old army friend of mine, Ross Ashe-Cregan, an accomplished climber. In the middle of our Antarctic expedition we would have to ascend the Beardmore Glacier, a river of ice one hundred and twenty miles long and criss-crossed with deep crevasses, one of which had swallowed up Shackleton's remaining pony, 'Socks'. It would be by far the most dangerous part of the journey and we had to know not just how to get through it, but also how to pull each other, and our heavy sledges, out of the menacing holes were any one of us to fall in. Reading Shackleton's description of the dire time he had on the same glacier certainly concentrated the mind on such preparation. With very little knowledge between us of polar exploration, we had to make a start somewhere and that weekend in Wales proved useful. Although we were pretty incompetent, we laughed a lot and begun to get an idea of what would be required; we had a massive amount to learn. Patrick, however, continued to strike me as a fish out of water. He was brilliant in our monthly meetings – full of ideas, funny and articulate, but walking to the top of a small hill in Wales he simply looked like he was hating it. Still, I kept reminding myself that we had plenty of time and, when pressed, Patrick continued to convince us all that he was up for it.

A few days later I received news that I was to be posted to Afghanistan for six months. I would be leaving in October and returning in late April 2006. I had been warned that this posting was likely, and although I would obviously be unavailable for six months, I would be back in time to attend Matty McNair's course on Baffin Island. Shortly before I left, Will was invited to take part in a travel programme on BBC Radio 4, during which he discussed the aim of the expedition. It was our first piece of publicity, and at last firmly placed the centenary project in the public domain.

Dressed in desert camouflage uniform and carrying a rifle, body armour and helmet, I departed England on a grey October morning in 2005 bound for Kabul. Joanna and I were used to these long periods of separation. Although it never got easier, she was very understanding, despite being left alone to cope with Max, twelve and Alicia, ten, who found my absences extremely difficult. The following six months were for me busy and exciting, involving extensive travel all over southern Afghanistan and regular meetings with Afghan elders and tribal chiefs. Essentially, as part of a small team, my job was to pave the way for the main British Army arrival into Helmand province, scheduled for the following summer.

Six months away also gave me a great opportunity to carry on researching Shackleton's journey in minute detail. I took with me *The Heart of the Antarctic,* as well as a couple of up-to-date Antarctic maps in order to understand fully the daily account of his ordeal. I had little contact with the rest of the expedition team, because of infrequent and unreliable email connection, but I assumed that plans were progressing. One piece of information that did reach me was that another great-grandson of Jameson Adams had joined the party as a result of Will's slot on Radio 4. So we now had two descendants of Jameson Adams, Dave Cornell and the newcomer, Henry Adams, who was in his mid-thirties, strong, fit and mad keen to be involved: he sounded ideal. As we already had a team of four, and wanted no more, it had been decided that Henry would become the reserve.

By January 2006 I was midway through my tour of duty when I received news of some significance which came as no surprise – Patrick had decided that the expedition was not for him. Dave, Will, Henry and Patrick had met up in the Cairngorms for a weekend of training with Ross Ashe-Cregan. On the second day Ross planned to take the team up the snow-covered slopes and rocks of Ben Nevis. Fifteen minutes into the climb Patrick described it all as 'sheer hell' and said that he'd had enough, and would meet them all later that evening in the pub. In fact, he was not waiting for them at the end of the day for he took the next train home to London.

This news was disappointing but it was far from the end of the expedition, or of Patrick's involvement with the plan. Instead of taking part in the physically-demanding walk, Shackleton's great-grandson would instead become the wordsmith of the project, crafting the expedition's literature, a role for which he was eminently suited. Whenever we needed to get our message on to paper to inspire the reader to part with money, Patrick delivered every time. And with Henry Adams as a reserve, Patrick's place was filled by someone who was a much tighter fit into the team, though Henry did admit later that he'd had mixed emotions about accepting the place after Patrick's resignation.

I returned to England in April 2006, just as the first British troops were entering southern Afghanistan. After six months away, I was given some time off but – very selfishly – I was to spend most of it on the previously-programmed training with Matty. Joanna and the children were amazingly supportive and understanding. No sooner had I got off one plane than I stepped on to another for a further three weeks away in Canada.

At the airport I met up with Dave and Will and met Henry Adams for the first time. I liked him instantly. He was a shipping lawyer living in Sussex, married to Alex, who was expecting their first child. He loved the outdoor life and was madly enthusiastic about the project and hugely excited to be given the opportunity to walk in the foot-steps of his great-grandfather, a man he had so admired all his life.

The polar training in Baffin Island was exceptional. Matty McNair was an inspiring teacher who took us through every aspect of the daily routine that we would encounter and put them into practice over the snow and ice fields where she lived. We covered nutrition, clothing, navigation, campcraft, skiing, sledge-pulling, medical issues and emergency procedures. No subject was left undone.

For the first time, the training also offered us the opportunity to live and work together for a lengthy period in a polar environment. It meant sharing duties, making decisions, interacting with one another in the confines of a tent and working day in and day out as a team. Each evening, relaxing in the tent, Matty was very good at getting us to debate and answer the awkward questions that we really had not yet faced up to – 'So, how are you going to raise the money? Do you think you can do the journey? What are your reservations . . . your strengths and weaknesses? What is the plan over the next two years? Who is the lead dog?'

That last question had certainly been niggling at me even before I went to Afghanistan. My doubts over the direction that the overall planning was heading were still there, and the more I listened to the muddled and fractious answers to Matty's questions, the more I sensed that time was moving too quickly for us to continue as we were. I sensed the frustration building between Dave, Will and I. One night, sharing a tent with Will I felt it was time to tell him that I did not think things were progressing as we would have liked, and I believed that if he stayed at the helm, I could not see the project succeeding.

'I am as passionate about it as you and Dave are,' I told him, 'and I know and respect the fact that it was your idea, but the lack of direction and inertia is creating a bad atmosphere among us. Unless you hand the reins to someone else then I think I will withdraw from the team. I absolutely appreciate this project was your idea but I just can't see it happening at the moment. So, I would be prepared to take on the leadership of the whole thing. I will need some help but you will have to agree to let go.'

Will admitted he, too, was not enjoying the current atmosphere, and was also considering calling it a day.

'I don't know right at this moment what I want to do,' he said, 'but I am not particularly happy about your suggestion. I will have to think it over.'

I sympathised with him hugely. For a few years, this had been his dream and here was I saying that perhaps he was not the best person to make it all come together. It was not surprising he wanted time to think about it and I could see that he was irked by my suggestion, which was quite understandable.

We returned to England having made significant progress. We had nearly burned down the tent through lack of attention to the cooker; we had navigated inaccurately, seemingly incapable of following a simple bearing; our skiing was slow; our sledges had been packed badly, dispersing the weight in an inefficient way; and through being idle I suffered from an excruciatingly painful attack of snow-blindness, which was totally my own fault. But through our collective errors we had all learned an enormous amount and now had a clearer understanding what would be required of us, not for three weeks, but for two months. But most significant of all, Will had let go of the reins and handed them to me. It was a huge gesture that must have been agony for him to make, but I sensed that perhaps there was a hint of relief as well. As I look back over the time frame of this whole project there was no more important moment than those tense and charged minutes in that tent with Will. But what I would always recognise and respect was that this expedition was his idea. Hopefully, with the help of the others, I would deliver it for him.

The first task was to form a fund-raising committee. We still had to raise in excess of £200,000 to cover our costs and the bank account was still empty – all expenses to date had come out of our own pockets. Dave Cornell took on the leadership of this and within a month had arranged for a small group of well-connected friends to meet with us in the hope that we could enthuse them with the project and persuade them to help. On one of the viewing evenings of the Polar Sale at Christie's auction house we gathered our guests in a small reception room, plied them with champagne and briefed them of our plan. I set out the historical context and the unique plans for the modern expedition and then Dave Cornell laid bare the costs involved. Professor David Drewry, an eminent geographer, also briefed them on a small science project that he was keen we undertake. There were many questions and polite alarm about the short time left to raise the money, but a week later all those who had been present agreed to help. We were not after their money – we simply wanted their advice, criticism, energy and, most importantly, their network of contacts who could become sponsors. The task ahead remained daunting, but at last it seemed we were on our way.

One family who Zaz Shackleton suggested we invite to listen to our presentation was the Fright family – direct descendants of Frank Wild, one of the four members of the original team. We were still very much on the lookout for a Wild and a Marshall and on that evening, Tim Fright, a great-great-nephew of Wild's, made it very clear to us that he would love to be involved. Just twenty-three, quietly spoken and with the slight but wiry physique of a jockey, Tim – actually a policy analyst – would prove to be surprisingly tough, just like his explorer forebear. He was a great find and, that very evening, he joined the team.

1907

Exactly a hundred years earlier, Shackleton was also desperate to announce his ambitious plans to the world and Captain Scott's return from the *Discovery* expedition was just the catalyst he needed. He charmed his way through Scottish and English society intent on persuading the monied, such as his Scottish colleague, Sir William Beardmore, to underwrite his burgeoning but still private plans; only as a last resort would he ask for the financial patronage of the Royal Geographical Society, for its president Sir Clements Markham would be disapproving of a private expedition and unlikely to support it. With sufficient backing and promises behind him to make a bold and official statement to the world, readers of *The Times* on 12 February 1907 learned of a 'NEW BRITISH EXPEDITION TO THE SOUTH POLE'.

One reader of that headline was not impressed, for he too had similar ambitions. Captain Scott read with disbelief that Shackleton was not only heading south to claim the ultimate prize but that he intended to use the *Discovery* hut as his base. As leader of that expedition, Scott made it very clear that the hut and even the ice-filled waters of McMurdo Sound were his property and trespassers were not welcome. The Royal Mail carried curt and intransigent letters between the two explorers as each held stubbornly to their positions. It took their mutual friend from the *Discovery* expedition, Edward Wilson, to calm the waters and prevent the disagreement reaching the public arena. Eager to get on with his plans, Shackleton unwillingly backed down. He would simply anchor his ship and build his hut elsewhere. His energy turned to raising more money, finding a ship and sourcing the finest equipment to go in it. With £7,000 (the equivalent of £552,000 in 2008) deposited into the expedition bank account by Sir William Beardmore and an office opened at No. 9 Regent Street, plans for his expedition were now firmly underway.

2006

The situation we found ourselves in by July 2006 was very similar. We had an idea which we needed to announce to the world and, like Shackleton, we had a lot of money to raise. Thankfully though, we didn't have to buy a ship. By late summer a clear plan for our expedition was beginning to emerge, but the team structure had yet to settle. On return from Baffin Island, Dave Cornell had decided that he was taking himself off the expedition team. He did not want to be away from his young family for further training periods, and then the two months of the polar journey, so he had decided to withdraw, but he would remain as the lead for fund-raising. It was a huge disappointment to everyone, but particularly to Dave. He was stepping down from walking in his great-grandfather's footsteps on an Antarctic journey never since repeated; and it was possible that he would never get another chance to do it in his life. I really felt for him but I was so impressed that he wished to remain totally committed to raising funds for a project that he wouldn't be taking part in. So with Patrick and Dave now off the team and newcomer Tim Fright deciding that the main journey was not for him either, only Henry, Will and I remained.

At first, the plans for the expedition seemed straightforward. On the 29 October 2008, exactly one hundred years to the day that Shackleton and his team set off on their journey, we would set off from the same hut at Cape Royds and follow the exact route that he took to the point where he made that extraordinary decision to stop and turn around, just ninety-seven miles from the South Pole. But having reached that same point, hopefully a century later on 9 January 2009, we were faced with a number of options. First, we discounted a return journey on the basis that we wouldn't have enough time to complete it before the short Antarctic summer came to an end – and none of us displayed much enthusiasm for a seventeen hundred-mile journey either. Next, we considered stopping at the point that Shackleton had and flying out from there; or we could go on to the South Pole and, in the centenary year, complete unfinished family business by covering those final ninety-seven miles. We debated the options for many hours and over time a solution began to emerge that would also involve Dave, Tim and Patrick. The three skiers – Henry, Will and I – would be joined by the others at the point that Shackleton stopped and turned back. It would be costly, but all they had to do was to fly there. Then we could all go on together as a group to the Pole and complete the journey. In concept it sounded simple, but the plan would be reliant on good weather and would also be very expensive. However, a hundred years on it was, just like Shackleton's plan had been, bold and imaginative.

By the end of 2006 we were making definite progress and the training programme over the remaining time was agreed in outline. In 2007, the 'Ice Team', as Henry, Will and I were now called, would travel to Finse in Norway, where Shackleton had trained for his *Endurance* expedition, and meet up for the final time with Matty McNair. In early 2008 we would concentrate on instruction in glacier travel and crevasse rescue in the French Alps and then, in the spring of the same year, undertake a dress rehearsal on our own in Greenland. The plans for the '97-Mile Team', as Dave, Tim and Patrick were now called, were also taking shape. The intention for them to meet up with us still remained but it seemed unlikely that we would all continue to the Pole at the same speed. The Ice Team would have just completed about eight hundred miles and would be eager to finish, whereas the 97-Mile Team would be starting out and need to acclimatise; our daily speeds would be very different. So Dave, the 97-Miler's leader, asked Matty to guide them as a separate group, which she agreed to do. The final details of the expedition were emerging.

With the training plans firmed up it was time to start talking to the company that would be flying us to the Antarctic and providing our support whilst on the expedition. Antarctic Logistics and Expeditions (ALE) has been providing that service for many years and is the recognised expert in that specialist field. Over many lengthy meetings with David Rootes, one of the company directors, we went through the detail he needed. Getting to the Antarctic would be straightforward. The Ice Team would take the four-and-a-half hour flight by Ilyushin aircraft to ALE's tented camp at Patriot Hills in the Ellsworth Mountains of West Antarctica from Punta Arenas in southern Chile. This has a blue ice runway which allows wheeled aircraft to land. But getting us to Shackleton's Hut, which was on the other side of the continent, would be challenging because of the distance involved, vagaries of the weather and crucially, the forward deployment of aviation fuel for the Twin Otter plane, equipped with ski fittings for landing, which would be needed for this section of the journey. David and his team had the 2007 season to deal with first, but were grateful for the early engagement as ours was a complex idea, resource-intensive and requiring a good deal of forward planning.

1907

Shackleton was also working at a frantic pace, having not allowed himself enough time to prepare for his recently-announced expedition, and Fridtjof Nansen told him so. In 1888 Nansen, a Norwegian, made the first crossing of Greenland; five years later he deliberately sailed his ship the *Fram* into the pack ice of the Arctic Ocean in order to be frozen in and then drift with the currents for three years towards the North Pole. He was widely recognised as the greatest polar explorer of that time and his greatness endures. Fortuitously, in 1907 he was filling a diplomatic post in London and was on hand to offer advice to Shackleton. Nansen was adamant that there was only one way to tackle a project of this magnitude and that was the Norwegian way, with dogs and skis. Deaf even to the wise counsel of such an iconic figure, Shackleton championed the use of tough, Siberian ponies and walking on foot. Nansen could not decide whether Shackleton was out of his mind or just naively nonconformist. But he knew that the British way to confront and endure hardship and suffering was with a big heart and unwavering reliance on the strength of the human spirit. So it was with little surprise that his advice was not heeded.

One thing Shackleton needed no advice on was where to source the best equipment and ships able to withstand the perils of the Southern Ocean. He knew that only suppliers from Nansen's homeland could provide the furs, sledges and vessels that he required. With barely sufficient time available to source the finest wolf and reindeer skin for the sleeping bags and mittens, Shackleton travelled frantically around Norway using his persuasive charm, that he knew few could refuse, to get his orders delivered on time. This was hardly the best way to prepare for a major polar expedition, but he made up for it with equal measures of hope and confidence.

CHAPTER 2

Unfinished Business

*'I would add one word on what I consider the requirements
necessary for a polar explorer; first Optimism, second Patience,
third Idealism, lastly I touch on Courage.'*

EHS, Adventure, 1928

2007

There was still an enormous amount left for us to do as we entered
2007, the penultimate year before our departure. I was satisfied
with the training plan and the concept of the expedition, but just
like Shackleton, worried about raising the money. Because of the
eye-catching plan 'DESCENDANTS COMPLETING UNFINISHED FAMILY
BUSINESS BY RETRACING SHACKLETON'S ROUTE ACROSS THE
ANTARCTIC IN THE CENTENARY YEAR', we begun getting interest
from companies wanting to be associated with the powerful
Shackleton ethos, and that also liked the idea of seeing their logos
captured in publicity photographs and on film.

Each night on return from work, I spent many hours handwriting
hundreds of letters asking for support. It was a laborious task, but

in these days of impersonal emails, I knew it would make a difference and over time I was proved right as money began to trickle in. Shackleton had been in exactly the same position, but he had focussed all his efforts on his affluent circle of friends and those who were swept along with his passion and drive to be the first to the South Pole.

Ever since I had taken on the role of driving this project forward it had gradually become more important to me than my responsibilities to Joanna and the children. It had become all-consuming and, looking back now, I realise that I lost track of where my real priorities should lie. 'Go out and achieve your dreams' would be a good motto for Joanna, who is herself fairly nomadic and well travelled, having lived in both India and California in her younger days. But I was getting it badly wrong. All of the expedition members with busy day jobs were squeezing everything we needed to do into the few remaining hours of each day, but I can see now that I was not dividing up the time sensibly and making my family feel important and special. Every spare hour was devoted to the project and 'bloody Shackleton' became a phrase frequently used by the children. No project of this size can be undertaken without the support of those closest to us, and I never really learned that room has to be made for them, no matter how consuming the passion. Half-Greek, and with a pathological hatred of the cold, Joanna wanted to be included in the planning and discussion, though certainly did not want to take part. But on too many occasions I turned my back on the signs that I was disregarding all else, and it is only now that I truly appreciate just what a rock Joanna was to me over those years in supporting me to fulfil a lifelong dream. Passion for something can so easily tip into obsession, which is a dangerous thing, especially when those affected are the very people who so loyally 'stand and wait'.

It had been more than eight months since our return from Baffin Island and, apart from a long weekend in Austria in December

2006, Will, Henry and I had been nowhere near snow, ropes or spending time together in the confines of a tent. So, as planned, the three of us set off for Finse in Norway to meet up with Matty for three weeks' intensive training, hopefully in bad weather. On our long drive from Dover to Oslo we stopped over in Holland to pick up our sledges, which we had ordered the previous year. At £1,500 each they were by far the most expensive piece of equipment we had to buy, but also the most important. Designed rather like a canoe, to ride over the frozen waves of snow and ice, they had to be strong enough to support a weight of around 300 lbs. It was a big moment to finally take delivery of them and strap them to the roof of Henry's car.

The training in Norway was invaluable. The weather wasn't as cold as we would have liked, as the winter was particularly mild, but any extended period of time spent together was crucially important now. We were getting on really well – helped by leg-pulling and general banter – and beginning to understand each other's foibles but, most importantly, learning to trust each other. The daily routine of any expedition in the polar regions is not complicated but it does demand high standards of personal discipline and team work. You need the discipline not to cut the corners, especially during the tedious jobs of the day, from pitching the tent, lighting the cooker, preparing the food, scraping off the rime (frozen condensation) from the inside of the tent, to looking after yourself and detecting the signs of frostbite in others. The list is endless but there is absolutely no place for being lazy and selfish. The polar environment can seduce you with its beauty and wilderness but then strike without remorse if through being idle you tempt it to challenge you.

Matty delivered all that we wanted. She criticised us for our many basic errors but praised us when things began to run efficiently. 'You get wet, you die' became a favourite mantra she drummed into us. And another, which I would have cause to mention two years later, 'The three golden rules of polar travel are, stay together, stay together, never separate.'

Two weeks later we returned to England with a growing sense of confidence in our ability to cope with the demands of the journey. Two-thirds of the expedition would simply be a test of our physical and mental strength. There would be long days of pulling a sledge towards a never-ending horizon, probably through weather conditions none of us had ever experienced before; but this should be achievable. What concerned me most was the remaining third of the journey, which was the ascent of the Beardmore Glacier. Shackleton's vivid account of his daily struggle made it abundantly clear that we would have to be ready to face similar difficulties and that would require specific training in the technicalities of glacier travel and crevasse rescue.

1907

In the final days of Shackleton's journey to Norway his attention switched to finding a ship, but running short of time he had to rely on the recommendation of others to find one suitable. One suggestion, the *Bjorn*, had both the cargo space, power and a proven record of withstanding pack ice. Shackleton was delighted when he saw her and returned to England tired but satisfied that preparations were going well. Back in the expedition office in Regent Street, the news awaiting him was bleak. Funds were running low and enthusiastic promises of financial support were proving to be hollow – the *Bjorn* was now unaffordable. Instead, he was forced to buy a Newfoundland sealer, the *Nimrod*, without even seeing if she was up to the task. But a few months in London's Blackwall docks and she was turned from being wholly inadequate to a vessel just about ready for the Southern Ocean – but she was all that Shackleton could afford.

Finally, he needed to select a captain and crew. He started first with acquaintances from the *Discovery* expedition but many were

Jameson Adams   *Frank Wild*

reluctant to accept his offer, conscious of appearing disloyal to Captain Scott. Frank Wild however, who had become a close friend, was keen to take part. Others were selected by interview or followed up from previous chance meetings with Shackleton – there was no shortage of eager volunteers. Those who were to play a notable part over the coming year were Frank Wild, Jameson Adams, Eric Marshall and George Marston. To complete the crew, Rupert England was selected to be captain of the *Nimrod*.

2007

With our Norway training behind us, our energy needed to revert to raising money. Over a number of months there had been a steady trickle of generous support and the fund-raising committee was proving its worth. We managed to get eight sponsors to donate £10,000 each. It didn't all come at once, but it did help enormously and the interest shown was a clear indication to us that we were planning something special. We had secured enough to employ a

PR company and start to build a comprehensive website, but we still needed a headline sponsor to fund the lion's share of the cost. Dave Cornell had made one important breakthrough, managing to get significant support from clothing manufacturer Timberland. Not only would the firm make a financial contribution, but because it was not keen to place its logo on clothing made by another company, it insisted that it make all the items that we would need. At first, Henry, Will and I were hesitant, as although Timberland made outdoor-style clothing, the firm was not known for its expertise in the specialised field of extreme-weather clothing. Nevertheless, they insisted, and promised to match any item we wanted to take. Luckily we secured the deal early, so had time to be carefully measured and fitted in order to trial the items during both the glacier training and the final rehearsal in Greenland, events both programmed for 2008.

My research into the original route was progressing well. I had read *The Heart of the Antarctic* many times now and could quote specific passages from Shackleton's diary. I was fast realising just what a tough journey it was going to be. I could just about comprehend the distance involved but it helped to be able to put it into perspective by reminding myself of the Yukon race that Will and I had done in early 2005. Then, we covered three hundred miles – just over a third of the Antarctic journey. I had also obtained some detailed maps of our start point on Ross Island and of the Beardmore Glacier, so was able to match them with the diary entries, which immediately brought the story to life. By marking Shackleton's daily locations I was able to plot the exact route and in particular note where he had had specific difficulty. It was crystal-clear to me that we would have to be well prepared for everything the Beardmore Glacier would throw at us. Just as Shackleton had been counselled by the expert of his time, Nansen, I went in search of advice. But unlike Shackleton, I intended to listen to it.

More people had stood on the surface of the moon than had attempted our intended route. Throughout the history of polar exploration, only twelve people have started from the Antarctic coast, crossed the Ross Ice Shelf, and ascended the Beardmore Glacier from its mouth to its source. The group we were retracing pioneered this route in 1908–09. Then in 1911–12 Captain Scott with Evans, Wilson, Bowers and Oates used the same route to get to the Pole, tragically perishing on the return journey. Nearly eighty years later, in 1985, Robert Swan, Roger Mear and Gareth Wood set off from Scott's hut at Cape Evans and followed in his footsteps to the Pole. But no one had actually set off from Shackleton's *Nimrod* hut to retrace his 1908–09 journey.

A number of scientists and glaciologists had worked at many remote field sites in this Antarctic region, but one stood above the rest. His name was Charles Swithinbank, a man who had dedicated most of his life to the study of Antarctic glaciology, particularly of the Beardmore Glacier. I would get no better insight to our route, and the character of the Beardmore, than from him and Robert Swan – but I had to find them first. Charles and I were both members of a couple of polar societies so I made contact with him through them, then out of the blue a close friend of Joanna's mentioned that she had been at university with Robert Swan and had often fed the then-penniless explorer as he planned and fund-raised for his 1985 expedition. Meetings were arranged.

Clutching maps and aerial photographs, I travelled to meet Charles Swithinbank at his home just outside Cambridge. Charles, now in his eighties, but still with that upright bearing and the weather-beaten complexion of an outdoors man, proved an invaluable help. It was a fascinating day, mainly spent poring over the line I had drawn on the maps which marked Shackleton's route. We intended to stay as close to it as possible, so I was keen to learn about the conditions we would face and in particular the threat from crevasses on the glacier.

'It is very unlikely that you will encounter anything as wide as this house for instance,' he said to my relief, 'but actually, the more dangerous ones are those just wide enough to break a leg or wedge you upside down by your rucksack or sledge-harness should you fall into one. You'll have fun getting out of those.' I half-smiled in response at the prospect.

Over lunch, Charles bombarded me with wise questions and listened intently to our plan, parts of which he picked apart.

'You'll not be able to start like Shackleton did on 29 October as ALE won't be set up by then. The very earliest they will get you there will be around early to mid-November but the Ross Sea should still be frozen for you to land on. So you should be able to get to the hut.'

This was key information and not something I had so far talked through with David Rootes. It was also rather a blow, as all my calculations had been based around a late October start and getting to the ninety-seven mile meeting point on 9 January 2009. This news knocked at least two weeks off the time available to achieve that.

Charles was supportive of our centenary journey. He said that it would do no harm and as long as the preparation was well thought through, then no lives would be put in danger. But he was concerned about our science project to collect ice samples from the Beardmore Glacier for Hull University. It sounded simple enough but none of us were scientists and he said that it could get in the way of everything else we had to do. Deep down I knew that he was probably right but Will, in particular, wanted to help David Drewry, who had spoken so enthusiastically about the opportunity at the Christie's launch a year earlier.

On the train back to London I reflected on Charles's advice. I was encouraged that he was supportive of our overall plans and I was confident that, with the right training, we could cope with the Beardmore. More than this, though, was the fact that I had spoken at length with a hugely respected polar figure who had actually been to the area we would be travelling through and nothing he had said rung alarm bells.

In June 2007 a date was arranged to meet Robert Swan. Robert was a great admirer of Captain Scott and while at Durham University he drew up plans to be the first to retrace Scott's 1911–12 journey. His idea was as bold as the original one had been. In 1985 he bought a ship, sailed it down to the Ross Sea, built a hut next to Scott's, overwintered and then set off along the original route with Roger Mear and Gareth Wood to the South Pole, without any communication with the outside world. It was a truly pioneering project on a grand scale. They achieved all they set out to accomplish but on arriving at the Pole discovered that their ship had sunk and that some of his team would have to overwinter for another season until a salvage operation could be organised. Then in 1989 he led another expedition to the North Pole, becoming the first person in history to walk to both points on the globe.

I was thrilled at the prospect of meeting Robert but nervous as well. Thrilled for, after Shackleton and Scott, he was the only person to have completed our route to the Pole and therefore could give us invaluable advice; nervous, because I knew that he was a straight talker and if he was unimpressed by our project, then he would make it plainly obvious. His book, *In the Footsteps of Scott*, was the only account, other than Scott's and Shackleton's own logs, that describes in detail the journey we were undertaking, so I made sure I had re-read it prior to our meeting.

Robert was everything I had imagined. A small, immensely powerful man with piercing blue eyes and the windblown skin of the explorer. Tough, direct, interested in our plans but enquiring, unquestionably passionate about the Antarctic and deeply respectful of those who had journeyed before us. He grilled me with questions about our training, what equipment we had, the types of sledge we would use, how would we prepare for the crevasses of the Beardmore, our fund-raising strategy, how well we got on with each other and even my age, which

The Arrol-Johnson motor car.

he thought was pretty much the 'top end' of the range for this type of journey. The list continued but, thankfully, he liked our plan and at the end of the evening he offered to help as a fund-raising patron, which was an enormous boost and finally told me that, at forty-eight years of age, I should be 'OK'. It had been an important couple of meetings, for no two other figures had the experience and knowledge of the polar regions than Charles and Robert. And to have them as supporters of our endeavour was a significant boost to morale.

1907

During the early summer of 1907, Shackleton carried out final preparations to his expedition. The equipment from Norway arrived just in time and the twelve Manchurian ponies he had purchased from China were scheduled to meet the expedition in New Zealand towards the end of the year. One item of equipment delivered to the docks to be stowed on board the already heavily laden *Nimrod* was a car. Sir William Beardmore, his main financial backer, had recently become the major shareholder in the Paisley-based Arrol-Johnson motor company and ordered a vehicle to be designed that could assist the expedition in transporting loads over the ice and snow. It was not something that Shackleton had particularly asked for but he was hopeful it would help move the heavy loads which would otherwise fall to the ponies. Shackleton's energy, meanwhile, was directed into 'the beastly process' of raising more money. He was heavily in debt and despite the potential book rights and income from lectures on his return, the financial position was still a huge worry to him.

2007

We were also worried about money, and still needed that major backer. The breakthrough we had been searching for came in June 2007. Former soldier and friend of mine since childhood, Bill Shipton, who I had drafted on to the fund-raising committee, believed he had a City contact who would be very interested in taking the headline sponsorship. Aside from the publicity to be gained from the potential media coverage, we believed we could also make an offer that would prove attractive to any interested sponsor. As the 97-Mile Team would be flying in to complete the last phase of the journey we could offer a place in that team to be filled by whoever the sponsor wished – and the person Bill had in mind, and who might jump at the offer, was David Royds, owner of Matrix Group, a London-based financial services company. David Royds is distantly related to Charles Royds, who was a member of Scott's *Discovery* expedition, after whom Cape Royds is named. They are both descended from the same Lancashire family.

An initial meeting was arranged and I asked Robert Swan to join us to help with the pitch for our case. Robert had on many occasions, in boardrooms all over the world, successfully persuaded corporate bosses to part with large sums of money; to have him at our side was invaluable. During the meeting the fly was cast. We explained what we wanted to commemorate and why we

thought it unique. We outlined the costs involved and highlighted the areas where we felt Matrix would benefit from association with the Shackleton name and the expedition. And finally, we offered David Royds a place on the 97-Mile Team and the opportunity to stand at the South Pole. The presentation was well received, Robert was very persuasive and there was definite interest, but understandably no concrete commitments were made. We would just have to wait.

Taking stock at the end of 2007, we were now in good shape. Our bank balance was beginning to grow to a healthy size. Our training was going well, but we still had more to learn on the planned trips to France and Greenland. Henry Adams was fast becoming an efficient quartermaster. He was in weekly contact with Timberland about our clothing and he had made good progress in gathering together all the equipment we would need. Shovels, repair kits, cookers, skis and tents all gathered in crowding piles at his house. Will had sourced all our food, chocolate and energy drinks from an expedition supplier and Dave Cornell and I were in close touch with ALE over the costs and details of the expedition once on the Antarctic. And by now, through growing media coverage, we were being approached by production companies eager to explore the options for making a television documentary about the expedition. It was all looking good but with under a year to go, I kept hearing Robert Swan's parting comment to me after our first meeting, 'Only two things stop an Antarctic expedition – the weather and money.'

2008

The training in France was a huge success. Camped for a week at the base of Mont Blanc and under the experienced eye of Simon Abrahams, a widely respected mountain guide from Chamonix, Will, Henry and I spent many hours discussing and practising all that would be required of us on the Beardmore. We agreed that whenever we roped up together I would lead, Will would be next and Henry would bring up the rear. That way we knew exactly what each of us had to do in an emergency and we kept practising the rescue drills until we were satisfied with the levels of trust in each other. We returned to England quietly confident that at last we had the technical skills to tackle any difficulty that the Antarctic might throw at us.

Soon after our return from Chamonix one of the independent film companies contacted me again, eager to explore the feasibility of making a documentary juxtaposing Shackleton's journey with ours. We explained that we were not keen to have a cameraman join us during the expedition, as it would intrude on the intensity of the isolation and further complicate the already expensive logistics burden. The film company fully understood this, so we devised a plan that involved one cameraman, Sean Smith, travelling with us as far as Shackleton's hut; we would film the journey and then Sean would meet us again a few miles from the South Pole to cover the last couple of days. Sean was an accomplished mountaineer of high regard and understood exactly why we were reticent about taking along an additional person. But he was keen to travel with us to Greenland to film our final training, which we happily agreed to.

During the spring months that followed we edged closer to finalising a contract with Matrix. We trod carefully, for we had no fallback and to lose Matrix's support at this late stage would be catastrophic. Until the money was in the bank we could not rest, but the signs were increasingly positive. The firm was ordering badges and labels to put on the sledges and clothing and it was content for us to refer to the project as the Matrix Shackleton Centenary Expedition. We were quietly optimistic, but far from complacent, as ALE was close to finalising its contract and about to send us a £300,000 invoice, this new figure included the cost of the 97-mile team.

There was little more I could do with regard to researching the original journey. I had the maps I needed, I had studied aerial photographs of the Beardmore and plotted our route. Using Shackleton and Swan's daily mileage statistics I also calculated that we would need to average between ten and twelve nautical miles per day if we were to hit the 97-mile point by 9 January 2009. And I had requested permission from the New Zealand Antarctic Heritage Trust to enter Shackleton's hut and for Sean to film inside it.

As summer approached, Will, Henry and I were ready for our final period of training in Greenland. Keen to test ourselves without a guide, we travelled to Milne Land, an island off the east coast which I had been advised provided everything we needed to replicate our journey: a flat expanse of sea ice, a crevasse-ridden glacier and a steep climb up on to a small ice cap. It sounded like the perfect stage for the dress rehearsal. With Sean joining us for the first week, the four of us travelled first to Iceland then flew in to Constable Point airfield on the mainland. From there we transferred all our equipment on to snowmobiles and trailers for an eight-hour drive across the frozen sea of Scoresby Sound, passing polar bear tracks and towering icebergs trapped in the sea ice, before we finally reached the edge of Milne Land. We pushed ourselves hard each day by covering more than the required daily mileage and up far steeper slopes than we would experience down south, all captured on film by Sean. It was exhausting work but vital that everything we did replicated as close as possible, or even exceeded, the actual journey. Most important of all was the period we spent amongst the crevasses of the glacier. Each night we pored over notes we had made in Chamonix. Then the following day, travelling roped up, without a guide to inspect our knots, we set off into the maze of obstacles and plunging chasms intent on reaching the glacier's mouth.

It was messy at first. As lead man I travelled too fast or too slow, Will as next in line got tangled in the slack rope or pulled ahead when it became taut and Henry as rear man got cold in the shadows waiting for us to get a move on. But over time our confidence grew as we threaded our way along and across the narrow ridges of ice. But it was slow and serious work requiring patience and care, eased by a good dose of laughter. Much later, I learned that Henry felt that he was untested goods in training. He knew that Will and I had learned a lot from the Yukon race and that both of us had pushed ourselves in other endurance events. The gap in experience fuelled him to train harder and to realise that perhaps he had more to learn about himself in doing the expedition than Will and I. That made him determined to do his best, so that he would be able to look back on the way he performed and behaved with pride.

We returned to England pleased with what we had achieved and feeling as well-prepared as we were ever going to be. The three of us were a very strong team now. Four years earlier we were strangers, and now it was almost as if we were brothers. The level of leg-pulling was high, which was a positive thing but I had also discovered what made Henry and Will tick – what annoyed them, how to recognise the signs that they were disgruntled or low and what they actually meant when they said they were 'fine'. Overall, what was really encouraging were the similarities between us. We were passionate about the project and determined to succeed, we were equally childish when needed, and serious when required and we were of similar fitness levels, although at fourteen years older than Henry I was conscious that by the closing stages of the journey I would be drawing more on my mental strength than on the physical. Following our return to England there were only five months left before our departure for Chile and then the Antarctic.

1907

In the build-up to Shackleton's departure, final preparations were drawing to a close and as the *Nimrod*'s departure date loomed, he and his ship were summoned to the Isle of Wight to be inspected by

Nimrod

King Edward VII, who was enjoying the social events surrounding the annual regatta at Cowes. It was a great honour and Shackleton could not disobey his sovereign. On 4 August 1907, the King and Queen Alexandra were piped aboard the tiny *Nimrod*, dwarfed on all sides by the leviathans of the greatest naval fleet in the world. From every mast and rigging line on every ship coloured bunting and signal flags danced in the sea breeze, some sending messages of good luck and Godspeed. To convey their hope and admiration for this great British endeavour, the King pinned an enamelled medal to Shackleton's chest, thereby making him a member of the Royal Victorian Order, and Queen Alexandra presented him with a Union Flag which she requested be planted at the South Pole. With the ceremony over, the *Nimrod* headed out into the Channel bound for New Zealand. Shackleton remained behind as he had more business to attend to, but would meet the ship later. At last the British Antarctic Expedition was underway.

2008

With five months left until our departure we were now confident that Matrix were right behind us. Timberland's clothing had been trialled with great success in Greenland and the minor changes we'd requested – an extra inch or so in the pocket depths, longer sleeves cuffs – had been made. Our permit to film in Shackleton's hut had arrived, our PR company was getting us good coverage in the media and the BBC had confirmed that it would be broadcasting a programme about our journey when we returned. ALE had also finalised the details of the logistics support: the Ice Team would be on the first flight from Punta Arenas in Chile to Patriot Hills, ALE's logistics base in the Antarctic. From there we would be flown across the vast Ross Ice Shelf by Twin Otter aircraft to land on the frozen sea right by Shackleton's hut. The 97-Mile Team would follow the same route as us to Patriot Hills and then fly on to meet us at the point where Shackleton stopped – hopefully on 9 January 2009. Having reached the Pole, we would be picked up and flown back to Patriot Hills and then return to Chile. Everything was coming together but a couple of surprises still remained.

Patrick had finally decided that he would not be joining the 97-Mile Team, which meant that another place was now vacant. It was getting late in the day to find someone else, although Dave and his team were still to do their final training. Then Matrix boss David Royds decided that rather than taking his place on the 97-Mile Team, he wanted to run a national competition to fill the slot. It was a brilliant suggestion. More than three thousand people applied and, after initial sifting, interviews and a weekend in the Brecon Beacons for the final five, the lucky winner was chosen – twenty-three-year-old Andrew Ledger, from Sheffield. Andrew, intent on joining the army, had been working as a labourer and found out about the competition to fill the final place by searching for 'dangerous jobs' on the internet. Such was the national interest in the event that he was paraded on BBC breakfast TV after his win. Matrix was delighted that it had received the media coverage it wanted and we were pleased that we had filled a place in the 97-Mile Team with a high-grade individual who was clearly very motivated, fit and appreciated the significance of the project he was joining.

By October 2008 all our kit and equipment was packed and ready to be freighted to Chile. The last items to be stowed were my skis, as I had asked Joanna, Max and Alicia to paint messages and illustrations on them which I could look at every day of the journey to spur me on. It was an idea that I had copied from Børge Ousland, the legendary Norwegian polar explorer, who had found similar memories from home motivated him through the low moments of his journeys. With little else to do I tried hard to maintain some level of fitness as well as eat as much as I could to create a reserve of fat, which I knew I would shortly need. But runs along the Thames towpath at this late stage seemed rather pointless and, because of the nervous energy building up inside me, I couldn't seem to add to the stone in weight that I had already put on. I was simply suffering from pre-match nerves.

The short time I had left belonged to Joanna and the children. On the last weekend before my departure date we celebrated Christmas at home, as I intended to be somewhere clear of the Beardmore Glacier on the actual day. Among the exchange of presents, Joanna gave me a large envelope which contained messages from friends and family members to be read on the journey. I was not allowed to open it until a suitable moment but she had asked them to be written so as to provide me with some inspiration and humour. It was a typically thoughtful gesture of hers and I was sure that the enjoyment I would get from them would far outweigh the additional kilo that I would now have to carry. I had no idea at the time just how helpful those messages were going to be.

In the days leading up to our departure I checked with Dave Cornell that he was content with the arrangements for his 97-Mile Team. It still consisted of him, Tim Fright and now Andrew Ledger, with Matty

McNair as their guide. There was still room in the plane for one more, so Dave was eager to find someone, even at this late stage, to share the cost. They were planning to conduct a final training period in Norway before Christmas and then fly out to Chile in the New Year. If Dave was unable to walk the whole route in his great-grandfather's footsteps then the planned rendezvous on 9 January 2009 was still firmly his focus, as it was for Will, Henry and I.

Our farewell party at Matrix's impressive offices was a great occasion. It was a fitting way to thank our families, sponsors and supporters but also the right setting for a special presentation to be made. Throughout the years of preparation Zaz Shackleton, Ernest Shackleton's granddaughter, had taken a close interest in our plans and been a huge support. She had in her possession a number of her grandfather's belongings, some of which had been with him on the expedition we were about to retrace. Apart from his Polar Medal, none was more significant than the compass he had taken with him on that long journey, and she wanted me to carry it to the South Pole, the place it never reached with Shackleton. It was the hugest honour, and when she presented it to me at the end of the evening there was a noticeable hush amongst the guests as they pondered the significance of the gesture. Rob Swan was also there. As well as proposing a toast to our safe return he presented me with a small teddy bear which he had carried to both the North and South Poles and he wanted me to carry it again for the children of the world.

'He will be particularly useful as he knows the way!' he joked.

1907

Having seen off the *Nimrod* on her journey south to New Zealand, Shackleton remained behind for two months desperately trying to raise more money and snatching rare moments with Emily and their young family. On 31 October 1907, as he boarded a train in London bound for Marseilles where he would join a mail ship destined for Australia, the whole project still teetered on a knife-edge because of the shortage of funds. But Shackleton's short stay in Australia proved to be valuable. There was huge enthusiasm for his venture in the country, and he departed with a £5,000 donation from the government (equivalent to £442,300 in today's money) and a group of eminent new Australian crew members, most notably a fifty-year-old, Welsh-born geologist named Edgeworth David, and one of his former pupils, Douglas Mawson.

2008

On 29 October, I set off for Punta Arenas in Chile, our launch pad to the Antarctic. Compared with Shackleton's three months at sea, my journey south took only a couple of days but I believe that our thoughts, hopes and anxieties of what we had so far achieved and what was to come were much the same. The first stage of our journey to the South Pole had begun.

CHAPTER 3

The Waiting Game

'We all looked forward eagerly to our coming venture, for the glamour of the unknown was with us and the South was calling.'

EHS, 1 January 1908

My long flight to the Chilean capital, Santiago, allowed me an opportunity to gather my thoughts and make a list of the final things that needed to be done both in Punta and at Patriot Hills. All being well, we would have only three or four days before our onward flight to the Antarctic, but it would give us enough time to get organised. All our freight had arrived so that would need sorting and we still needed to buy certain items of food. Top of the list was 'Buy Salami' as we weren't allowed to import this meat product from the UK. Salami would be our main savoury high-fat snack food each day, as it does not freeze – but I knew that Will, who had travelled ahead of us by a week, had that in hand. I was also keen to send a photo back over the satellite telephone to Bill Shipton, who was managing our website, and, crucially, I also had to make contact with Al Fastier from the New Zealand Antarctic Heritage Trust. Al held the key which would let us in to Shackleton's *Nimrod* hut. He was leading the conservation team at Cape Royds until about 5 or 6 November, but then he would be moving on to Scott's *Terra Nova* hut at Cape Evans. This was only about ten miles further along the coast, but I knew he had no form of transport so if we were delayed, we would have to collect him somehow – though heaven knows how it would be possible. Making contact with him over the next few days by satellite telephone was therefore vital. The 'to do' list grew as I worked my way through some of the important paperwork I needed; permit to visit the hut, next-of-kin and medical forms for ALE, insurance details, family contact details in case of emergency, copies of photographs taken on the route by Shackleton and Robert Swan and a list showing the contents of our medical kit. I dozed off with images in my mind of Shackleton's last-minute preparations and his departure from New Zealand on 1 January 1908.

1907

Crowds gathered at Lyttleton Harbour, on the eastern coast of New Zealand's South Island, on New Year's Eve 1907 to witness the final preparations being made to the *Nimrod*. Makeshift stalls for the Manchurian ponies had been built, more coal had been loaded, pieces of the prefabricated hut were lashed down, the crate that contained the car was re-stowed and last-minute arrangements were made to house nine dogs. It was obvious even to the layman that she was lying very low in the water but, despite the chaotic scene, everything was finally ready and the *Nimrod* exuded the optimism of the age. Minutes before departure on 1 January 1908 a wealthy, but very breathless, New Zealand farmer named George Buckley bounded up the gangway of the crowded ship, having raced from the train station. In return for being taken on the outward leg of the voyage he had given the expedition £500. His journey back to Lyttleton would be aboard the *Koonya,* which was to tow the

Nimrod to the edge of the pack ice and then return to New Zealand; by being towed, the *Nimrod* was saving three tons of coal a day. In the final hours before departure, Shackleton was deep in thought in his cabin, just as he had been before the *Discovery* sailed five years earlier. For this was the time that the last letters with guaranteed delivery could be written to loved ones. He placed a sheet of the expedition paper on the blotter and started writing tender words to his darling Emily, 'Oh Child I do want so much to have you with me now . . .'.

With a rousing cheer from thirty thousand people, and drenched by the spray from two huge underwater explosions to mark their departure, the British Antarctic Expedition was given the send-off it deserved. Small craft raced alongside the *Nimrod*, sailors sat astride rigging lines in ships at anchor in the bay and pleasure craft listed heavily to port and starboard as their passengers fought for the best view of this historic sight. Ready to commence the tow, the *Koonya* drew alongside, fastened her line and headed out to sea. The noise from the crowd was soon lost but aboard the *Nimrod* the crew gazed over her stern to savour their last fading view of land and civilisation. Looking the other way, one pair of eyes was fixed on a point beyond the bow and towards the horizon. Shackleton was returning to his new home, lured on by the siren calls of his white mistress.

2008

I met Henry and Sean, who had flown in via Madrid, at Santiago Airport. We sat in the departure lounge carrying down jackets and small plastic suitcases – mine containing the satellite telephones and video cameras, Sean's carrying his lenses, battery packs and a large camera. It was a good moment to see the team almost complete. The short onward flight to Punta Arenas arrived mid-afternoon on 30 October. Cold air that had raced over the freezing water of the Magellan Straits, probably from Antarctica, whacked into us as we stepped from the plane. We headed over the tarmac to the arrivals lounge where Will met us. At last the team was complete.

It was good to see Will. He seemed relaxed and had entered expedition mode by starting to grow a beard. He had lots to tell us.

'First thing is the flight to Patriot Hills is already delayed,' he said. 'One of the Twin Otters, which go ahead to help set up the camp, has an engine fault. Not sure how long we will be waiting but it looks like 6 November at the earliest.' It was boring news, but it wasn't the end of the world and the delay would give us plenty of time to thoroughly sort out our equipment and pare it back to the absolute minimum in order to save weight.

'Next thing is I have met up with our freight and unpacked it. It is in the ALE warehouse and we need to go there tomorrow to start sorting out the food bags and the team kit. Most of the ALE staff have arrived and we will be called forward for a number of briefings over the next day or two as well.

'And, General' – now my nickname – 'you'll be interested in this. I have been introduced to a couple of people at their family house just outside Punta who have a visitor's book which has an entry in it written by Shackleton as well as other polar explorers from over the ages. I have arranged for us to go there tomorrow afternoon.'

Will had clearly been busy, but there was still a fair few hours' work to be done on distributing the packeted food into weekly bags, weighing every item of equipment and looking at it ruthlessly, still asking the question, 'Is this really essential?' Settled into our guesthouse, it was a great feeling to be all together in Punta and now a significant step closer to setting foot on the Antarctic. For Shackleton, his final journey south was far from straightforward.

1908

For ten never-ending days the *Nimrod* and *Koonya* battled with the power of the Southern Ocean. Rarely had those experienced sailors

The Koonya *just visible above the towering swell.*

seen such seas. Everything on board was deluged as the *Nimrod* lurched from crest to trough of the angry, frothing waves. The wind scraped the spray off the sea and blasted it through fabric, rigging line and bulwark. The ponies whinnied through fear and cold. One fell and had to be destroyed – only nine remained. The dogs barked and howled. Nothing escaped the wet and the wind. Below deck, men lay drenched on their beds as each swirl of freezing water washed their sickness up and down the corridor in time with the relentless rhythm of the storm. They prayed that they might die rather than have to endure any more.

Then on the tenth day, as suddenly as it had formed, the storm died away. A homing pigeon, owned by the *Lyttleton Times* and released by Shackleton on 4 January, arrived on land with news of their journey. On the horizon ahead of the *Nimrod* lay the first icebergs that marked the edge of the sea ice. For some it was their first sighting, but for others like Wild and Shackleton it was a familiar marker. On 15 January 1908, preparations were made on the *Koonya* to release the tow rope but not before George Buckley, clutching a final bag of mail, had been rowed across to start his return journey. With a wave and a cheer both crews departed on their separate ways.

George Buckley being rowed from Nimrod *to* Koonya.

2008

The following morning we headed off to the warehouse to start sorting out our kit. Will held up a blue bag from the pile at his feet.

'You have nine bags like this which need to contain seven breakfasts, seven suppers and seven puddings each – so nine weeks' meals in total. You will notice I have dated them and chosen a start day of 8 November – let's hope that's right. In the tenth bag, which I have marked "emergency", you need to put eight days' worth of food.'

I stared at the mountain of green packets at my feet and started to read some of the labels – shepherd's pie, Thai chicken noodles, rice pudding and apple flakes, chilli con carne and porridge with raisins. We sorted the packets into piles for each meal and then started to fill our blue bags. Next we added packets of high-fat-content ghee butter and olive oil and then large plastic bags of powdered energy drinks. But the most time-consuming chore had yet to be started. During the day we would graze from a bag of flapjacks, nuts, chocolate and salami and most of that we still had to buy.

Later in the day we set off to the ALE office for our first briefing. Waiting in the small reception area I couldn't help looking at all the framed photographs that covered the walls with messages of thanks from successful expeditions over the previous years. It was an impressive roll of honour, mainly Norwegians and Canadians. I wondered if ours might be up there the following year.

ALE's briefing was very thorough and professional. Steve Jones, the operations manager at Patriot Hills, needed to be satisfied that we were absolutely prepared for the journey. Most important of all was the communication plan. We would be required to call Patriot Hills by satellite phone every day giving our position and how far we had travelled in the previous twenty-four hours. We would also tell them of any medical problems we might be having. If we missed two communication schedules or 'scheds', then the ALE search plan would be activated. The rest of the meeting focussed on what equipment we were using, what spares we were carrying, the likely weight of the sledges and then Steve briefed us on the outline plan to get us to the hut at Cape Royds.

'I am not sure yet when we will all leave here. But once we get to Patriot Hills, I will be looking to get you away as soon as possible. Your onward journey will tie up two of the three Twin Otters and there are lots of other expeditions and climbers I need to send off as well. So simply put – I want to get rid of you as soon as I can.' We were pleased to hear that we were a high priority.

'However,' Steve went on, 'you are going a sod of a long way to your start point – just over a thousand miles, and I can tell you now that the weather will play its part. So *be patient*. We will do our best for you. Swan did the journey in seventy days so you will have plenty of time, don't worry.'

ALE carried huge responsibilities and quite rightly the meeting had been carried out in a very detailed manner in order to satisfy the staff that we were not a liability. If our expedition went to plan then we would be on the ice for the firm's entire summer season and at our most distant spot would probably be at least a week away from rescue or medical help, so this was serious stuff.

1908

Having sailed into the still-weak pack ice, Shackleton was looking for somewhere to drop anchor. Although he was not in command of the *Nimrod*, he reminded Rupert England of where he should attempt to land. Under the terms of the agreement with Scott, not only was the *Discovery* hut out of bounds but Shackleton was also to keep to the east of the 170° line of longitude, as Scott regarded anything west of the line as 'his territory'. Eager not to breach this agreement, Shackleton was forced to consider selecting a site on the unstable surface of the Ice Shelf. He could see that already it had changed hugely over five years. Vast areas had calved off and were now drifting out to sea. It was too risky; he ordered England to alter course to take him back towards McMurdo Sound to find a site on land rather than on the unpredictable barrier ice. England, as captain, should not have been ordered to do anything and many hours were spent in the privacy of the cabin they shared trying to come to some arrangement whereby both their objectives could be satisfied. Eventually the expedition was offloaded, the cautious England and the impatient Shackleton parted company and the *Nimrod* set sail back to New Zealand in mid-February – carrying a letter from Shackleton to his agent, insisting that England be replaced as captain. Both men were glad to see the back of the other, but as the *Nimrod* passed from sight it suddenly dawned on the fifteen men left behind that they were the only human beings on an unmapped continent, literally at the bottom of the world. The feeling of vulnerability and isolation caused some to ponder on their chances of survival.

'What if the *Nimrod* never reaches New Zealand?' Shackleton heard Eric Marshall mutter.

'Easy,' answered 'Putty' Marston, the expedition artist and joker. 'We have a rowing boat. Some of us will row it there and get another ship.' It was a sensible question and one that Shackleton had already considered but which had conveniently been turned into a light-hearted moment.

Offloading stores from Nimrod.

2008

In the afternoon the four of us took a taxi to the edge of the town to meet up with Will's contacts who owned the visitors' book. The family house was a small, timbered building nestled in a stunning position on the coast overlooking the Magellan Straits and Tierra del Fuego. At the start of the twentieth century the family had been influential figures in Punta Arenas and everyone passing through the town, including polar explorers from the heroic age to the 1950s would have made a point of meeting with them. We were warmly welcomed and immediately offered cups of maté, the South American infused tea.

'Well, there's the book,' said our hostess, pointing to an open book on a side table lit by the late afternoon sun streaming in through the bow window.

Will, Henry and I took a few paces over to the table and gazed down on the page. I recognised Shackleton's handwriting immediately. But this was no short entry consisting of a date and a signature – he had written out the lines from a favourite poem and had dated it July 1916. The date indicated that it had been written at the end of the *Endurance* expedition, while arranging the rescue of the men from Elephant Island, which was finally successful on 30 August 1916. Knowing when it had been written and the remarkable journey that he had just endured, the words resonated within me as Henry read them aloud.

> We were the fools who could not rest
> In the dull earth we left behind
> But burned with passion for the South
> And drank strange frenzy from its wind
> The world where wise men sit at ease
> Fades from our unregretful eyes
> And thus across uncharted seas
> We stagger on our enterprise

We took it in turns to read it to ourselves. Also slipped in to the page was a striking photographic portrait of Shackleton that he had given his host. I reached into my trouser pocket and with a bit of ceremony, placed Shackleton's compass on the visitor's book and opened the hinged lid. I explained to our hostess just what this item was, an explanation that drew quiet gasps of disbelief. Sean had assembled his camera by now and was keen to get a shot of the book and the compass together. I sensed that this handwritten poem was a rare gem of 'Shackletonia' that had never before reached the public domain.

The following day was spent back at the warehouse slicing chocolate bars into bite-sized chunks, taking wrappers off as many food items as possible, partly to reduce weight but also to make them easier to eat by not having to unwrap something in gloved hands in a fifty-knot wind. Outside I tested the solar panels, which we would be using to charge our battery-operated equipment, by angling them towards the sun just to ensure they were working. They had been fine in England just three days before but there seemed an obsessive need to check everything just one more time. Later that evening back at the guest house I removed the memory card from my camera and slotted it into the small, handheld computer which I then attached to the satellite phone, so I could 'upload' pictures to our website back in England. Again, I had practised this procedure with Bill Shipton, but it still needed to be checked. It was a maddeningly slow process due to the signal being periodically interrupted because of the loss of satellites passing overhead; not a problem we would encounter on the Antarctic, I sensed.

It had been another useful day making the final adjustments to our food and equipment. In particular I was pleased that we had provided Bill with a photograph, text and a recorded message to place on the website. I was very keen not to overburden myself with an endless requirement to send daily messages and photos back each day for the website, but it was important to keep our huge number of supporters, now worldwide, abreast of how we were getting on. All that we needed now was for the aircraft to be repaired and then a break in the weather at Patriot Hills and we could get underway. I went to sleep with Robert Swan's prophetic words ringing in my head. Money was no longer an issue, but the weather was.

1908

At Cape Royds, Shackleton had found an ideal site to set up his winter base. Over the days that followed the *Nimrod*'s departure the hut was erected, unfit animals were exercised and stores were unpacked; boxes left outside were carefully arranged so they could be easily accessed in the wild blizzards and darkness that the imminent winter would bring. The location of the hut was perfect. It provided everything required to survive – shelter, water and food. It was nested in a shallow bowl of ground surrounded on three sides by a shield of dark volcanic rock formed from the ancient lava flow from Mount Erebus. Close by was a small freshwater lake and, within walking distance, a colony of Adélie penguins.

The men quickly made the interior of the hut home-like. Despite the inexperience of some, they all knew that any fool could be uncomfortable. Shelves made from empty packing cases were screwed to the walls and the main dining table was attached to pulleys so it could be hoisted up to the rafters after use, creating more space. The wiring for the acetylene gas lighting system was threaded around the sleeping bays, and thick curtains were fastened on rings so they could be opened and closed to create a degree of privacy around each bed space. Room was found for the sewing machine, a printing press, a simple science lab and a kitchen with a coal-fired stove. Tinned food was arranged in neat rows; jar labels of familiar brands were a constant reminder of home. Hams and legs of mutton were hung from the rafters and tin plates and mugs, already chipped, gathered warmth by the stove. And a framed photograph of the King and Queen, from the *Illustrated London News,* was hung on a wall. It was cramped, but cosy and relatively warm. Only Shackleton had his own cubicle. Outside, kennels were made for the dogs and now their puppies, mangers were constructed

Winter quarters at Cape Royds.

for the ponies and the car was housed in a makeshift garage of packing cases. All was ready for the approaching Antarctic winter.

2008

For us, the morning was interrupted by a phone call from ALE telling us that first the Iluyshin was due into Punta Arenas airport later that day and that the Twin Otters were on their way to Patriot Hills. Second, we needed to go to their office for our medical brief. The arrival of the Russian plane was a step in the right direction at least, but it seemed that because of high winds, preparations were slow at Patriot Hills so a delay to our departure still seemed inevitable. We passed the morning putting the finishing touches to our kit in the warehouse. There was really no more that we could do. Thirty blue food bags stood neatly in a row beside our sledges. Our skis, sticks and the tent were all squeezed into one bag and the group kit was boxed up ready for final distribution at Patriot Hills. Henry had meticulously weighed each item so that he knew what to give us so we carried equal loads. All that remained now was for the whole consignment to be weighed and put on the Iluyshin.

If there was one area of our preparation that I felt had not been covered properly it was our medical training. I was the only one with any previous tuition and that had been pretty rudimentary: one day spent with an Army medic, which had been useful but not enough. I was confident that we were carrying a comprehensive medical kit to deal with pain relief and other minor ailments but the thought of stabilising someone with a serious spinal or neck injury following a fall into a crevasse and then getting them to a place where a plane could pick them up was not something I wanted to dwell on too much.

For the next hour we listened intently to the ALE doctor as he described the signs and symptoms of frostbite, backed up with a detailed slide show of previous patients of his who had got it very wrong. As far as I saw it, frostbite was a self-inflicted injury. Never for one moment did I underestimate just how ruthless and patient we would have to be to avoid any cold injury but I could see how easy it would be to ignore the signs when you were utterly exhausted and couldn't face stopping in order to force the blood back into the tips of your fingers. It would also be up to each of us to look out for the signs of frostbite in each other.

Next the ALE doctor examined the contents of our medical kit. I had packed a range of painkillers, which included five phials of morphine and muscle relaxants, antibiotics, creams, splints, bandages, airways, iodine spray, a thermometer, aloe vera, sun cream, syringes, scissors and a suture kit. The doctor was impressed with what we were carrying and I handed over a list of all the items so he knew what we had with us. On the walk back to the guesthouse I realised I was more concerned about a serious fall on the Beardmore Glacier than I was about frostbite. But I kept reminding myself that we were very well prepared and had come through four years of training without any injury. But now that we were about to depart I was aware of how vulnerable the Ice Team would be, for help in an emergency would be only by phone, with actual hands-on assistance possibly a week away.

With our equipment all packed and ready there was little else to do but sit and wait for news of our departure. We had been promised a seat on the first flight, because of our need to get to Cape Royds, but we began to notice more and more expeditions gathering in the town, all waiting for the mounting backlog to clear. The supermarkets were filling up with small groups of easily-identifiable people wearing thick pile jackets with sponsor's logos emblazoned over them. Punta Arenas is not overwhelmed with fine restaurants so it was unsurprising that each evening the same groups would congregate in the same places to stuff themselves to keep their weight on. It was a time to chat and find out each other's plans. There were Finns, Spaniards, Brazilians, Brits, Russians, Czechs, Canadians and Americans, all with different dreams. Some would be man-hauling unsupported to the Pole from Hercules Inlet.

Others were doing that but kiting back as well, and then there were the mountaineers aiming to climb Mount Vinson to finish off their tally of the seven highest summits on the seven continents. There was even a Czech photographer who was heading off to photograph a vast colony of Emperor penguins. It was a rich and colourful tapestry of people drawn to the bottom of the world, each with a passionate desire to fulfil an ambition; we were no different.

One was Mark Langridge, a fellow British Army soldier, who wanted to be the first man to ski without any outside assistance to the South Pole and back, along the recognised route from Hercules Inlet. His was an awesome challenge as he would set off pulling a sledge filled to the brim with food and fuel for ninety days, and weighing 156 kgs. His plan was to depot his rations every five miles on the outward leg so that his sledge would only carry essentials for the return journey as he retraced his route back from the Pole through the depots of food and fuel. It was an immense undertaking, as he had very little margin for delay. He had planned for his outward journey to take fifty days and the return leg forty. And knowing that the cut-off date had to be the end of January, he could afford hardly any delay due to bad weather; any nagging injury would stop him dead in his tracks. Therefore, every day spent waiting in Punta was one day less available to him for travel. Although I sensed his growing frustration, Mark remained astonishingly buoyant and positive. As the delay mounted he calculated how many more miles each day he would have to cover to keep on track to fulfil his goal – it never seemed to worry him as the figure steadily increased. He exuded optimism, the premier quality that Shackleton believed a polar explorer should have.

1908

By March, Shackleton was content with the progress his team had made. The expedition leader's frustration that had emerged during the closing stages of the sea voyage had now faded with the departure of Rupert England and the *Nimrod*. With the hut built and a daily routine now established, he felt more in control. But he was still troubled. He needed to maintain the morale of his men through the coming winter. He knew, too, he hadn't brought enough ponies (the car was also proving useless) and also that no one really knew how to handle the animals. Fewer ponies meant he would have to take fewer people on the journey, and gnawing away at the back of his mind was the uncertainty of whether he was up to the physical demands of the journey ahead. No matter how dismissive he was over his sickness on the *Discovery* expedition, he knew it had exposed his vulnerabilities. But he knew also that the men must not see his black mood. There was a need for strong leadership.

'Before the onset of winter I wish for there to be an attempt to reach the summit of Mount Erebus,' Shackleton announced after supper one evening. It was a bold and clever proposal. Bold, because not only was it a first ascent, but no one had any climbing experience and they had no bespoke equipment. And clever, for if successful then it would be a great boost to morale before the winter and credit him with a significant achievement so soon into the expedition. The air was thick with pipe smoke and the smell of coffee but through it he could scent a positive reaction to his announcement. He continued.

'I would also like for us to print a book whilst we are here. I was the editor of the *South Polar Times* when I was at Hut Point with Scott and it would be a wonderful record of our time if we produced something similar here. We will all contribute and Putty,' here he turned to the expedition artist, 'I would like you to provide the illustrations.'

2008

Daily updates of news for our departure were still not good. The preparation of the ice runway at Patriot Hills was proving to be slow work, because of the strong winds. Even if the drifted snow

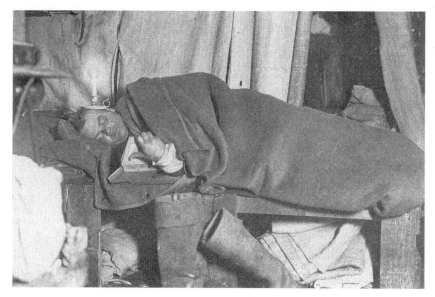

Putty Marston reading after lights out with a candle on his head.

that had collected from the previous year had been cleared, the Iluyshin would not be able to land with a crosswind in excess of eighteen knots.

Morale among the three of us was beginning to fray. I was in no doubt that eventually we would get going, but because of the distances we had to travel and the importance that we attached to reaching S88° 23′ E162° on 9 January 2009, we had set ourselves an immovable target, which every day of delay was making more and more difficult to attain. If the delay continued, the 'difficult' would become 'impossible'. I noticed the rising level of frustration in everything we talked about. There were endless discussions about the weight of our sledges and had we pared back the load to its absolute minimum. Henry was quizzed over and over about the need to take extra items such as cookers, ski bindings and spare boots. We had satisfied ourselves on countless previous occasions that everything we had packed was crucial. But now that we had time to dwell on it, the nightmare scenario of having to cover more miles per day than we had planned for was fast becoming a reality.

I spent hours studying the maps, concerned about my ability to navigate the team across the Ross Ice Shelf to arrive at the foot of Mount Hope. These were all natural anxieties felt before any event that requires extreme physical and mental demands to accomplish. Once we were underway I knew that these thoughts would drop away. I kept hearing Shackleton reminding me to be patient.

During the days of the waiting game spent in endless coffee shops we met and chatted with a number of interesting people – other fellow travellers, but also those working for ALE. One such individual was Shaun Norman, an ex-London-based New Zealander who had spent twenty-five summers and three winters in the Antarctic working at McMurdo Sound, the South Pole and on Deception Island. He had driven dog teams along the Antarctic Peninsula for The British Antarctic Survey in the 1960s and early seventies and even descended into the crater of Mount Erebus. Every line under his grey beard told an intriguing story.

He was interested in our plans, for he had also worked in the Ross Sea region and around the Shackleton and Scott huts. One afternoon, I asked him to come to our guesthouse to tell us what he knew of the route we would be taking. I laid out the 1:250,000 scale map on a small table and asked him to describe what we could expect. He started on a positive note.

'Firstly, I hope the sea is still frozen. It should be. But every day we are delayed here is one day closer to when the sea will break up.' Pointing with a gnarled finger close to the contours of Ross Island he continued, 'You should aim to land about here, right under the eye of Erebus, and then you'll only have a short walk to the hut. Be careful of the Adélie penguin colony, as it's protected. The hut is great. I slept in it many times, long before it became a protected site.' For a moment I looked at Sean with envy at the thought of him unfurling his sleeping bag in the *Nimrod* hut and it was a good few seconds before I was back from my daydream to carry on listening to what he had to say.

'You will make good progress across the sea for the first couple of days,' said Shaun. 'The sledges will glide very nicely over the thin layer of snow and patches of sea ice. You will pass Scott's *Terra Nova* hut, Inaccessible Island, the Erebus glacier tongue and then after a couple of days you will see the McMurdo station and the *Discovery* hut. It's pretty straightforward up to that point.' Nothing he had said so far had alarmed us.

'Next you need to pass round Observation Hill. Look out for the cross on top – put there as a memorial to Captain Scott. Once you get round the hill you will reach the small cluster of green huts of the New Zealand Scott Base. Then you are almost on to the Ross Ice Shelf and heading for the Williams Field air base.'

'Is it obvious when you leave the sea ice and get on to the Ice Shelf?' asked Henry.

'Yes, but not in a dramatic way. It's certainly not a climb up. You will pass through an area of broken and disturbed ice which marks the tide line. But it is pretty narrow and should only take you a few minutes. Then you will be on the Ice Shelf proper and heading towards the air base, which you will see in the distance about five miles away. Once you are through that you are on your own. Next stop, four hundred miles away, Mount Hope.'

I reminded Shaun that we were following Shackleton's route so we would have to pass to the west of White Island and then head past Black Island and Minna Bluff.

'You could always try and pick up the Antarctic Traverse.'

We had heard of the Antarctic 'road', or traverse, but had no real idea of what it looked like, where it actually went nor how we would find it on the ground.

'It's a surveyed track that goes from McMurdo to the Pole and is used by a fuel convoy that takes aviation fuel to the airfield at the science base,' said Shaun. 'It crosses the Ross Ice Shelf and then goes up the Leveret glacier and on to the Pole. It doesn't go in exactly the same direction as you guys but it might help for a day or two if you can find it. It is marked by a series of green flags on bamboo poles and follows roughly this line . . .' Shaun took my pencil and drew a scribble across the map to illustrate the rough route. I looked at Will and Henry and sensed they were mulling something over. Should we use it or not? It might help us make up some distance quickly but how easy was it to find? But it wasn't there in Shackleton's time, so would it be right to use it? It was a tempting thought.

'Now, I suggest you keep away from the western edge of White Island by some distance as this is a shear zone where two ice sheets meet and oppose each other, creating crevasses – big ones.' This was the first time that I had heard mention of crevasses on this part of the journey. Shackleton had commented on them in his diary when crossing this point but he had passed through them without roping up and had avoided trouble.

'You should be fine and not need to rope up, but just keep away from the island by a good few miles. If they are there you'll see signs on the surface and how the snow lies will give them away,' Shaun said, trying to sound reassuring. 'The rest is plain sailing. Providing the snow is not too deep you will make good time across the Ice Shelf. I haven't been on to the Beardmore but I assume you have got crampons?' he asked.

We nodded.

'How about your crevasse rescue skills?' he continued.

'We have practised a good drill and are happy with all that,' Will answered with confidence.

We spent the rest of the afternoon feeding off his enormous breadth of experience. He quizzed us extensively about all aspects of our preparation and the journey ahead, without once trying to catch us out or appearing dubious or negative about our plan. He was just being thorough as Swithinbank and Swan had been.

1908

No time was wasted between Shackleton's announcement of the Erebus ascent and the departure of the team. Over three days the individuals were selected, equipment and food were packed and loaded on a sledge which they would all man-haul. Jameson Adams had been put in overall charge but, confusingly, Shackleton had chosen Edgeworth David to lead the summit party. On the morning of 5 March 1908 the party of six leaned into their harnesses, the sledge runners squeaked on the snow and they headed off towards the forward slopes of Mount Erebus, which dominated the skyline ahead of them. The snow was deep but over the following five days they made brisk progress up the gradual incline until they were forced to depot the sledge. Had the volcano required any climbing expertise then this short journey would have ended in disaster. Unable to carry any of the heavy items to provide shelter from the wind and low temperatures, the team hung cooking equipment and

The Erebus party packing across the old crater 11000 ft above sea-level   March 1908

sleeping bags off numb shoulders and plodded on through the knee-deep snow like an army in retreat. Five days after setting off, this amateur party became the first men to peer over the crater lip through the sulphurous smoke rising out of Mount Erebus. With the use of a hypsometer, Adams recorded the height they had reached as 13,500 feet. The return journey back down to the sledge and then onwards to the hut took only one day. A welcoming party cheered the weary mountaineers into the warmth of the hut to hear the detail of their ordeal. With his swollen fingers wrapped around an enamel mug of Lipton's tea, Shackleton sat and listened to their story, quietly delighted by the expedition's first significant success.

2008

While all the maps I'd spent the afternoon poring over with Shaun were still spread out on the table, I took the opportunity to input the data for all the waypoints along the journey into my handheld GPS. There were some obvious ones: Cape Evans, White Island, Mount Hope, Buckley Island, the point ninety-seven miles from the Pole, and the South Pole itself. But some of these were hundreds of miles apart and knowing how vital it was to break down the journey into measurable stages, I needed to enter some more. So I picked points adjacent to mountains and glaciers that we would be able to recognise from the map – Mount Discovery, Socks Glacier, Adams and Marshall Ranges. It was a slow and painstaking process to first work out the precise latitude and longitude of the point I had chosen and then to enter it into the GPS. One digit entered incorrectly would send us way off course. I checked and double-checked the information and got Will to look over my work before he entered the same data into the spare GPS.

Lying in bed that evening and listening to the rain driving into the draughty windows of my room I read the appendix to *The Heart of the Antarctic* where Shackleton explained how he navigated and measured distance on his journey. I read with interest, looking for references to his compass which I could see out of the corner of my eye on my bedside table. 'The latitude observations were taken with a three-inch theodolite, which was carefully adjusted before the start for the Southern journey . . . the remainder of the distance marched toward the South was calculated by sledge meters and dead reckoning. At noon each day the prismatic compasses were placed in the true meridian, and checked against the theodolite compass and the steering compass.'

On 6 November we had been in Punta for a week and were already four days past the day we had hoped to leave. We had received our emplaning instructions from ALE, weighed and labelled all our kit, visited every tourist site, been to the cinema more than once, eaten as much as we could, attended a Remembrance Day service in the Anglican church and even listened repeatedly to President-Elect Obama's victory speech on the television. Emails were piling up on the expedition website asking for news but there was little to give, apart from a sense of frustration growing by now into mild despair. Would we still be able to stick to the schedule, and rendezvous on 9 January? The timing was going to be very tight. There was nothing else to do but wait for the phone call. After a further four days of waiting, early on 10 November it finally came.

'Get ready. The bus will be with you in one hour. We aim to fly at nine and be in Patriot Hills by mid-afternoon.'

With two months' worth of salami in one bag and the satellite telephones and video cameras in an other, I felt like an astronaut heading out on his final walk to the rocket. Sean followed behind with two huge camera bags slung over each shoulder. The Iluyshin cargo plane looked an ominous sight. It was vast and I tried hard to imagine it landing under control on a runway of sheet ice. We climbed aboard and squeezed down the side of the plane, over rudimentary canvas seats, until we were all packed tightly in. I couldn't stretch out at all. Inches from my knees and face was a cargo net holding together all the freight for the numerous expeditions and the first load of food and equipment to set up the tented camp at Patriot Hills. We all buckled ourselves in and waited to take off. Some took out earphones and iPods, others turned on head torches and starting reading books; many others simply folded their arms and tried to grab some sleep. The noise from the engines grew louder, heralding our departure. At last we were on our way to the Antarctic, a four-hour flight for this stage, but then another twelve hundred miles before we reached the *Nimrod* hut. As I felt the aircraft's wheels lift off the runway, I knew we would soon be a significant step closer.

Ten minutes later, the Russian loadmaster signalled that we could unclip our belts. I was first off the chair, climbing the cargo net to claim a comfy spot. Encased in the warmth of my down jacket I wriggled into position, hoping to sleep for the next four hours. From my vantage point I had a final glance around the huge cabin. Shafts of light from the many head torches flitted around until finally settling down on the pages of books. I noticed one person was reading the journals of Captain Scott. We had our copy of *The Heart of the Antarctic* with us, but now was not the time to read it. We would save that for when we could see with our own eyes what Shackleton was writing about.

I was woken by a tap on my foot with the news that we had ten minutes before landing. Although it had been early morning when we had left Punta Arenas, I was now conscious of the shafts of bright light pouring in from the cockpit area and above the doors. It was a reminder that we had left behind darkness – constant daylight would now be our companion.

We all returned to our seats and sat patiently, waiting for the thump of the wheels hitting the ice. The engines began to scream and suddenly we felt the impact of the undercarriage as we landed. The screaming continued as the engines reversed their thrust in order to slow up the barely controllable slide along the sheet ice. At last the beast seemed to be nearing a stop. The plane turned slowly around and made its way back up the runway, finally stopping beside the waiting snowmobiles and ALE staff. The plane's side door opened and a small ladder was let down. I squinted my eyes. All I could see was blue and white. A head poked in and I noticed the cloud of condensing breath pouring from his mouth and nose. We gathered up our bags and shuffled towards the door. As I got closer, the white and blue came into focus. The sky's colour was intense and below it I could make out the snow and, closer still, the brilliant shimmer of the ice runway, where I watched my fellow passengers inching their way across, fearful of slipping and sustaining injury before they had even set off on their expeditions. Then it was my turn. As I placed my right foot on to the glistening surface I will never forget that memorable greeting.

'Welcome to Antarctica,' a stranger said.

Henry, Will and I grinned and Sean started filming. There was not a hint of wind, the sun was high and intense and wherever we looked, the snowfield carried the eye to the distant Patriot Hills or to the flat line of the horizon. Bags, boxes, sledges and skis were all offloaded and retrieved by their owners. Because of the two-week delay, everybody was eager to get going straight away. Most of the teams were setting off from Hercules Inlet, the recognised start point of the trade route to the Pole. Mark Langridge was the first to be flown onwards. He had to get going as soon as possible, as every hour was now critical to him. I watched him collect his fuel, make final preparations to his sledge and then push it over to the waiting Twin Otter. I didn't envy him. He was attempting something that no one had ever achieved. We said goodbye, exchanged satellite phone numbers and agreed to keep in touch, intending to speak on Christmas Day. With him on his way, we returned to our kit and found a suitable spot to pitch our tent.

1908

In the permanent darkness of winter on the other side of the continent, the only signs of life were the smoke rising from the prominent chimney and the dim glow of light through the shuttered windows of the hut. Outside, the ponies faced away from the wind and neighed pathetically when the vicious gusts became too much and penetrated their simple stables. The dogs lay curled up, nuzzled into their tails as the drifting snow gathered around them. Inside, Shackleton kept the men busy with preparations for the coming spring. Harnesses were strengthened, sledge runners were smoothed down and sledging rations were divided up. Adams made daily visits to the weather station on a small ridge behind the hut and other science projects filled the darkness of the days. One evening, Putty Marston sawed through one of the packing cases, which had 'VEAL' stencilled on the side, to use as the front and rear binding of a copy of *Aurora Australis*, the name of the book he was helping Wild and Joyce to print.

L–R: Sir Philip Brocklehurst, Shackleton, Marston and Wild working on a sledge runner.

'I think we should give that copy to George Buckley when we return,' said Shackleton, as he watched the pages being printed. 'He was great company on our sea voyage and he has been immensely generous. I would like us all to sign it when it is finished.'

One hundred years later the 'VEAL edition' of *Aurora Australis* was sold at auction in New York for $70,000.

2008

Steve Jones, the ALE operations director, had promised us that he would get us away as soon as he could. But the meteorological forecasting desk was not yet fully set up and it would be a while before the 'met man' could download weather maps from the internet in order for Steve and the pilots to make a 'go or no-go' decision. So, as expected, we would not be flying for a good few hours at least. We returned to our tent and prepared supper from a bag of food that we had specially set aside for our time at Patriot Hills. It had a week's worth in it, just in case of delay, but I prayed that we would not need the full amount. As I scooped up Antarctic snow in my plastic cup and tipped it into the kettle, I considered for a brief moment that this was our first meal on the continent and a further reminder that we were edging closer to the start of our journey. While it melted I took delivery of all our naphtha fuel for the journey which I decanted into five-litre plastic jerrycans, and smaller bottles for everyday use.

Our first evening on the Antarctic continent should have been very special and although it did feel so, we were eager to get going, so a rising level of frustration began to take hold, made worse as we heard the Twin Otters ferrying more teams to Hercules Inlet to start their expeditions. We kept running over the number of days we had left in which to complete the journey, working back from 28 January, when the Antarctic summer gave way to autumn and ALE's operation at Patriot Hills closed down. I had planned on us taking seventy days for our journey to the Pole, so we still had a few days in hand, but the realisation of the scale of the onward journey to Ross Island and the unpredictable weather was leaving us with very little margin for further delay. What was becoming abundantly clear now was that our aim of reaching the 97-mile point, where the original team turned back from, on 9 January 2009 was slipping out of reach. We had so wanted to be at that point exactly one hundred years to the day. The following morning, 11 November, we awoke to glorious blue sky and low winds. As we walked to the control room for our weather update, I thought of all the other expeditions already underway. Lots of satellite pictures showing the weather patterns were now coming in, but the news was not good. While we at Patriot Hills were enjoying fine conditions, the Ross Ice Shelf was covered in a bank of low cloud, especially over the area of our intended refuelling point, about 500 miles away. There was nothing we could do other than be patient and use the time constructively. So we agreed to report back in the afternoon for a further update, and left the warmth of the cabin.

I decided to pass the morning by going for a ski, in order to get an idea just how difficult it was going to be to haul a 140 kg sledge over the snow. This was a critical moment and as I laced up my boots and fastened the harness around my waist I began to feel very apprehensive. There was no turning back now, but just how difficult was it going to be? I was about to find out. I'd put as much as I could into the sledge until I was confident that it was pretty much at its full weight. The nine bags that each held a week's worth of food were untouched and there was also the emergency bag that held food for a further eight days. We had shared out the fuel, so we each carried five of the jerrycans. The three solar panels were stowed aboard, then finally I zipped up the sledge's green canopy. I clipped the toe of each boot into the ski bindings and for the first time looked down at my children's artwork on the skis. As I was putting on my gloves I looked ahead to select a distant point to aim for. Then it was the off, and Sean captured the moment on camera.

I planted both ski sticks and, using the purchase of the skins on the underside of each ski, I started to crouch down at the same time as pushing off on the sticks. The sledge begun to move, slowly at first as I gathered enough speed for the runners to overcome the friction. At last I felt I was underway. The tightening of the harness around my stomach and hips was sudden as my muscles tensed up. With every push I felt my forearms and triceps taking the strain as I tried to maintain the momentum. Because of the earlier high winds at Patriot Hills the surface of the snow had been sculpted into wave-like obstacles called sastrugi, which made it impossible to get any form of glide going. I began to get alarmed. We were bound to experience conditions like this on the journey and right now I was finding it damned hard work – and I had to keep this up for nine hundred miles. I sensed it was counter-productive to contemplate the journey on such a grand scale, for I was in danger of psyching myself out at this early stage. Nevertheless, the couple of hours I spent heaving my sledge over the rough and jagged sastrugi was a stark illustration of the physical trial that lay ahead. I glanced back to watch the sledge climbing one side of a small ridge before it teetered and dropped down the other side like a small boat at the mercy of a high sea. But across the smoother areas, where I could ski more freely, I was pleased to notice just how well our sledges performed. We had packed them carefully to make sure that the weight was predominately in the middle and it was great to feel them move with uninterrupted ease. As long as the surface stayed flat then all would be well. But only a fool would expect that.

Around midday I returned to the tent to find Henry and Will stowing kit inside their sledges. They had both been off for a trial ski and had returned feeling just as anxious as I was. Over a handful of salami, nuts and a flapjack, we discussed how surprised we had been at the effort required to move our sledges. The most sensible thing to do was to laugh it off, which is what we did. There was no use getting worked up over the weight. We knew that our sledges

Will and me pulling tyres, but being mentally prepared was equally crucial.

Alicia painting my skis with motivating messages and drawings. Little did I realise just how important they would become.

RIGHT: Crevasse rescue training in Chamonix.

OPPOSITE TOP: We crested a small slope and there she was – Shackleton's hut.

OPPOSITE BOTTOM: Inside Shackleton's hut, the past was vividly alive.

BELOW: The sheer scale of our project was both exhilarating and daunting.

Everywhere you looked there were items that had been touched, drunk from, opened, read and used by the *Nimrod* expedition members.

Underway at last. Our first night camped on the frozen Ross Sea, under the eye of Mount Erebus.

Will, Henry and I beside Vince's Cross. Scott's *Discovery* hut, the point from where Shackleton was rescued in March 1909, is in the foreground.

Everything we needed to survive for seventy days. Day by day we ate our way through our burden.

Time for personal administration, checking progress on the map and writing diaries.

At the mercy of your imagination. The importance of positive thinking soon became apparent.

'We got a photograph of the wonderful red granite peaks close to us, for now we are only eight miles or so off the land.' EHS, 3 December 1908 and 14 December 2008 (below).

Two weeks into the journey the fine weather changed, forcing us to sit out a storm for two days.

The cairn I built on Mount Hope to commemorate Shackleton's discovery of the Beardmore Glacier.

would be heavy and we had pared them right back to the minimum, already having discarded items we had originally thought it important to have.

The afternoon hours crawled by, but eventually it was time to return to the operations cabin for the long-awaited update. Henry and Will chose to stay behind; I think they sensed the news would not be good. On my walk over I could feel that the wind had increased and saw that the sky was overcast and threatening. The wind was not an issue, but the low cloud was.

'We are getting a good picture of the Ross Ice Shelf now and it's not great, I'm afraid,' said Steve Jones.

The weather man took over the explanation, 'We are in touch with McMurdo Sound and they report an area of high pressure, but it's the bit in between that is not helpful. A huge area of low cloud and poor visibility hangs over the area where you will have to refuel. That is the problem.'

Terry Welsh, the Twin Otter pilot assigned to our flight, had arrived for the update. 'Well, I won't fly without as much certainty as I can get and what I have just heard is not enough, I am afraid,' he said. 'We can take camping stuff to weather out a storm but landing in low cloud and no visibility in a place so remote is not wise.'

So that was that. From what I had heard there was no room for manoeuvre and Terry, who had clocked up more than ten thousand hours' flying in the polar regions, was quite understandably not going to take any foolhardy risks, no matter how much pleading he faced.

'So, no flight today, I am afraid,' said Steve. 'We shall have another look tomorrow morning. In the meantime, bring the others over to the mess tent tonight and join the camp staff for scoff.' I thanked him very much for the kind and helpful offer and sloped off to our tent with the gloomy news. The campsite suddenly seemed deserted, for during the day all the others had been flown out. Until the Iluyshin returned with another load of climbers and expedition teams, we would be on our own, waiting. But at least we would not have to cook tonight.

Supper in the mess tent was a treat. Will, Henry and I stayed as long as we felt was reasonable and then set off into the brilliant bright light for our second night on the Antarctic. As we got ready I reminded myself of the quality that Shackleton had said was so important in a polar explorer – patience. But it was of little comfort. I took out the diary that I had started in Punta Arenas and finished off my entry for the day, trying to be as optimistic as I could, 'Despite the delay, every day is a day closer to when we fly.'

1908

Shackleton had spent the remainder of the 1908 winter turning over in his mind the preparation required for the southbound journey to the Pole. He decided that to leave before the end of October would risk inflicting too heavy a demand on the ponies, as the temperatures would still be very low. He also wanted the team to undertake a number of short expeditions across the sea ice and the barrier, to help depot food for the main journey. This would give everyone experience of foul weather, hauling sledges and even trialling the car. With the successful summiting of Mount Erebus, his mind turned to another project. He decided that Edgeworth David, Mawson and Mackay would attempt to reach the magnetic South Pole but it would have to be done at the same time that the southern journey was underway. There was so much to think about and by the sun's return in mid-August, heralding the arrival of spring, Shackleton had a clear plan. He put his men straight to work.

2008

The following morning I awoke in good time for the scheduled briefing at 8 a.m. With Sean now filming our every move, I followed my tracks from the day before to the operations cabin. Brushing loose snow from my boots, I went inside. There was no sign of Paul, the weather man. Steve looked at me, eager to break the news but he had to wait until Sean was ready to capture the impending disappointment on my face.

'Still not good, I'm afraid, Henry. Clear as a bell on Ross Island but clagged in all the way from here to there. But the winds are strong, so anything can happen. Come back in two hours. There was no invitation to a breakfast fry-up in the mess tent either. I headed back to the others feeling very demoralised. They were equally dejected but cheered up a little when ten minutes later I handed them a packet of steaming porridge and a hot drink.

'My main concern,' I said, 'is that we are running out of time to complete the journey now. My calculations have been based on a total time of seventy days. Today is 12 November. We know that ALE have to close this camp by 28 January. That means we have to be underway by 18 November, which is in six days' time. So if we are further delayed here, then need a day to get to the hut, then allow a day at least to film there and then get underway, that will mean we have hardly a day to spare for bad weather or slow progress.'

I turned to Sean. 'At this rate we won't be able to hang around for long at the hut to film, I'm afraid.'

'Yeah. Let's just wait and see,' he replied. 'We must spend at least some time there, as it is such an important part of the whole story. But I understand how eager you are to set off.'

Sean was a wise and very experienced mountaineer and he knew how futile it was to plan too far ahead when at the mercy of the weather. It was typical of his easy-going nature not to make it an issue. After breakfast there was little point in getting kitted up to go off on another training session, so I joined the others and dozed for an hour before it was time to get another weather update.

At ten o'clock the three of us shuffled over to the cabin, followed by Sean. I opened the door and went inside. Terry, the pilot, was already there poring over a satellite picture on Paul's laptop and Steve Jones was smiling.

He waited until all three of us were squeezed into the cabin before starting his update.

'It's looking good. The high winds have shifted the cloud and there is a clear window all the way to McMurdo. And they have confirmed fine weather their end. It's up to Terry, but I am happy that you leave.'

Terry was the judge and jury. He had heard the evidence and was now mulling it over. Despite his experience of flying for ALE, he had never flown from Patriot Hills to Ross Island before and he didn't relish being stuck on the Ross Ice Shelf. I stood there prepared to take any risk necessary to enable us to get to our start point, but he looked at the situation through a different lens. The decision lay with the pilot.

'Mmmm'. Then there was a pause. 'McMurdo say it is fine their end and set to remain that way for at least forty-eight hours?' He asked, wanting a reply from Paul, the forecaster.

'Correct, Terry. They confirm that.'

'OK then. Sounds good to me. Let's do it.'

I glanced at Henry and Will at the same time as clenching both fists and squeezing hard. At last we were off.

'Right,' said Steve. 'Pack your stuff and be ready within the hour to move your kit to the Otter. We will give you an early lunch in the mess tent and a packed meal for the journey.' Filming as he went, Sean captured the look of excitement and relief on our faces as he followed us jogging back to the tent, which we dismantled immediately and stowed with the rest of our equipment. Everything we needed for the next two months was quickly and neatly packed in three sledges. I thought how neat, tidy and simple it all seemed as we dragged them over to the waiting plane. We returned to the mess tent for our early lunch, which has similarities to a condemned man's last meal. Wiping away the condensation, I peered through the windows and watched our sledges being lifted into the plane, along with barrels of aviation fuel. Moments later ALE's director David Rootes came into the tent with the news that I had been dreading.

'Your sledges are very heavy,' he said. 'Three hundred pounds, I reckon. Too late to do anything now but Terry says he will need a long take-off.'

The weight of our sledges had become a huge factor. In stark terms, the weight held the key to success or failure. We had pared it down to the absolute minimum but still it posed a formidable burden. 'Keep positive,' I told myself.

At last everything was ready. We set off to the waiting plane with David Rootes, who wanted to wave us goodbye. Before climbing aboard I turned to shake him by the hand.

'It's great to be finally underway, David, but I think we will be pushed to meet up with the others on 9 January now,' I said with one foot on the ladder.

'Oh yes. You can forget about that,' he replied. 'It will require a stunning effort.' David had no idea just how significant those few words would become. Henry, who had also heard the comment, exchanged a sidelong glance with me and grinned. The gauntlet had been thrown. If meeting the others on 9 January was possible but it required a 'stunning effort', then that was all we needed to hear. Unknowingly, David had set us the ultimate challenge. He would never know just how often we would remind ourselves of those few words in the weeks to come.

1908

Leading up to October 1908, Shackleton's aim was to depot as much food and equipment along his planned route as possible.

A pony lies dead having ingested the sand.

Depots were laid beyond the *Discovery* hut and marked with an upturned sledge and a black flag on a bamboo pole. The ponies were regularly exercised, but Shackleton was not keen for them to be overused, as he was now down to only four: Chinaman, Quan, Grisi and Socks. Disaster had struck after only one month of their arrival when three ponies had been found lying dead where they were tethered. A rudimentary post-mortem showed that the animals' stomachs were filled with the dark volcanic sand. A basic error in animal husbandry had occurred. No one had thought to give them any salt in their diet; they had licked the ground in search of it, ingesting the sand instead.

Shackleton's original plans had hinged on being able to use the ponies for at least two long journeys, but as they began to die he had to radically change his ideas. He would take the remaining four with him on the southern journey, which left the northern party to use the car, or else haul their sledge on foot. Faced with only four ponies, Shackleton was also forced to reduce his team to the same number. From a shortlist of six names he chose Frank Wild, Eric Marshall and Jameson Adams.

The car preparing to assist the Northern Party.

2008

The door of the Twin Otter closed shut. Inside it was cramped. Bending double, I forced myself into a seat next to Will. The air was heavy with the smell of aviation fuel and as we taxied to the end of the ice runway I settled down for a long and very uncomfortable journey. But at last we were on our way to Cape Royds. Terry turned the plane and paused to increase the power of the propellers to the required speed. And then we were off. The take-off distance seemed endless, but eventually the skis lifted from the surface and we were climbing into the freezing Antarctic air. Ahead lay a five-hour journey, after which we planned to stop and refuel from the second Twin Otter that was following right behind us. I sensed a feeling of excitement amongst us but as it was so noisy there was no chance to chat. Instead, I gazed out of the window at the endlessness below. We were still climbing, but no matter how far I could see to the horizon, I knew we would have to travel way beyond that point on our journey. Viewing the continent from ten thousand feet was the perfect way to begin to contemplate our utter insignificance and microscopic presence in a wilderness of such grand scale.

The minutes passed slowly at first. The air in the fuel drums begun to expand, causing them to force out the dents with a loud 'crump'. Then we all sat bolt upright as a loud 'pop' cracked the air. At first it was hard to tell what had happened, then we realised that someone's sleeping mat had burst because it had been loaded fully inflated. An unfortunate error and one that preyed on Henry's mind, as it turned out to be his.

Helped by a few hours of sleep, the first stage of the journey passed by quickly. The refuelling stop was going to be our first taste of the Ross Ice Shelf, or Great Ice Barrier, as Shackleton called it. He had a terrible time crossing it because of the depth of the snow and the exhausting effect it had on the ponies. We were equally nervous that facing similar conditions with our sledges at their heaviest we would get off to a very slow start. We were about to find out what lay in store. We landed on an area free of sastrugi and waited for the door to open. Henry was the first to step on to the surface. I focussed on his feet, to see how much he sunk into the snow, but he remained on the crust.

'It's fine,' he said with a grin, and then headed off to make sure everywhere else was as firm. Although we still had another five hundred-mile flight ahead of us, it was a huge relief to know that, with luck, most of the Ice Shelf would be the same. But to expect similar snow conditions across two hundred thousand square miles was probably stretching it a bit. Refuelling over, we climbed back on board and watched the other plane head back to Patriot Hills. For us, another five hours and we would reach the hut.

There was plenty to think about on this leg of the journey. The immediate plan on arrival was to find Al Fastier, as he had the key to Shackleton's hut. I knew from our earlier phone calls that he had left Cape Royds and was now working on the artefacts in Scott's *Terra Nova* hut at Cape Evans. Steve Jones had very generously said that I could use the Otter as a taxi if necessary and go to Cape Evans to pick up Al, if it helped. Next, I did some calculations to work out how long we could stay at the hut before leaving. On arrival we would enter the New Zealand time zone, and so travel forward to 13 November. If we spent twenty-four hours at the hut and left on 14 November, then we would have seventy-five days to complete our journey, based on ALE ending the season on 28 January. We had enough food and fuel for seventy-one days. In a nutshell, we didn't have much of a margin in case of delay. Sean had been filming me doing my sums so I leaned over to him.

'Sean, I would like to leave tomorrow morning at ten o'clock,' I shouted. 'You'll be able to film tonight and tomorrow morning, but I really think we need to get going.'

He nodded.

I stowed away my notebook and gazed again out of the window. Below was an intimidating sight. Will was asleep, but I had to wake him. He looked at me rather startled so I mimed to him to look out of the window. We were both transfixed. Ten thousand feet beneath us was an area marked by dark gashes across the surface of the snow. Deep, deep wounds, never to heal, caused by the mighty power of the Ice Shelf's indiscernible movement. Everywhere we looked there were crevasse fields the size of a small parish. What we were about to undertake was brought sharply into focus in those few moments. None of us said a word. As odd as it may sound, it would have seemed disrespectful.

I reached into my jacket and pulled out a map of the Ross Sea, for on the horizon now we could make out mountains, pale mauve against the blue sky. The excitement replaced the fear. Features that I had only ever seen on a map and read about in the diary were now appearing below us through both windows. Black Island, White Island, Minna Bluff, Mount Discovery and suddenly, through the starboard window, I could see Mount Erebus. Terry did well to keep us level as we launched ourselves from one side of the plane to the other. The US administrative base of McMurdo Sound was rather a shock. We could clearly see the roads, cabins, vast vehicle parks and the jetty for the tankers and cruise ships that dock in the summer months. But we were soon past that and into the final few miles of the journey. Terry flew us low down the coastline towards Ross Island. The sea was clearly frozen solid and I could make out seals sunbathing on the ice. There were no leads of open water visible, which meant that we would be able to land as close as possible to the hut. But where was it? Holding my excitement at bay for a few minutes, I searched the coastline for the Adélie penguin colony and Pony Lake – from there I would be able to locate the hut. The penguin colony was a lighter colour than the surrounding black volcanic rock, so it was easy to spot. Then I saw the lake.

'There's the hut. There it is. There it is,' I screamed, like an excited child. 'My God, we've made it. Five years. This is it.' For some reason, the three of us shook hands and squeezed each other tightly as a sign to mark the achievement of having got this far. Terry circled the hut and then the sea, looking for a clear area on which to land. Mount Erebus dominated the skyline as we flew lower, then the skis made contact with three feet of sea ice and we were down. We taxied towards the edge of Ross Island and came to a stop. I just gazed at Mount Erebus again. This was the same view of it Shackleton must have had when he finally berthed the *Nimrod* in 1908. I reckoned we had stopped exactly where he had offloaded his stores. I looked up to the crater rim and thought of the first ascent party. There it was. We were really here.

Within minutes we were all standing on the sea ice, grinning away. Sean's camera had been running non-stop for the previous hour capturing our excitement. There was no sign of Al, so we decided to go and view the hut first. Then I would call him on the satellite telephone and arrange to pick him up.

So we set off. It was a glorious evening, the sun was high and bright in a pure blue sky and there was no wind. A fine wisp of sulphurous smoke was lifting from Mount Erebus. A couple of Adélie penguins stood their ground as we walked towards them but then they flopped on their bellies and, using their flippers as paddles, moved at speed across the ice towards the collective protection of their colony.

Barely noticing the point at which sea and land met, we were soon on the black volcanic rock and ash. It was a short walk uphill before we crested some high ground to look down into the sheltered bowl where Shackleton had built his hut. And there it was, unchanged from the grainy photograph I had stared at perhaps a hundred times as I leafed through *The Heart of the Antarctic*. I saw the packing cases, the prominent chimney and the weather station. As we got closer, all the items I had seen only in modern photographs came into view: the puppies' kennels, the spare wheel for the Arrol-Johnson motor car, the mangers for the ponies still full of snow from the previous winter. I had expected it to be bigger, but it looked perfect. Shackleton had chosen a great spot. I walked around the hut slowly, viewing it from all sides and from different distances. Pausing often to sit on a rock, it was easy to imagine Jameson Adams going off to check the thermometer in the weather station and Frank Wild feeding the ponies their hay. There were even bales of it still along the outside of the hut. But we were eager to see inside so I called Al on the satphone and arranged an immediate pick-up. The *Terra Nova* hut was only a few miles away. In no time at all Terry had completed the round trip and returned with Al, his small team of conservators – and the key.

It was great to meet Al at last. I had been in frequent email contact with him over the previous few months, as he was critical to this phase of the journey. Even if disaster befell us on day one, at least we would have seen inside the hut and all of the effort would have been worthwhile. Before he asked for it, I showed him the permit I had been granted by the New Zealand Government to enter the specially-protected area. He thanked me and we continued talking as we walked towards the door.

'Before you go in I'll take the shutters off the windows. I suggest you three go in on your own, which will allow you to be alone for a while. It's quite a feeling, I assure you. Then I will come in and explain about the layout and what we are doing with the artefacts.'

Al removed the three shutters and then came round to the door to unlock it. Will was first in. As he pulled the door towards him I wondered if it creaked like that a hundred years ago.

'Oh . . . my . . . God,' Will said quietly, pausing between words. I followed him in but stopped the moment I set foot in the room to allow my eyes to adjust to the gloom. It was like entering a Pharaoh's tomb. First I noticed the stove, and then, to the right, the shelves of food, cured hams hung from hooks, enamel plates stacked ready for the next meal. Moving round, I picked out some leather boots, a bedspace with a reindeer skin sleeping bag and then the framed photograph of King Edward VII and Queen Alexandra that I had read about in the diary. I looked up. Above my head hung pairs of socks in need of darning, above them two sledges were stored across the rafters. There was too much to take in. The warmth of the place and its atmosphere were intriguing. It was easy to imagine being welcomed in by Shackleton and offered a tin mug of steaming tea. You could hear the chatter and the laughs and the odd cough. You could smell the tobacco smoke, damp wool drying and coal burning in the stove. The past seemed vividly alive and it was easy to feel that this was still the home to untroubled spirits who had passed away the dark and unforgiving months of the Antarctic winter in 1908.

I started to pace carefully among it all to look in more detail at the thousands of artefacts placed carefully around the interior as if they had simply been left behind in early March 1909 when the *Nimrod* returned the expedition members to New Zealand. None of us said anything for quite a while. With small reverential steps I just wandered, looked and imagined. And then I slid my right hand into my trouser pocket and grasped the compass. Without taking it out I continued to meander around, peering into every dark corner and under every bed in case I missed one single detail. It seemed unthinkable that the compass had been in the hut before and it probably lived in Shackleton's trouser pocket as well. After a few steps I took it out and ran my thumb over the familiar engraving on the lid –BR. ANT. EX. 1907. Then I opened it up. The spinning card seemed alive, driven by an invisible heartbeat in a room where everything else was motionless and locked in time. I waited until it had stopped, but this time I ran the same finger over the initials that had been scratched in the lid – EHS. Then I placed it on the corner of one of the beds and left it there for a moment.

Al came into the hut and started to explain how the conservation team from the New Zealand Antarctic Heritage Trust carry out the painstaking business of treating, cleaning, preserving and cata-loguing all of the artefacts. He also had a copy of the floor plan of the hut which clearly showed where everyone had slept. Henry turned around and looked straight at the area where Jameson Adams, his great-grandfather, had had his bed and stored his belongings. Chatting later to Henry on the journey about the impact of that moment, he said that he found it elating yet daunting. He had never really felt relaxed whilst in the hut, since he knew that we were about to travel in the footsteps of such indomitable men.

Al also had copies of photographs taken in 1908, which showed exactly where a lot of the items had been placed, and this had helped him lay out the interior as faithfully as possible. But this was no museum. It was like walking into Badger's house in the Wild Wood – cosy and welcoming and safe. We were in no hurry so we continued to explore. I was now noticing the smaller items such as safety pins, boxes of matches, buttons, frayed boot laces, blue bottles of medicine marked 'Diarrhoea'. Wherever I looked I was seeing something that one of those explorers had once owned, held, opened, drank from, ate off, wore, lit and read. I had slept beside Shackleton's grave on South Georgia and now I was standing in the hut where he had spent every night of the Antarctic winter in 1908 planning his great journey. I could hardly get closer to my mentor. The only thing left to do was to walk in his footsteps to the Pole.

Al had to return to Cape Evans, but before he left he invited us to stop off and have a look at Captain Scott's *Terra Nova* hut when we passed by the next day. Sean carried on filming as Will, Henry and I put up our tent and made final preparations for our departure the following morning. Lying in our sleeping bags that night it was hard to believe that our journey was about to start. After the years of planning, training, fund-raising and, to be honest, selfish indulgence, we were ready. The tent should have been filled with excited banter and leg-pulling. Instead it was quiet and still. Of course I was excited; but also nervous, unsure, doubting and hesitant. I wondered if Shackleton had felt the same on the eve of his departure.

1908

In early October 1908, David, Mawson and Mackay set off on the northern journey to be the first to the magnetic South Pole, accompanied by others at first and using the car, but it was not long before the vehicle had to return and the party of three were left on their own. With them firmly on their way, Shackleton's attention

29 October 1908. Ready to commence the Southern journey.

turned to the final preparation for the southern journey. Food for ninety-one days was packed and stowed on to four sledges, which increased in weight to about 500 lbs (about 225 kgs) each as tents, sleeping bags, cooking utensils, stoves, oil, navigation equipment and a maize grinder were added. A final overhaul of the equipment was carried out and the ponies were kept carefully supervised, for an injury at this stage could prove to be catastrophic. Everything seemed ready for the start. At dinner on 28 October, looking up from the last full meal he was likely to have for months, Shackleton noticed a shaft of evening light shine through the window and illuminate the photograph of the King and Queen that hung over Marston's bed space. He regarded this as a great omen and recorded the event in his diary that night. After dinner the hut became quiet to allow the four men a full night's sleep, but they lay on their beds until it was late, writing their last letters home in the event of them never returning. The following morning, after breakfasting at 7 a.m., the men harnessed the ponies. The car set off first, towing the sledges across the sea ice, closely followed by the support party with their load. At 10 a.m., Shackleton, Wild, Adams and Marshall turned briefly for a final glance at the hut then tugged on the halters that they were holding and set off with their ponies beside them. The first steps of the British Antarctic Expedition were truly underway.

CHAPTER 4

The Antarctic Malt Whisky Appreciation Society

'It is possible that we have reached the windless area around the Pole, for the Barrier is a dead, smooth, white plain, weird beyond description, and having no land in sight, we feel such tiny specks in the immensity around us.'

EHS, 18 November 1908

It had been impossible to sleep. It was 14 November 2008 and our bodies were still adjusting to the difference resulting from the change in time zone that had taken place only twelve hours earlier. Added to that, the day had finally come when we would set off on the most mentally and physically demanding journey of our lives. The enormity of the task seemed overwhelming; I found it impossible to relax. Whilst Will and Henry slept, I slid out of my sleeping bag, put on my cold boots and left the relative warmth of the tent; outside I stamped around to reverse the flow of blood which had shunted away from my cold toes. The sun was bright in a clear sky and positioned over the crater rim of Mount Erebus. The sights were no different to when Shackleton had been there. The Adélies were milling around in their colony and paid no attention to me, even when I walked as close as I could until forced to stop by the signs forbidding me to venture into their protected area. As all penguins do, they looked at me inquisitively for a brief moment, then shuffled away, head down, looking as though they were off to complain about something.

I sat down on the black rock and gazed out across the pack ice of the Ross Sea to the distant peaks of the Dry Valleys, along which Mawson, David and Mackay had set off to locate the magnetic South Pole in October 1908. Their achievement was astonishing, and had been unfairly eclipsed by Shackleton's South Pole journey. Sitting quite still, I reflected on what Shackleton wrote in his diary on 29 October 1908.

'Last night as we were sitting at dinner the evening sun entered through the ventilator and a circle of light shone on the picture of the Queen. Slowly it moved across and lit up the photograph of His Majesty the King. This seemed an omen of good luck, for only on that day and at that particular time could this have happened, and today we started to strive to plant the Queen's flag on the last spot of the world.'

Last night I had looked at that same photograph on the north-facing wall of the hut and in a few hours I, too, would start to strive to place not a flag, but Shackleton's compass, on the last spot of the world. I returned to wake the others and to start preparing breakfast.

I had arranged with the Patriot Hills staff to make my daily phone call to them at eight o'clock in the morning on our time. It would be before breakfast for us and late afternoon the previous day for them. So, taking a battery from one of my chest pockets, where it was kept warm and dry, and inserting it into the satellite telephone, I waited for the display to tell me there were the required number of satellites overhead before dialling the number. This was to become a familiar routine and the call was answered straight away.

'Patriot Hills, Victoria speaking.'

'Hi, Victoria, the Matrix Shackleton Expedition calling in with our first report. Our location is South 77° 40.114′, East 166° 25.477′. We are setting off in a couple of hours. All is well. No medical problems. We had a very moving time in the *Nimrod* Hut yesterday and Sean did a lot of filming. Terry is fine and the Otter is performing well.' Victoria, the radio operator, repeated our location and then asked what Terry's plans were for his return journey, as they needed the Twin Otter back at Patriot Hills.

'We will be leaving at ten o'clock this morning,' I replied.

'That's fine. OK. Have a great journey. Good luck and we look forward to hearing your daily calls and charting your progress. Out.'

I re-stowed the phone in my sledge and the battery back into the warmth of my chest pocket. The satellite telephones were the most important piece of equipment we carried and ALE required us to carry two of them. It was vital that we kept to the daily scheduled calls, or 'scheds'. If two were missed, then ALE would come looking for you – possibly the most expensive taxi ride in the world, if the call-out was simply because the phone batteries ran out. So it was crucial that they were painstakingly looked after. I carried three and Henry carried two, together with the spare telephone.

I spent the next two hours needlessly fiddling around with my sledge and equipment. I placed my lunch bag and two vacuum flasks at the front of my sledge along with goggles, mittens, video camera and balaclava. The down jacket I was wearing would be the last item to be stowed and removed only seconds before I set off.

I checked that the solar panels were securely fastened and angled towards the sun; a small blue light reassuringly indicated that they were charging. There was nothing else to do but wait until ten o'clock – the hour that Shackleton and his team set off. This was it. It was a golden moment, rare in a lifetime when you wake one morning to find that a dream has become real, and that moment had finally arrived.

We stood to have final photos taken by Sean. I grinned with excitement but it was a thin façade. Just under the surface my mind was rattled. I was nervous about lots of things; of failing the team; of getting injured; of letting down all those people who had supported us; of plainly not being physically up to it – put simply, I feared failure and how would I cope with the disappointment. I also felt disheartened, because that ten-day delay in Punta Arenas did now make it highly unlikely that we would reach the important rendezvous on 9 January 2009. We had set ourselves a hugely ambitious target, to stand at that lonely spot exactly one hundred years later to the day. But it was what this expedition was all about – to stand where Shackleton, Wild, Marshall and Adams had stood and to honour their astonishing achievement. We had to do all that we possibly could to accomplish that. But before I left home, to reassure my wife Joanna that I wouldn't be reckless in pursuit of that goal, I stole the words that Shackleton said to his wife on return to England in 1909, 'I thought you would prefer a live donkey to a dead lion.'

I looked at my watch and it was ten o'clock. The three of us leaned into our harnesses, pushed down on our ski sticks and slid one ski in front of the other. We were under way. My first thoughts were focussed on the weight of my sledge and how it felt. I was hugely relieved to find that it was not prohibitively heavy, but we all reminded ourselves that we were on sheet ice with a very thin layer of packed snow, so the conditions could not have been better. Regardless, it was a great sensation not to feel daunted by the burden we were pulling. Seven miles ahead of us was the ink-black shape of Inaccessible Island – hopefully, our first campsite. Appropriately named, it was sheer-sided all round and very imposing. To our east was the glorious sight of Mount Erebus with its fine plume of smoke dissipating into the brilliant blue sky. She would be our guardian for some days to come as she watched our progress from afar.

Although there was no small crowd to see us off, in spirit my feelings were no different to Shackleton's when he wrote, 'A clasp of the hands means more than many words, and as we turned to acknowledge their cheers and saw them standing on the ice by the familiar cliff, I felt that we must try to do well for the sake of everyone concerned in the expedition.'

Our first stop, only six miles away, was Captain Scott's *Terra Nova* hut built in 1911 at Cape Evans. We wanted to take Al up on his offer to call in on him and his team of conservators. We passed the Barne ice cliffs and made good time, reaching the hut by early afternoon. As arranged, Al was there to meet us and give us access.

The *Terra Nova* hut has a special place in British polar history because of its association with Scott's race to the Pole against Roald Amundsen in 1911/12, Amundsen's victory and then the death of Scott's party on the return journey. Despite the confidence and hope of the expedition members, captured so poignantly in Herbert Ponting's photographs, it is a place from where five men departed but to which they never returned. Al had warned us that the atmosphere inside was completely different to the *Nimrod* hut, and he was right. I suppose that visitors armed with the knowledge that five of the team had perished on the expedition would always find it a miserable place. But the wretchedness was palpably strong.

Snow was still piled high up the windows, letting in very little light. A significant drop in temperature was noticeable as I cautiously pushed open the door. It creaked as the light poured in. We stepped inside and my eyes adjusted to the still-gloomy interior and strained to make sense of all that I saw. We stood in silence, as we had done the day before. I had vivid impressions in my mind of Ponting's iconic black-and-white photographs of Captain Scott writing up his journal at his desk, of 'the tenements' (the bunk beds), of Dr Wilson colouring a sketch and of Meares and Captain Oates at the blubber stove. Then I realised I was standing right where Herbert Ponting would have placed his tripod to take the photograph of the *Terra Nova* crew sitting around the table celebrating the Midwinter Day Dinner on 22 June 1911 that marked the countdown to the coming spring. I slowly scanned the interior taking in all I saw. But I couldn't shake the sense of pathetic sadness from my mind and the despair that must have been so prevalent among the expedition members as they eventually returned to Britain without their leader and four gallant friends. It was a difficult place to leave, but we had to get on. We were keen to get a few more miles under our skis before pitching camp for our first night. So we bade farewell to Al and continued on our way towards Inaccessible Island.

Midwinter Day Dinner 22 June 1911. Scott (left) and
Wilson (right) at the head of the table.

We covered 7.7 nautical miles on the first day, which we were pleased about, although in the future we would have to be doing about double that. It had been relatively easy and the weather had been very kind to us. The temperature reached -10°C and the wind blew twelve to fifteen knots from the north-west but the sun was still high in the sky when we finally came to a stop.

We pitched our tent, cooked supper and lay in our sleeping bags soaking up the fact that this was our first night of the expedition – our journey was firmly under way. Everything had turned out as expected. So far, the anxiety over the weight of our sledges had lifted and nothing seemed to have caught us out. It was very early days, but we seemed well prepared. Henry said that he too was excited, but also unsettled, totally devoid of rhythm during the first day as his mind raced over millions of issues. Despite all our training he felt like a total beginner. He was right and honest; none of us knew what the next two months were going to be like. Before turning in for the night Will read out the relevant entry from Shackleton's diary. I was very familiar with these entries, as they had been an invaluable source of information when I was planning the journey, but it carried far greater meaning when you could actually see the land that was being described and you were sharing the same experiences. I finished off my own diary entry for that first day quoting Shackleton, for I could not have put it better, 'At last we are out on the long trail, after four years thought and work. I pray that we may be successful, for my heart has been so much in this.' Then I went straight to sleep.

Breakfast the following morning was dreadful. Much to our surprise, the snow that we had melted was noticeably brackish. Either the salt had leached up through the ice, or fine spray had been borne on the wind from the sea and settled on the snow. Whatever the explanation it was hugely debilitating, for although it was just about bearable to eat the porridge it was no joke having to drink two litres of salty energy drink during the day. The daily temperature hovered just below freezing and under the persistently bright sun, we worked up a huge thirst pulling our heavy sledges. Interestingly, I had found no mention of this phenomenon in Shackleton's diary during my research. As a result we were ill-prepared and I spent most of the day dreaming of a long cool glass of Coke. Pathetic really, after just one day of mild discomfort.

I was eager for us to cross the Ross Sea as fast as possible and I had planned to get on to the Ice Shelf within four days. This allowed for a steady start, which we would gradually build on as we became fitter and more in tune with the daily demands of the journey. The Ross Sea area was busier than I had expected. Scientists raced past us on snowmobiles, cabins on skis dotted the coastline and helicopters passed us overhead. This annoyed me, but we seemed to be moving well across the sea ice and, by late in the evening of our second day, we had already reached McMurdo Sound and the site of Captain Scott's *Discovery* hut, built at Hut Point. This was a significant location, as it was where Shackleton had experienced his first taste of the Antarctic when travelling with Scott in 1902. And it was the trek over new ground, across the Ross Ice Shelf, that lit the Antarctic fire within him to return on his own terms. This was also the base that Scott had forbidden Shackleton to use for his *Nimrod* expedition. With the intention of visiting the hut in the morning, we camped just under the wooden cross erected by Captain Scott to commemorate the disappearance of Able Seaman Vince in a blizzard in March 1902. But it wasn't long before people started to drift out of the McMurdo base to pay us a visit.

'We heard that you would be passing through. Nothing like this has ever happened here before, you know. You have no idea how exciting this all is. And you are all related to Shackleton? Awesome,' commented an admirer from somewhere inside an oversized parka. We had clearly caused quite a stir among the staff of the huge science and administrative base which supports the US National Science Foundation. We chatted for a short while and then made our excuses to dive back to the warmth of our tent. They promised to return in the morning to let us have a look around Scott's hut and wave us off.

We had made excellent progress on only our second day and covered eleven nautical miles. Tomorrow we would be off the sea ice and on to the Ice Shelf, where we would find out whether we would have to contend with deep snow. By now our routine was well established. The tent went up and the stove roared into life and broke the silence. We took it in turn to cook supper and breakfast. I much preferred cooking supper, for this meant you were the first into the tent at the end of the day and once the stove was lit you could relax until the snow in the kettle had melted and boiled. It was your job to ensure that you made enough hot water for the evening meal, and also to fill the six vacuum flasks. This involved keeping the kettle topped up with snow and the stove working at full efficiency, which usually took about two hours. For those not cooking, this was a useful time to examine feet, clip nails, check for blisters, write your journal, review photographs, charge camera batteries, chart progress on the map and read Shackleton's diary entry for that day. Will also had to sort and store his ice samples for the Hull University research. There was always lots to do and it was unusual to be asleep before midnight. Our second day had come to an end.

The following morning the weather had changed. It was overcast, flat light and windy. As arranged, we were shown the interior of the *Discovery* hut, which was very disappointing. There were very few artefacts left, having been plundered over the years due to the hut's close proximity to the McMurdo station. Nevertheless, it was still a special moment to wander around the interior knowing that Shackleton had first trodden those same creaking floorboards in 1902 with Captain Scott, and then seven years later, in March 1909, staggered into it with Frank Wild in the hope of finding the *Nimrod*.

While we finished packing our sledges a small crowd of well-wishers was gathering to wave us off. I gave them a short résumé of what we were setting out to achieve, and why we wanted to celebrate the centenary of the *Nimrod* journey. They were intrigued by the contents of our sledges, which we were asked to open and I added further delay to our departure by producing Shackleton's compass, to gasps of disbelief and wonderment. It was some time before I was allowed it back from the photographers. We were sent on our way by the cheering crowd and headed off under Observation Hill towards the New Zealand station at Scott Base, a couple of hours' away. Pausing briefly to reciprocate another enthusiastic farewell from the small contingent of Kiwis, we then hit the tide line between the Ross Sea and the Ice Shelf. This was marked by a strip of ice rubble formed by the pressure and movement of the sea ice against the barrier. It posed no real obstacle for us and we were soon through it and on our way towards the Williams Field air base, the only feature we could see, five miles away. We worked our way past a number of C-130 aircraft, fire tenders, trucks and even joggers, who looked at us incredulously, but were nevertheless very supportive. Finally, we crossed over the hard-packed runway and headed off to the distant horizon, cutting a fresh trail through the virgin snow at last, leaving signs of civilisation behind.

Over our right shoulder was White Island, in the far distance was Minna Bluff and behind it was the towering peak of Mount Discovery. Behind us, still keeping watch from the day we set off, were the two polar sentinels, Mounts Erebus and Terror. At this early stage we were travelling for thirty-minute legs before stopping for no more than ten minutes for a quick bite to eat and drink. It was a good way to break into the journey but the intention over the following three weeks was to increase the time of each leg to one hour. Our sledges and skis were gliding well and we felt strong, but I was becoming concerned about my lack of appetite.

We had been warned that it would take a couple of weeks of the journey before we could eat all of our daily ration of food – and the advice was correct. I was finding it difficult to consume all of my lunch bag during the day, which was not good as I knew I needed to keep taking in the calories. But I simply was not hungry. Like an animal preparing for winter, I began to keep a store of half-eaten bags in the bottom of my sledge, to be devoured at a later date.

We now had a well-practised routine at the end of each day's travel, which at this stage was around 7 p.m. From the moment the lead man planted his poles and removed his harness, signalling the end of the day's work, the priority was to get the tent up and the cooker on. Personal administration would have to wait. Henry had been in charge of evenly distributing the team kit among us and had generously elected to carry the tent himself. It was a typically selfless gesture, as he knew how much of a bore the tent was to carry, because it took up the entire length of the sledge and got in the way if you needed to find something else during the day. It was a team effort to erect the tent, then shovel snow around its skirt to secure it and then to place in the support for the guy ropes, which were either metal pegs if the snow was packed hard, or the skis and ski sticks if it was soft. First to go inside was the cook, who would take off his boots and hang his damp socks on the drying line that ran down the centre of the roof of the tent. Next, he would put on a pair of dry socks followed by his tent 'booties'. These were like down-filled slippers and were probably my most favourite piece of equipment.

By the time the cook had moved to the front vestibule of the tent the others would have gathered from their sledges the cooker, fuel bottle, kettle, empty flasks and packets of food for supper and breakfast, which they would place in the cooking area. One of us would have neatly piled heaps of snow for the kettle in the corner by the cooker. It was then simply a matter for the cook to light the stove, pour into the kettle a water 'starter' from a small flask we had nicknamed the 'twelfth man' – you can't boil snow on its own, it burns on to the pan – and wait for the snow to melt.

It would not be long before the other two would have gathered up their sleeping system and tent bag and made themselves comfortable inside the tent as well. Out of the wind, with the sun on the outside and the stove roaring on the inside it soon became warm enough to hang up socks, gloves and anything else that needed to dry. It was pretty cramped inside so we had to be tolerant of each other. But we had spent enough nights together during our training to be comfortable in each other's company, especially in a confined space. After we had eaten our evening meal it was time to write diaries, brush teeth and, very occasionally, wash. Sleeping bags were unrolled and we climbed into 'scratcher heaven' (a military term) as soon as we could, for the temperature dropped off quickly once the stove was turned off.

Progress over the next few days was very encouraging. We passed White Island and Minna Bluff but still Erebus and Terror watched over us as we made infinitesimal inroads across the Great Ice Barrier. To the west we could just make out the peaks of the Transantarctic Mountains piercing the horizon, but ahead of us was just a flat line. We were being blessed with low winds and a firm surface but on some days it was far too hot and we devoured our drinks at each stop, finding it difficult to make the two-litre ration last the day. We could have made more in an emergency, but it was not practicable to stop and brew up during the day.

These were perfect conditions to use the solar panels. I travelled with three of them strapped to the outside of my sledge and during the day they would suck up enough energy from the sun to charge a twelve-volt battery in ten hours. We would then plug in our telephone, cameras and iPods to the battery and recharge them. It was very simple and efficient, and with the temperature around -5°C, impressively quick. We began to settle into the routine of the journey, but there were still a couple of things it was taking time to get used to. The lack of appetite was expected, but I was beginning to realise just how important was one's mental approach to the journey. Although we were a team, because we travelled in single file, we spent most of the day by ourselves. You were at your most solitary when leading for an hour's leg, for you had no one in front of you; just the immeasurable horizon marking a point where shades of white met shades of blue. I found it an exhilarating feeling to spend that hour imagining I was doing the journey solo – 'Alone, alone; all, all alone, alone on a wide, wide sea', Shackleton wrote in his diary whilst on the Ice Barrier, quoting the *Ancient Mariner*. When at the front, looking ahead, without being able to see Will and Henry, one could contemplate the utter insignificance of one's presence on the vast continent and very soon be reduced to a feeling of sheer irrelevance.

Key to this mental approach was discovering and understanding the importance that one's imagination played, and especially the power of positive and negative thoughts. With no one to talk to for most of the day it became the norm to drift off into a dream world. If I was thinking positively then the miles passed by with little effort. Conversely, a black mood meant a black day. These were rare, but I found it difficult to shake off the gremlin once he was sitting on my shoulder. It took me a few days to learn just how important the first five minutes of each leg were, for they governed how the hours would pass. It was soon evident that having a fertile imagination and a mental list of things to think about helped enormously to pass the time. The extent of my imagination improved as the journey progressed, but Shackleton's endeavours were always prominent in my mind. Memorable family holidays, films I had enjoyed, a planting programme in our Herefordshire garden and how I would paint the landscapes around me were other examples of recurring thoughts. But the image of Shackleton and his ponies travelling beside me on this stage of the journey was by far the most powerful.

Crossing the Great Ice Barrier, deep snow and blizzards took their toll on the ponies.

My intense yearning to feel completely isolated was magnified by the intermittent intrusion of man's presence. It took a long time for me to become less and less resentful of the aeroplanes as they scarred the pure blue sky with their vapour trails en route back and forth to the Pole. But it was a far greater intrusion when we came across signs of human activity in our path. Henry spotted one first.

'What's that?' he said, pointing his ski stick at what looked like another flag way off in the distance. But it was on its own and seemed to be much bigger – it had to be something else.

'No idea,' I replied. 'But wouldn't it be fantastic if it marked one of Scott's or Shackleton's food depots?' I added rather stupidly, knowing full well it wasn't.

About a mile from it we stopped for a snack and pondered on what it might be. When we finally arrived it turned out to be a meteorological mast supporting a solar panel, thermometers and an anemometer passing weather data to somewhere in the world. What did surprise us, though, was that a small plaque secured to the mast informed us where that far-off place was. The mast was the property of the University of Wisconsin. Initially we laughed about this absurd chance encounter but, petty as it might seem, I was hugely irritated by the intrusion. Why, on so vast a landscape, was this thing positioned directly on our line of march? Why couldn't it be a mile to our east or west? For the rest of the day my mind churned over, searching for answers to this maddening encounter. A couple of hours later I glanced back and thankfully the mast had disappeared from view. We were back on an unblemished canvas.

It took us eight days to cover the first one hundred nautical miles and during that time we had ascended only one hundred and ninety three feet. We were pleased with our progress but, alone with my thoughts day after day, I couldn't stop thinking about the true scale of the journey ahead of us. Mount Hope marked our exit point off the Ice Barrier but it was still two hundred and sixty-three miles away and the Pole was a further six hundred miles beyond that. However, I had learned through the experience of long endurance marches in the army that it was a mistake to think so far ahead – far better to chip away at the distance in ten-mile chunks and take each day as it comes. Otherwise the sheer enormity of the task would consume me and allow those gremlins, who were waiting for any opportunity, to ruin each day.

Crossing each degree of latitude on a polar journey is traditionally the cause for a small celebration. For each one crossed you are sixty nautical miles closer to your destination. We passed the line of 79°S after eleven days' travel and it was our first really tangible measurement of progress. That night, replete and lying warm in our sleeping bags, much to the surprise of Henry and I, with great ceremony Will produced a litre of malt whisky that he had kept hidden away. He unscrewed the top, releasing oaky fumes that drifted around the tent. We held out our plastic mugs and, once he had poured out our ration, dropped in a piece of snow. It smelt heavenly.

'A little celebration is in order,' he said. 'I would like to toast the crossing of the seventy-ninth degree and mark it by forming the Antarctic Malt Whisky Appreciation Society. We should meet every Thursday night until our supplies run out and award ourselves a two-hour lie-in the following morning.' It was typical of Will. He enjoyed fine wine and whisky and surely there was no better place to be warmed by it than in the Antarctic. His idea of a two-hour lie-in, or a 'double scratcher', as it became known, was equally popular. Grinning rather inanely, we lay savouring our dram as one of us read aloud Shackleton's diary entry.

Forty miles to our west, the Transantarctic Mountains were still a hazy mauve blur on the horizon. Some days they were lost in the low cloud altogether. But over time we would watch them come closer and then, eventually, appear in front of us. But we had many miles to cover before that happened. We were capitalising on the fine weather and making encouraging headway towards the daily mileage that we were required to do if we were to come close to making 9 January on time. Everything was going well. Our appetites were growing, so it became easy now to consume the lunch bag each day. And the snow conditions were allowing us to glide relatively well, with only the occasional field of mild sastrugi to slow us down. The days were passing by with ease and we were well settled into our routine. Then, after two weeks on the Ice Barrier, the storm came.

The first sign of trouble appeared late in the day with an increase in the wind speed and a fast-advancing band of low cloud. The surface spindrift began to move like a plague of grey snakes sidewinding directly towards us. The day lost none of its brightness, but it wasn't long before the sun and blue sky were obliterated by a swirling mass of low cloud. We stopped to put on our windproof smocks then pushed on for as long as we dared into a strengthening headwind, but it was soon apparent that we should stop again and pitch our tent. To wait until the wind strengthened would be unnecessarily risky, as we had no spare and one rip or tear would have presented a real crisis.

It needed all three of us to put up the tent and we wasted no time before diving in to escape the freezing effect of the wind chill and already drifting snow. Inside it was noticeably noisy. The gusting wind battered the sides of the tent, competing against the roar of the stove. At last we were experiencing some proper Antarctic weather, but foremost in my mind was just how long it would last. I had heard and read about people being stuck for weeks on end in these unpredictable blizzards and this was exactly what we did not need – yet another delay just as we were starting to make real progress. My thoughts turned briefly to the ferocious blizzards that trapped Shackleton and Scott on this same Ice Barrier. Desperate and life-threatening days for them; just inconvenience for us. As I turned in for the night and pulled my eye mask down, I sensed we would see little change in the morning.

I awoke tired and grumpy. My hunch proved correct. Our night had been very disturbed as the wind continued to pummel the tent. It was as if the elements were furious that we were there. How dare we intrude. As I lay awake in the morning, knowing full well that we would not be moving, I reminded myself of what Robert Swan had drummed into me before we left England, just in case I thought to change my mind. 'My boy, it is imperative that you respect the Antarctic, for it will prove to be a merciless opponent if you don't.' Wise words from a man who truly understood the character of this beguiling continent. We would be going nowhere. At 8 a.m. I made my daily call to the logistics base at Patriot Hills stating our position and distance travelled the previous day.

'Hi, Victoria. Location is South 79° 48.052′, East 167° 47.430′. Distance travelled 13.4 nautical miles. No medical issues, all is well but we are caught in a storm and won't be moving today,' I informed her.

After repeating the location and distance she replied, 'Yes, I can hear the wind. It sounds strong. The other teams heading out from Hercules Inlet are also stuck in bad weather. Eighty knot winds. Some have not travelled for four days. Speak to you tomorrow. Out.'

'What did she say?' asked Will, hidden from view inside his sleeping bag. I relayed her news.

'Well, today will be a nice rest but any longer will be a real bore. I'm going back to sleep.'

He was right. The rest would do us good, but one day would suffice. We all slept until lunchtime but I couldn't help worry that we might be stuck here for some time. Shackleton had placed patience second to optimism on his list of qualities required of a polar explorer and he was right. We had had to be patient in Punta Arenas, and now we would have to be patient again.

The high winds persisted without let-up. We passed the day by dozing, playing cards, chatting and reading. I had thought long and hard about which book to take on the journey as I had visions of lying in my sleeping bag every night being able to finally read T.E. Lawrence's *Seven Pillars of Wisdom*, but at the final moment it was discarded because of its weight. But the hours spent deciding what to read had been wasted, for at the end of each day we were so tired the thought of lying awake and reading a book was laughable. Likewise, Shackleton only seemed to read when trapped in his tent during the blizzards, '. . . and in our one man sleeping bags each of us has a little home, where he can read and write and look at the penates and lares brought with him. I read Much Ado About Nothing during the morning.' The delay had been welcome, but we needed to get on. I sensed myself getting frustrated at the lack of progress but it was pointless. The wind would choose when to allow us on our way again.

Outside, our sledges were proving to be very effective barriers to the drifting snow. Thankfully, the southerly wind had maintained its course so the drifting had been consistent. High dunes of spindrift, three feet high, formed around each side of the tent, protecting us from the ingress of snow. Visibility was down to a few hundred yards. It was impossible to face into the wind without goggles, as the ice crystals blew into your eyes like a blast of grit. We hadn't seen land for two days now. We seemed cast adrift and at the mercy of the winds. As I climbed back into the tent having satisfied the call of nature, I noticed the sky clearing to the south – hopefully bringing with it change.

I was wrong. The following morning, the weather was even worse. The wind had been unremitting throughout the night. As a result I had slept fitfully again and, knowing we would not be moving, I started the day in an irritable mood. I called Patriot Hills for the morning 'sched' and informed them that we were delayed again. I heard that the weather was still no better on their side of the continent either. But that was little consolation. I lay on my back staring up at the line of socks and gloves gently swaying on the drying line inches from my face. I cupped my hands behind my head, closed my eyes and my mind drifted off to join Shackleton sitting out a similar gale. In the same month and exactly one hundred years ago, his diary revealed that conditions hadn't changed at all. 'Lying in our sleeping bags all day except when out feeding the ponies, for it has been blowing a blizzard, with thick drift, from south by west. It is very hard to be held up like this, for each day means the consumption of 40lb of pony feed alone . . . They [the ponies] have been very quiet, standing tails to the blizzard, which has been so thick that at times we could not see them from the peepholes of our tents.' I thought back to something else that Robert Swan had said to me before we left. 'Remember. No travel, no food.' I hadn't taken him at his word yet, but in theory he was right.

In the late afternoon we sensed a definite drop in the wind and the visibility began to improve. We decided that whatever the conditions the next day, we would set off again. We'd had quite enough rest and we knew that we had a lot of digging to do before we could collapse the campsite and move on, so we agreed to an early start. The following morning it was still windy but the sky was not as angry, so we were up early to dig out our sledges and remove the drifted snow from the side of the tent. We had to take extreme care doing this as an overzealous swipe of the spade could easily rip the material. We tried to lever the wind-packed snow off the tent fabric, which was now stretched as tight as the skin on a drum. It was a slow business. The wind was far from finished, but by nine o'clock we were under way, eager to make up lost time.

The conditions improved throughout the day. Off to the west, through breaks in the cloud we again caught glimpses of the Transantarctic Mountains, but still ahead of us lay the ever-familiar flat line of the horizon. The wind had polished and packed the snow hard during the storm, so we made swift headway over the firm surface. In places I remember it resembled burnished alabaster. It was so energising to be on the move again and I sensed that for each leg, now forty-five minutes, we seemed to be moving quicker than normal. At the end of the day my senses proved right. We had covered sixteen nautical miles, our furthest to date and crossed the 80°S line of latitude. This was a very gratifying moment as we were into the eighties at last and had only ten more degrees to complete the journey now. But ten degrees, I reminded myself, is six hundred nautical miles. We were barely a quarter of the way.

1908

At this stage of the Great Ice Barrier Shackleton started to have serious trouble with his four ponies. He had been following the same route he had taken with Scott and Wilson in 1902 but the snow was deeper now and the ponies, often buried up to their bellies, were finding it desperate work pulling the heavy sledges. Only three weeks after they left the hut at Cape Royds, Chinaman was showing signs of distress and routinely fell back behind the others. He became lame, off his food and tiring fast. So badly was he suffering that when they came to camp on 21 November 1908, he was shot. It was a sad but ominous moment, as it was obvious that Quan, Grisi and Socks were also feeling similar strain and would not last long. The daily grind was also being felt by their handlers. Marshall, ill-equipped for dental work, took two attempts to pull out one of Adam's teeth, splitting it on the first. Shackleton was suffering from snow-blindness and Wild found the fatty food made him unwell. But on 26 November, after four gruelling weeks on the Ice Barrier, there was cause for celebration, as they had passed the 'Furthest South' point that Scott and Wilson had reached in December 1902. The achievement was marked by two tablespoonfuls each of curaçao – an orange liqueur – and a smoke, before they settled down for the night, each wondering now what the days ahead would bring, for no one in history had ever ventured so far south. Despite this record, the demands being made on the tough Manchurian ponies was too great. On 27 November Grisi was next to go. Four days later Quan was led behind a specially built snow wall where a single shot from Shackleton's revolver ended his misery.

Campsite on the Ice Barrier. Snow wall on the right was used to shield the death of Quan.

It must have been a dreadful moment, not only to end the lives of such loyal and hard-working animals, but also to realise that with their passing his primary method of travel had gone. 'The killing of the ponies was not pleasant work.' Shackleton wrote, and on the day of Quan's death, 'We all felt losing him, I particularly, for he was my special horse ever since he was ill last March. I had looked after him, and in spite of all his annoying tricks he was a general favourite. He seemed so intelligent. Still it was best for him to go, and like the others he was well fed to the last.' That night Socks stood cold and pathetically alone, hopelessly whinnying for his lost companions. Shackleton's plans had suffered a major blow. Within the space of just over a week he had lost three of his four ponies and he was having to cut down on his already-meagre sledging ration of food. The ponies were, however, a source of food. So before the animals were left and depoted for the return journey, a quantity of meat was cut off and carried on the sledge; even their ground-up maize would supplement the food supply. Socks had been Wild's pony from the start so he continued to lead him along whilst Shackleton, Adams and Marshall leaned into their harnesses to pull the other sledge.

2008

We read about those moments as we lay in the tent each evening. The images I formed from Shackleton's daily descriptions were so powerful that they kept me going day after day. I passed many hours imagining the original team battling along beside us, still so full of hope despite their hardship and setbacks. I would talk to Shackleton about his thoughts, hopes and disappointments, and with every slide of my ski I could feel his compass in my trouser pocket. In many ways I seemed to be developing a bond with him through this shared experience.

Positive progress over the following days was evident by the renewed interest we were taking in our time and distance calculations and by the space beginning to appear inside our sledges. For as each week passed we were able to roll up one of the empty blue food bags with some ceremony. While there was a considerable expanse of the continent still to cover, we began to realise that the 9 January rendezvous was not an impossibility after all – but we would have to maintain our current daily mileage, which would be a considerable challenge on the Beardmore. We knew that Robert Swan and his team had raced up the glacier, so hopefully we would find a similar route and our equipment would hold up to the rough terrain. But it was still some way off, and without question would be the toughest stage.

Three weeks into the journey and we had covered close to two hundred miles and ascended only one hundred and ninety feet above sea level. I was beginning to feel at ease with the barrier and actually began to look forward now to each day on the march. I had quickly learned that there was no point in trying to battle with the surface, it was better to try to overcome it with style and skill. I was picking my route in a far more efficient way and going with the grain of the sastrugi. My skiing technique was improving and periodically I would feel a weightless glide, as if there was a helping hand at work, pushing at the small of my back for a brief moment.

As the journey wore on I became particularly intrigued by my increasing ability to pick up the minutest imperfection on the surface of the snow. Involuntarily, it seemed, my eye would be drawn to anything that seemed out of place – a speck of oil from someone's ski binding, a spot of blood from a gobbet of spit or even a single crumb from a biscuit. And in the air I was clearly seeing minute pieces of fluff from a hat or balaclava as they drifted past me on the incessant wind. The purity of all that was around us was so intense that any imperfection, however small, was an unnatural intrusion and immediately noticeable.

One sun-drenched afternoon, I was skiing contentedly along at the back of the group having just led a stage, lost in the thought of what vegetables to plant in our garden in Herefordshire the following spring. Suddenly, I stopped dead in my tracks. Just ahead of my ski tips I could see two small shadows darting across the snow to my front. Quite startled, I turned my head towards the sun to find the cause, and there, barely twenty feet away, were two of the purest white birds I had ever seen. Very like magician's doves and with beady, black eyes they stared down at me, continuing their flight for a few moments. Then they arced effortlessly upwards and peeled away towards the sun. They remained in view for some time as I watched them head off towards the distant mountains, just visible forty miles away on the western horizon. I shouted to Henry and Will but my excitement was no match for the headwind (and, I later realised, their iPods) so they missed the very unusual sight in this vast, empty landscape, of seeing other living creatures. It wasn't until we stopped at the next break that I was able to tell them about what I had seen and I sensed a twinge of disappointment from them at not sharing the sight; although it took some convincing for them to believe me.

I spent the rest of the afternoon mulling over what I had experienced. I could simply brush this off as an unusual sighting of two inquisitive birds which had probably flown over to see if we were a source of food. But I was not content with that explanation. That was unimaginative and too simple. I do not have a particularly strong faith but I found it impossible not to be moved, in some spiritual way, by such an incident. My mind was racing and I was far more inspired by thinking that this could be the spirits of Shackleton or Scott and this was a sign that they were keeping a watchful eye on us. I found it hugely comforting that perhaps some greater being was amongst us and I wrote in my diary that night, 'I took it as a great omen of good. Were these the spirits of those who went before us? Guardians of the Great Barrier checking on our progress? It is hard, in a place like this, devoid of life, that on seeing these lovely creatures not to imagine some other force at work.' I learned later that they were a pair of snow petrels that had very probably come from nesting sites known to be in the Transantarctic Mountains. I was humbled by the thought that they were over two hundred and fifty miles from the sea and their only supply of food – but such was the scale of the place we were in. One year on, though, part of me still believes I witnessed more than just two birds.

The days seemed to be getting better and better. The snow was very forgiving, the wind far from cruel; ironically, I wished for more sun cream and a floppy hat as the Antarctic sun sapped our strength. The mountains in the distance were now creeping round to lie ahead of us, which was a clear indication that we were making headway. Our morale was high. I was feasting on a diet of positive thoughts all day long and you could tell from the banter in the evening that we all felt the same and were in great spirits.

As the journey progressed, it became obvious that we were getting noticeably fitter. It was as though we were spending seven hours each day in a gym doing circuit training with only a ten-minute break between each session: no wonder it was having an effect. Yet at the start of the third week I noticed that I was beginning to drop back – not by much, but as it was so early in the expedition, I thought it a worrying sign. When I was in the lead I seemed fine. I easily kept to the required mileage and, on occasions, even pulled away from the other two. But when I went to the back, no matter how hard I tried, I would slow down. I was certain that there was no difference in our speeds, yet I couldn't seem to close the gap. The distance between us was never far but it begun to concern me, not because I thought I was less fit but I couldn't work out what was going wrong and the anxiety made it worse.

Day after day the sun continued to arc round us with barely a dip in its course. With little or no wind it became a menace. Most days were now unbearably hot and the nights uncomfortable as well. On one particular windless day Will removed his shirt completely and skied for over two hours with the sun hot upon his back. The cooling effect from the air was comfortable but it masked the burning. He put his shirt back on after a couple of hours but it was too late, the damage had been done and he would pay the price over the next few days. Henry and I had stripped down to our long johns but remained covered on top, and all of us travelled with neither gloves nor hat – but still we sweated. Our sunglasses misted up with sweat and our sun cream began to run low. We later heard that back in Britain during that same November week, the temperature went down to -11°C. It had been only -2°C on the Great Ice Barrier of the Antarctic.

At the end of those hot and sweaty days we needed little encouragement to wash. The process was simple and short. Just before climbing into our sleeping bags we would pour a cupful of hot water into a plastic bag, just enough to soak a small flannel. Using a miniature bar of soap we would then wash our groins, armpits and, using a separate flannel, our faces. We were not as fastidious as perhaps we should have been, and there was a noticeable drop-off in the frequency of washes as the air temperature fell and we became more tired. It was a lazy approach, as personal hygiene is vital in all extreme environments, especially when the risk of rashes and infections is high. But one thing we did do every night was brush our teeth. I knew, from countless days spent on exercise in the army, that no matter how dirty you actually are, having clean teeth creates a comforting illusion of overall cleanliness. I would brush mine while outside the tent on my night-time walk at the very end of each day. I would lean forward and sweep the head of the brush through the snow before applying the paste. It became an evening ritual that I loved, for I knew that it would be part of the journey that, if I wanted to, I could remind myself of every evening for the rest of my life.

On 10 December 2008, the twenty-seventh day of our journey, we passed the 'Furthest South' point that Shackleton had reached with Captain Scott on 30 December 1902. From the warmth of our tent Henry read aloud Shackleton's account of when he reached the same place again in November 1908. 'A day to remember, for we have passed "Furthest South" previously reached by man.' I loved that sentence for its simplicity and understated significance.

We spent the next half-hour discussing what a moment that must have been for Shackleton. But however hard we tried to imagine his feelings on that day, his own words describe them more eloquently, 'It falls to the lot of few men to view land not previously seen by human eyes, and it was with feelings of keen curiosity, not unmingled with awe, that we watched the new mountains rise from the great unknown that lay ahead of us. Mighty peaks they were, the eternal snows at their bases, and their rough-hewn forms rising high toward the sky. No man of us could tell what we would discover in our march South, what wonders might not be revealed to us, and our imaginations would take wings until a stumble in the snow, the sharp pangs of hunger, or the dull ache of physical weariness brought back our attention to the needs of the immediate present. As the days wore on, and mountain after mountain came into view, grimly majestic, the consciousness of our insignificance seemed to grow upon us. We were but tiny black specks crawling slowly and painfully across the white plain, and bending our puny strength to the task of all ages. Our anxiety to learn what lay beyond was nonetheless keen, however, and the long days of marching over the Barrier surface were saved from monotony by the continued appearance of new land to the southeast.'

One of a number of evening rituals would be to plot our position on the map from the GPS reading I took at the end of each day. I had brought three maps with me. The first one we used was a 1:250,000 scale of the Ross Sea area, which covered only the first week of our journey. On a map of that scale each day's progress was clearly visible. It was a great feeling to run my pencil along the straight edge of the spare compass to join up the new cross with the one from the previous day. We then had to wait for a further ten days before we joined the second map, which covered the latter part of the Ice Barrier, Mount Hope and all of the Beardmore Glacier. The third map I used was a pilot's map which covered the entire length of the journey but on a scale so small that our daily plots were very close together and it appeared we hadn't moved at all. But it was all we had for the crossing of the polar plateau and the Pole. And I kept reminding myself that Shackleton had nothing.

1908

Following the death of his three ponies, Shackleton and his team pressed on towards new land. Each day that passed, the Transantarctic Mountains that lay to the west appeared closer and began to be seen in front of them, forming a menacing barrier of granite and ice that Shackleton had to find a way through. To the east, the surface was by now becoming a mass of icy rubble, crevasses and ridges. He was being forced off his line of march and had no option but to head for the high ground ahead of him. 'There is a red hill about 3,000 foot in height, which we hope to climb tomorrow, so as to gain a view of the surrounding country', was how he described what unfolded before him.

2008

By early December a hundred years later, there was mounting excitement among us. We knew that, after nearly a month's walk, we were approaching the closing stages of the Ice Barrier and the second stage of the journey was about to begin. We had only forty miles to go but we would cover that in three days and then the same 'red hill' – or Mount Hope – and a pass which Shackleton had called The Gateway would be in front of us. But this beguiling barrier was not finished with us yet. What better way to tease us than to draw a curtain across the great sights which had just come into view, and which we had waited so long to see? Everything was now so tantalisingly close, when thick low cloud plunged us suddenly into a white darkness. It seemed so cruel. We had to resort to navigating solely with the compass rather than picking a distant point on the horizon. The lead man skied with his head bent, trying to keep the needle fixed on the bearing. It was a tedious way to ski. Heading into a featureless wall of white nothingness with a stiffening neck and stumbling over seemingly huge obstacles that in normal light would have been hardly discernible. A glance behind would reveal a meandering line of tracks in the snow as we corrected and overcorrected in a blind attempt to keep to the bearing. Buoyed on by knowing we were so close to Mount Hope and our exit, we persevered through the white-out for two days. Each morning we awoke hopeful for a clear sky and view of the mountains which we knew were hiding so close now. But it was not to be.

Two days later, and with only fifteen miles left to go, we were fumbling our way through the flat light when glimpses of blue sky began to appear beyond the motionless cloud. Above us the sun seemed as though it was trying to help, but I didn't trust it. We pushed on, remarking to each other at the breaks how saddened we were that we had to imagine the same sights that Shackleton described in his diary. They lay somewhere directly in front of us, but hidden from view; we would be kept waiting until the bitter end. But as the day wore on, the strength of the sun increased and its influence over the low cloud prevailed. Slowly, as the air temperature rose, so the cloud began to dissipate – like a fine muslin curtain being torn slowly apart. Through these misty windows we could see the mountains and ice fields gradually emerge, thrillingly close. As each minute passed greater sights were revealed until the curtain was finally lifted to reveal The Gateway and Mount Hope's red slopes in all their glory. Despite having to wait until the last moment, the manner of this grand unveiling was worth the wait.

We stopped, sat down on the front of our sledges and stared in silence at the panorama, comparing it to the photograph that Shackleton had taken from almost the same point and which I was carrying in the same pocket as the compass. Like sailors, it was as though we had been at sea for a month and were now reaching familiar dry land. Looking back on this day of the journey, I remember thinking just how close we felt to the original team at this point. We were looking at exactly the same piece of high ground that they had seen. It was not difficult to imagine them talking about which route to take to get them to the highest point. It was also the first time when poor Socks would be required to haul his load uphill as they left the flat surface of the Great Ice Barrier.

Where we had stopped we noticed that the surface of the Ice Barrier was noticeably different. At this point it was having to absorb the unbelievable pressures of the ice flow from the numerous glaciers that crashed into it as they flowed down from the high ground. But it was a motionless crash. There was no noise and no suddenness about it – just thousands of years of minute movements

Shackleton's view of Mount Hope (left) and The Gateway (right).

that produce this chaotic junkyard of ice. The results were rifts and fissures and heaped icy rubble that was to serve as a warning of what was to come. We picked our way through and kept heading for the red hill and the obvious Gateway to its west. This was the first time on the journey that I suddenly felt respectful of the forces of nature at work around us. Our journey to date had lacked any real danger, but now I sensed change. For the first time we were right among signs of the churn taking place. And all this disturbance meant only one thing – the threat of crevasses. Taking no chances, we steered wide around all obstacles we could see, keeping one eye on the high ground to our front. The red hill became closer and grew higher. Patches of cloud still drifted past, blocking our view, but the overall panorama was a glorious sight.

1908

For Shackleton, this stage of his journey was a key moment. He was desperate to find a way through the mountains that barred his way. After breakfast on 4 December, leaving Socks behind with enough food for the day, the four intrepid explorers set off, each with four biscuits, four lumps of sugar and two ounces of chocolate to last them until the evening. The approach to the red hill was guarded by crevasses which forced them to rope up. After a very light lunch they started to ascend the forward slopes until they were high enough to see new land beginning to appear over the ridge lines and peaks all around them. With each step they took over the red granite scree they climbed higher, heading for a ridge from where they hoped to see even further. As they crested it they stopped, stood still and just stared. For there, stretching away from them as far as they could see was a glacier of such immense proportions that it must, they thought, lead straight through the mountain range and on to the Pole. Perched on granite boulders and eating the remains of their meagre rations, their minds were momentarily blocked from intense hunger by the discovery of this great highway. With their hearts pounding from the effort of the climb and feeling weak but elated they gazed into the distance, no one uttering a word. Scanning the panorama, Shackleton noticed a prominent peak on the western side of the valley that had the only cloud in the sky hanging over it, as if tethered like a balloon to the summit. He made a mental note that it would be a prominent reference point to head for. On his way back to the campsite in the afternoon, he felt filled with the optimism and hope that the view from the red hill had given them. 'A very good name for it. I must remember that – Mount Hope,' he muttered to himself as they retraced their tracks back to their solitary pony waiting patiently at the campsite.

2008

The closing hour of our day's work was spent starting the climb towards the high ground that led to The Gateway. It was our first significant ascent of the journey and noticeably hard. We finally felt the true deadweight of our sledges and it came as a huge shock. It was hard to get a grip on the steep slope despite the skins on our skis and at times I was forced to herring-bone my way up, and by the end of the day I was tiring quickly. Our progress was suddenly much slower, but we managed to cover about a quarter of the distance to the high ground before pitching camp for the night. More low cloud was moving in and the wind was increasing each minute. We wasted no time in putting up the tent and getting the stove on. Inside; warm, fed and relaxed we reflected on the journey to date, for after thirty-one days we had finally left the Great Ice Barrier. She had been a considerate opponent and allowed us on our way with very little interference. The weather had been hugely forgiving and, in spite of the storm, we had made the most of it by covering the distance a week faster than I had planned. We had definitely grown fitter, but were also driven by a determination to succeed and to make up the lost time. The 9 January meeting still remained our goal.

Camped in The Gateway, our thoughts in the evening turned to those who had gone before us through this narrow pass: only Shackleton, Scott and Swan. The presence of those great polar explorers was tangible. What a moment of great anticipation this must have been for Shackleton – the first in history along this route. At last he was leaving the Great Ice Barrier behind. It had been a far more formidable opponent for him than it had for us. It had claimed the lives of three of his valuable ponies. Food was beginning to run low but still the optimism burns like words of fire in his diary – from somewhere very close to where we had pitched our tent he wrote, 'Our way lies to the South. How one wishes for time and unlimited provisions. Then indeed we could penetrate the secrets of this great lonely continent. Regrets are vain, however, and we wonder what is in store for us beyond the mountains if we are able to get there.' I closed my eyes, turned on to my left side and buried my head into my down jacket, which served as my pillow. What a feeling it was to finish the day on such an historic spot. We had just joined the list of extraordinary men who had crossed the Great Ice Barrier and journeyed through this narrow windy pass en route south.

The following morning the intention was to continue climbing for a couple of hours when we would reach the top of The Gateway. Thereafter, just as Shackleton had done, we planned to camp and then scramble up to the high point of Mount Hope to get our first view of the Beardmore Glacier. But even the short distance to the top of The Gateway was hard going. Henry and Will powered on as if in four-wheel drive, but the gradient was too steep for me to tackle head-on, so I set off across the slope to zigzag my way up. It was more time consuming but far less demanding and, therefore, much more enjoyable. The weather had not improved from the night before so it was unlikely that we would see much of the glacier from our vantage point. But as this was such an important stage of the journey we had decided to wait for twenty-four hours in the hope that the weather would improve; we simply had to see the same view that Shackleton had seen on 4 December 1908. So, after having covered only one mile, we pitched our tent again and climbed back into our sleeping bags to play another waiting game with the weather. Regardless of the delay it imposed, we had to explore this historic spot. It was one of the special points on the route.

I was restless. Despite the gloomy conditions I wanted to explore, not rest. I told the others that I was going to recce a route for tomorrow's scramble up to the high ground. Grunts of acknowledgement emanated from the interior of Henry's scratcher.

'I won't go far and will be back this afternoon,' I said as I unzipped the entrance to the tent and stepped outside. I put on my windproof smock, grabbed my lunch bag and skied off to the base of the high ground where I could see a route up through the loose rock and scree to a small plateau. It was an exhilarating feeling to move without the burden of the sledge. After twenty minutes skiing easily uphill, I reached the point where the snow stopped and the scree begun, but the incline was now quite severe, so I removed my skis with great care. One slip and they would have careered off down the slope. Our boots offered no real grip at all on the very icy slope, so it was a relief to finally get purchase on the rock, despite it being very loose. I trod with care so as not to damage the small metal pin at the front of my boots, which was the only method of securing the boots to the ski binding. We were each carrying a spare set of boots, but it would be cavalier to take risks with key pieces of equipment at this stage, so I was careful. To walk and climb after a month on skis was a strange feeling of freedom because I was now on land rather than snow and ice. It was such a change. I felt free and eager to climb away from the flat Ice Shelf.

I scrambled a short distance up to the plateau from where I should have seen my first glimpse of the glacier, had there been no cloud. Instead, all I could make out was the bottom of the mountains on the western and eastern sides. Behind me, to the north, I could just about make out the Ice Barrier and the direction of our approach over the previous two days, but the cloud made it too difficult to identify clearly the route we had taken.

Disappointed, I decided to push on upwards in the hope of finding a suitable spot for the next day from which to see the glacier and the next stage of our journey. The boulders were getting bigger as I edged my way to the front of a shelf that overlooked the whole area. Below me I could just make out our tent, a miniscule dot in the centre of The Gateway. I gazed into the gloom wondering just what my nemesis had in store for us over the coming two weeks. To the right was Cape Allen and the Granite Pillars and, somewhere in the cloud on the opposite side of the mouth of the Beardmore, would be the unmistakable shape of Mount Kyffin. Shackleton must have reached somewhere close to the point where I now stood when he wrote, 'At 1 p.m. we had a couple of biscuits and some water, and then started to make our way up the precipitous rock face. This was the most difficult part of the whole climb, for the granite was weathered and split in every direction, and some of the larger pieces seemed to be just nicely balanced on smaller pieces, so that one could almost push them over by a touch. With great difficulty we clambered up this rock face, and then ascended a gentle snow slope to another rocky bit, but not so difficult to climb.'

It was frustrating not to be able to see the mouth of the Beardmore as Shackleton had done, but hopefully the weather would clear tomorrow and we could all return to the same spot to see, with our own eyes, what he had seen. I was enjoying being on my own. I sat down on a smooth boulder, took a piece of chocolate from my pocket and munched it while for a long moment I looked out over the great glacier below me. We had reached an important stage of our journey and my mind drifted back over key moments of the past month. I recalled how despondent we had been as we set off, knowing that because of the delay we were almost certainly not going to arrive at the arranged rendezvous on 9 January 2009. But now, perhaps we might just make it. Morale was high, but we were not complacent. We felt a real sense of accomplishment about what we had so far achieved; pushing on across the Ice Shelf solely intent on honouring Shackleton's achievement. We had also been blessed with fine Antarctic weather which we had taken advantage of, but the short storm had taught us not to drop our guard. The same, or worse, could easily pin us down on the glacier that we were about to ascend. We were working well as a team. We were efficient, we laughed a lot and – importantly – we understood what an utter privilege it was to be retracing this great journey. Our respect for Shackleton and his team was growing daily as we turned page after page of his diary each night. I had thought about him and his team constantly on the Ice Barrier, trying to delve between the lines of his understated and optimistic writing. I was in awe of how he, as the leader, had managed to keep the level of belief so alive within his team when disasters had already befallen them. Being the first to plant your nation's flag at the South Pole must have had an unimaginable power over them but to journey into the unknown, not knowing what crisis the day might bring or what lay over the next rise must have been a great strain on their mental fortitude – but it is impossible to find reference in his writing of the fear of the unknown. Those men seemed close to being indestructible.

I stood up and, without hesitation, stooped to pick up a large, flat-topped, rock which I placed on top of a boulder, then I selected another one, and another and started to build a cairn. I had a real urge to create something to commemorate the discovery of the Beardmore Glacier. It didn't take me long to gather a series of rocks that gradually decreased in size so they would all sit neatly in a pyramid-like pile. I then found a flat-faced piece of slate-like rock on which, using the metal tip of my ski stick, I scratched the names of the team: SHACKLETON, WILD, ADAMS, MARSHALL. I placed it at the foot of the cairn. I was rather ashamed with what I did next, but I wanted there to be a record of Will, Henry and I having passed this way as well. So, on a separate rock I scratched 'SCE [Shackleton Centenary Expedition] 15-12-08'. Mischievously, I deliberately didn't put the year in full in the hope that perhaps one day the cairn would be discovered and thought to have been built in 1908, though the acronym SCE made it look rather suspicious. When I had finished building the cairn I felt rather hypocritical, because throughout the journey so far I had yearned for isolation and was scathing about any unnatural intrusion. Yet here I was, creating an artificial monument and leaving a permanent record of our presence there. The desire to recognise and mark Shackleton's achievement had prevailed, but I remain troubled about whether I did the right thing.

Despite the overcast weather I felt no urge to return to the tent so I set off to explore, scrambling over the rocks and across the snow. It was not dissimilar to rock pooling on a Cornish beach. Jumping from boulder to boulder, stopping to gaze in astonishment at the rocks cleaved in half by the power of erosion and periodically picking up and examining samples of quartz and granite; I was in my element. A couple of hours passed swiftly by and it was time to head back to find my skis and then, onwards, to the tent. I covered the short downhill journey to the campsite quickly. Planting my skis in the snow, I heard the comments even before I had unzipped the entrance to the tent.

'Ah, General. We were beginning to think you'd met an unfortunate end,' Henry said.

'Yes, my fault. I'm sorry. I got rather carried away. I have recced a route for us tomorrow which will give us a great view of the glacier – as long as the weather clears,' I replied. 'Have you guys been in your scratchers since I left?'

'Yes,' Will answered with a contented grin. 'A bit of iPod action and dozing has helped pass the time. Any complaints?'

'None at all. I reckon that if the weather is still gloomy tomorrow then we should still go up first thing and try and get under way by lunchtime. The view is still worth the climb and there is something I have made that I want to show you.'

Henry and Will quite quickly guessed it was a cairn but I refused to say more. Much to their amusement, I spent the rest of the evening examining the few rock samples I had collected. I wanted a memento from Mount Hope and, in particular, I wanted to present Zaz Shackleton with something from the journey when I returned the compass to her.

When we were back inside our sleeping bags after supper, I read out the diary entry for the day Shackleton climbed Mount Hope. Hopefully, tomorrow we would see what he had described. It was the perfect end to a very special day when I felt closely connected to the past.

For some unexplained reason I awoke at 4 a.m. I lifted my eye mask slowly and immediately noticed how much brighter it was than when we went to sleep. Trying to avoid waking the others, I reached up and slowly unzipped the entrance to the tent to see if the cloud had moved on. Before I had reached the bottom of the zip it was obvious that it was a flawless day. All the cloud had lifted and you could see as far as your eyes would allow. Mount Kyffin dominated the skyline, standing guard over the mouth of the Beardmore, which stretched away far into the distance to yet another horizon. Our patience had been rewarded and I returned to the warmth of my sleeping bag grinning like a schoolboy, knowing that we would be in for a treat once we had climbed back to the spot I had chosen the day before.

Four hours later we wasted no time in melting the snow for our breakfast and flasks. We left the tent up, put on our skis and set off following my tracks from the day before. Very quickly we reached the point where I had set off on foot up the scree slope to the small plateau and the boulder field. I sent Will and Henry on ahead to the edge of the rock face so that they would stumble on the cairn. Will came across it first.

'Ah, very good, General. A fitting memorial. Good effort,' he said approvingly.

Behind the cairn stretched the Beardmore. From our eyrie it looked smooth and welcoming, but we were not fooled. Despite having to deal with the obvious challenges that lay ahead, this was such an exciting moment. At last we could gaze on the same view that had so lifted Shackleton's spirit. I thought back to the diary entry I had read out last night and now repeated it aloud, 'From the top of this ridge there burst upon our view an open road to the South, for there stretched before us a great glacier running almost South and North between two huge mountain ranges. As far as we could see, except toward the mouth, the glacier appeared to be smooth, yet this was not a certainty, for the distance was so great.'

We each savoured the moment in our own way. We sat, stared and thought our own thoughts in silence. For a moment, I felt so close to the original team for, like them, we were about to embark on the toughest part of the journey.

CHAPTER 5

Battle with the Blue Ice

'Falls, bruises, cut shins, crevasses, razor-edged ice, and a heavy upward pull have made up the sum of the day's trials, but there has been a measure of compensation in the wonderful scenery.'

EHS, 10 December 1908

Over the five years of planning this expedition, the Beardmore Glacier had become my nemesis, for it posed the single greatest threat to us completing the journey. Named by Shackleton in recognition of one of his financial backers, Sir William Beardmore, it is one of the largest glaciers in the world – more than one hundred miles long, twenty-five miles wide and an ascent of six thousand feet from mouth to source. Due to its remote location, it has rarely been walked upon save by a handful of explorers and glaciologists.

The greatest danger to us lay in the myriad traps that had been set on the surface – crevasses narrow enough to snap a bone, or wide enough to swallow a car for ever. And because we were at the bottom of the world, where scale and distance exist on an unimaginable level, we would be additionally vulnerable, as rescue in the event of a serious injury would be many days away. However, we had focussed a considerable part of our training, especially in Chamonix, on glacier travel and crevasse rescue techniques so I was confident that we were very well prepared and equipped to deal with whatever difficulties we might face.

I had spent a sizeable amount of time researching the character of the Beardmore by reading the accounts of those who had been there before us – Captain Scott, Ernest Shackleton, Robert Swan, Ranulph Fiennes and Reinhold Messner. The list was short and rather imposing but since Shackleton and Scott only Robert Swan, our fund-raising patron, had ascended it the way we intended. I found it rather unnerving to think that we were endeavouring to complete a journey only ever undertaken by such an exclusive list of formidable polar legends. That fact alone made the prospect of even starting this journey such a daunting challenge.

By mid-morning we reluctantly left our viewpoint, scrambled down the loose granite scree of Mount Hope and skied back to where we had left the tent and our sledges. We packed away the tent and harnessed up, intent on making for the Granite Pillars which marked the western entrance to the glacier. I clipped the trace to my harness and, as I lifted my head to look out across the valley to where we would shortly be heading, I could see ahead of me the blurred outline of Shackleton's team making tracks in the snow as they made their way down to the glacier and on to the 'Highway to the South . . .' What a moment that must have been for them. Despite the loss of three ponies and with only Socks remaining to haul one of their sledges, 5 December 1908 must have been an exhilarating day, perfectly described in the name Shackleton chose for the mountain at the glacier's mouth. The fading dream that they might still make it to the Pole came alive once more, and was captured by Wild, 'I really believe we shall reach the Pole, but we shall as surely miss the ship.'

We covered the distance past the imposing features of Cape Allen and the Granite Pillars making good time, for it was downhill and the surface conditions were perfect. Despite the covering of snow I noticed signs that alerted me for the first time that we were about to ski on to the face of this great glacier. Patches of ice, aquamarine in colour, only a few square yards in size, started to appear. I also noticed a few stones, some as big as footballs, lying on the snow but a considerable distance from the valley side. It was obvious that they had rolled down, or been prised from the cliffs by the erosive power of freezing water. But it must have taken many years of travel on the surface of the glacier for the rocks to be where I now saw them. I stopped for a moment and bent down to pick up a small stone as a memento of my first steps on the Beardmore. But then I felt rather guilty: in an unthinking moment, I had interrupted a journey that, up to then, had probably been under way for fifty years or more as the small splinter of rock hitched a lift on this great river of ice.

After an hour we had reached the Granite Pillars, where we stopped for the usual snack. I set up the tripod and camera for a team shot to send back to the website, marking our first day on the Beardmore. Shortly after this we continued along a new bearing which took us out to the centre of the glacier. I had planned to take this route because the surface in the middle would be the least disturbed, away from the rubble and chaos caused by the numerous smaller glaciers that fed into the Beardmore along both sides of the valley.

It wasn't long after we set off, still on skis, that we started to notice our first crevasses. These were not gaping chasms, but narrow fissures often well disguised with a covering of snow which acted in most cases as a bridge – but which varied enormously in the loads they could support. This was no time to be complacent or lazy, so we stopped immediately and agreed to rope up. We had practised a set drill for travelling this way in Chamonix. I led, Will came next and Henry was at the back. It was a system that worked well and each of us knew exactly what was required from one another in the event that one of us, together with a sledge, fell through a snow bridge and was left dangling in a dark, bottomless void. On my visit to the eminent glaciologist Charles Swithinbank, I had been reassured that it was highly improbable that a man and his sledge would plummet hundreds of feet into a yawning chasm but much more likely that a knee or ankle might be twisted or broken by stepping through a soft snow covering into one of the many narrow cracks and fissures. The time had come to use some of the equipment that, up to now, had simply been deadweight at the back of my sledge. We each took out our lightweight climbing harness, stepped into them and fastened them tightly. While checking that the karabiners, ice screws, prusiks and slings were all securely fastened it hit me that this was what all our training had been preparing us for – a safe ascent of the Beardmore Glacier. There was no guide or instructor to look over our shoulder. We were on our own and would have to rely on each other for everything. Henry moved up the line, double-checking the various knots we had tied and the proper alignment of the fifty-yard rope that linked us all together.

'Not sure this auto-block is properly tied,' he said to me.

'Yes it is,' I replied sharply. Then I checked again and discovered he was correct. Not needing to say a word, Henry looked at me, smirked and slightly raised his eyebrows as I secured my sledge to the rope the right way. After so many years training together we knew each other so well. The relationship was now firmly rooted in friendship and a common goal, which we were approaching like three brothers. But now it was specifically about trust in one another – trust in each other's abilities, trusting our judgement and the trust not to cut corners.

1908

Lifted by his discovery of the glacier from the slopes of Mount Hope, Shackleton and his men set off from the top of The Gateway to join it. But their eagerness was to be short-lived. As soon as he and his team reached the glacier it became apparent that progress would be slow. The unshod Socks was sliding on the blue ice, unable to get enough traction to pull his sledge and the men were forced to travel roped up because of the web of crevasses that lay in their path. Day after day the surface became more treacherous. The only solution was to unload the sledges and move the stores in relay, until the going got better. For every five miles gained, they travelled fifteen as they fetched and carried stores back and forth. It was slow and painful work. Shins were scraped as they dropped through soft snow bridges and elbows were bruised from countless falls. The Alpine climbing rope which linked them saved them from certain death as time after time it pulled tight as each man occasionally slipped into crevasses determined to catch their prey. Frank Wild described their first day on the glacier, 'At 5.30 p.m. there were so many crevasses around us we could not find room to pitch a tent, and as the outlook ahead seemed to be worse still, we had to go back a quarter of a mile to find a camping place. Now we have both tents on a patch of snow some ten yards across and on all sides of us are hell holes. However when things get to their worst they must mend, so we are looking forward to better times tomorrow.'

2008

With the surface now getting more uneven for us too, and increasing patches of blue ice making continued use of skis slow and awkward, we decided to travel on foot and, for the first time, to use our crampons. After a final round of checks I led off, reminding myself that as the front man my job was to find the safest route and be ever-watchful for the telltale signs of hidden crevasses. It was a great feeling not to be travelling on skis; I felt much more in touch with the surroundings. But it did make us more vulnerable. Travelling on skis over this type of ground is safer because the body's weight is distributed over a wide area and the skis themselves can act as a bridge when crossing over narrow crevasses. On foot it is quite the reverse and it wasn't long after we set off that we received an abrupt reminder of just how careful we would have to be.

The area of glacier we were travelling over had a considerable covering of snow on it, which made it difficult to spot where the holes and cracks lurked. When in doubt, I used my ski sticks as probes to test the strength of the snow where I wanted to place my feet. Very often the stick would break through the crust and expose a dark hole, forcing me to step elsewhere. I became intrigued by these holes and wanted to see more. It was rather like teasing an animal to see how angry you could make it. I found myself hacking away at the snow covering just to see how wide and deep the hole was. These were lift shafts to an underworld inhabited by 'Crevassians', as I came to call them. But it was only a matter of time before each of us had been caught out.

The Antarctic can take your life in one of two ways. It can wear you down over a prolonged period of time through starvation, cold and exhaustion, often in the face of appalling weather. Or it can take you into the throat of a crevasse in a split second. There is an alarming suddenness to breaking through a snow crust, with your leg disappearing into a chasm up to your hip. One minute you are making good progress and the next you are reminded just how exposed you are to the designs of nature. It was relatively easy to extricate oneself when this happened, but each time it did so, you sensed your luck was running out and it may not be long before a big one got you.

Shackleton wrote in his diary that 'Wild described the sensation of walking over the surface of half ice and half snow, as like walking over the glass roof of a station.' He added that 'one gets somewhat callous as regards the immediate danger, though we are always glad to meet crevasses with their coats off, that is, not hidden by the snow covering.' Well, we were coming across a good many with their coats still on, and hidden from view. The prospect of playing a form of Russian roulette for the next hundred miles begun to take root in my mind.

To continue on foot would have been foolhardy and slow, for it only took a twisted knee or ankle, which seemed certain to happen, to place the whole expedition in jeopardy. There was still a sufficient covering of snow so we halted, put our skis back on and resumed our course towards the middle of the glacier. It might appear that we couldn't make up our minds whether to walk or ski, but remaining flexible would be key to our safety and perhaps even our survival. Although it was tedious and time-consuming to keep changing, we would have been in grave danger if we had not been bothered to act when we knew it was necessary. Being lazy and taking short cuts on an Antarctic glacier would be utter madness. If you did so, you deserved all that you got.

That first night we camped between Mount Kyffin to the east and the Granite Pillars to the west. It was such a thrill to have finally made it to the Beardmore, as this marked the second phase of our journey. We would be passing mountain peaks and glaciers all carrying the names of extraordinary individuals from the heroic age of polar exploration and we would be able to see and experience first-hand all the sights and difficulties described in Shackleton's diary. That night we read of his snow-blindness and the decision taken to lay a depot on their first day on the glacier, 'We are leaving a depot here. My eyes are my only trouble, for their condition makes it impossible for me to pick out the route or do much more than pull. The distance covered today was nine miles with four miles relay.'

Between mouthfuls of porridge at breakfast the following morning, I made a suggestion to Will and Henry, 'I think we should continue to travel roped up, on skis, for at least the first three hours today. By midday we should have reached the centre of the glacier and we can reassess the situation then.' They nodded in agreement.

We set off into a gentle fifteen-knot wind which died off during the morning, allowing the sun to keep us warm for the rest of the day. As predicted, the glacier surface became much smoother but large patches of blue ice began to appear by mid-afternoon which, if they continued to get bigger, would require us to put our crampons back on. Despite the skins on the bottom of my skis I was sliding all over the place and was desperate for greater grip. Blue ice forms on the surface of glaciers where the snow fails to settle and compress, due to the high winds. The action of the wind creates shallow cups and ridges – very similar to the effect it has on the sand of a windswept beach. It is as beautiful as the surface of a calm sea rippling in sunlight, but on a glacier it is solid, slippery as glass and as hard as steel.

We were surrounded on both sides by ice walls and peaks that had hardly ever been seen before and certainly never climbed by anyone. Behind us we could still make out Mount Hope and, in the distance to our front, 'a big mountain with a cloud on the top . . .' as Shackleton described it from the same summit and later named as 'The Cloudmaker'. No matter which direction I looked I was overwhelmed, not so much by the beauty, but more by the privilege of just being there. I was feasting on sights rarely seen by any man. Shackleton described a similar feeling in his diary. As he gazed on the glacier from the crags of Mount Hope he recorded, 'It is all so interesting and everything is on such a vast scale that one cannot describe it well. We four are seeing these great designs and the play of nature for the first time, and possibly they may never be seen by man again.'

After seven hours of travelling we started to look for somewhere to stop and set up our camp. Although we had travelled on skis all day, patches of snow were becoming less frequent and we needed a good supply of it to melt for our food and drinks. In due course we found somewhere suitable, pitched the tent and Will dived in first to get the stove going. It had been a great start and I wondered if the glacier was not going to be such a formidable opponent after all. I stepped out of my harness, sat down on my sledge and took the GPS out of my pocket. I turned it on and waited for it to tell me how far we had travelled that day. It always seemed like waiting for an exam result.

'Scores on the doors for today was 15.1,' I announced to the others.

'Good work, fellas. Still on track for 9 January,' replied Henry.

'Yes. I think tomorrow we should set off on crampons. There is so much blue ice around now I think we are wasting our time staying on skis. We'll be able to see all the crevasses as there is no snow covering. What do you think?' I asked.

'Definitely,' said Henry, already starting to coil up the rope. Will answered too, but I couldn't hear him over the roar of the stove inside the tent. I turned to my sledge and as I gathered together my sleeping bag, my right foot shot straight through the surface and my leg disappeared up to my hip. Henry rushed over and helped to haul me out. Although we laughed it off, I was struck by the suddenness of the event and how easy it is to let your guard down. It wasn't a deep crack, but if I hadn't got the message that we would have to be utterly respectful of this glacier, then I had now.

The following morning, our second full day on the glacier, we secured our skis to the top of our sledges and put on our crampons. In order to save weight we were using aluminium ones rather than the stronger, but significantly heavier, steel variety. I felt that there was no need to rope up, as we could clearly see where all the cracks lay due to the scanty covering of snow. I confirmed the direction of travel from the compass and pointed out a prominent peak to head for, about twenty miles away. As long as we stayed in the centre of the glacier and the blue ice remained flat and obstacle-free then we would be fine.

The first half-hour of the day's travel was hugely enjoyable. We seemed to bounce along the surface, hardly noticing our sledges as they ran friction-free over the ice. The noise we made as we walked was very different to what we had been used to, and every new sound stood out in the total silence. As each tooth of our crampons bit into the diamond-hard face of the glacier there was a grinding squeak accompanied by a faint tinkle as shards of ice slid out across the surface. My ski sticks were also a help, but the pointed tips provided little grip unless I punched downwards in time with each step. Over time this constant jarring caused significant pain in my elbows, but it was essential to maintaining any semblance of balance on the virtually impregnable surface. I paused briefly and looked back to the others.

'This is fantastic. If we keep this up, we'll be doing twenty miles a day no problem,' I said when we all met up. My buoyant mood was short-lived.

'Er, General, you've lost some teeth from both your heels,' Henry pointed out.

I sat down on my sledge and examined each crampon. Sure enough, I had already broken off a couple of teeth. We'd only been going half an hour. I wasn't too concerned, as I was still getting a strong grip, but it wasn't a great start as we still had about a hundred miles to go and a six-thousand foot gradual ascent until we would be clear of the glacier. Unsurprisingly, Will and Henry soon realised that they were also facing the same problem.

Despite my relaxed attitude over the early failure of the crampons, I had been very surprised at just how tough the blue ice was. Being far from smooth, the edged cups were so hard and uneven that they snapped off the crampons' aluminium teeth with ease, as it was impossible to place a boot down flat enough to ensure that equal pressure was spread across all points.

But we were in great spirits. The weather was glorious, there was no wind and the distant peaks and glaciers looked stunning.

A seemingly minor problem was not going to slow us up or dampen our high spirits.

We continued on, making good progress, but it soon became clear that our crampons were simply not up to the job. I started to get edgy as I noticed them beginning to fracture under the strain of the ice surface. Then, in mid-afternoon, my left crampon snapped completely in half. Now I was furious. How stupid we had been to bring the lighter-weight sets. We faced many miles still to go and there seemed no way we could cover the distance without them. Seated on my sledge, cussing and swearing, I saved time by replacing the broken crampon with my left ski and carried on in a very ungainly manner, skiing one stride, walking the next. I eventually caught up with the others at the next snack break and showed them the quandary I was in. Predictably, they were facing similar setbacks and becoming equally frustrated and impatient. It was not looking good.

We ended the day pitching our tent on the only patch of snow we could find. While waiting for the kettle to boil, we tackled the task of creating a new design of crampon from the small heap of twisted metal and straps that were piled in the centre of the tent. Survival in any extreme environment is often about problem solving, and this was the first real test of our resourcefulness. After a good couple of hours I had created a design that I hoped would cope, and which would get me through the next day. Although we had to take the situation seriously, those hours passed by quickly as we joked and laughed at the bizarre contraptions we were making.

Before turning in for the night I went outside for my usual wander about. I looked forward to this part of the day whatever the weather – in fact, the windier and colder the better. It was an important time for me, to be able to move into my own space, away from the others and reflect on all aspects of the journey and give thought to where we were. This entire experience was such a privilege that it would be a crime to waste any single moment of each endless, permanently light day. I was still frequently imagining Shackleton camped beside us. I would walk over to his tent and listen in on what they were discussing, taking care not to startle Socks, who was tethered to a sledge. At other times it was simply contemplation of our utter insignificance on this infinite landscape. On this occasion I didn't go far, as the tent booties I was wearing were no better than carpet slippers and had absolutely no grip at all on the unforgiving surface. I was eager to spy out a route for the next day as we needed to get clear of the pressure ridges and broken rubble that were now appearing on the glacier surface. With utmost care I climbed to the top of the nearest ridge and could see better ground some distance away in both directions, west and east. But to cut across the grain of this icy wreckage would take at least a day's travel in the wrong direction, probably more. My instinct was to get back to the centre of the glacier and to keep heading towards Buckley Island, which marked our exit.

I lay awake that night angry with myself that my research of the Beardmore had not been more thorough. I had allowed us to be drawn off our route into the chaos and our equipment was evidently not up to the job. After such a great start on the Ross Ice Shelf this was all very different. We were in no danger at the moment, but one simple fall on this surface resulting in a broken wrist or ankle and we definitely would be.

1908

Shackleton's progress up the glacier was also slow and awkward. The days of relaying the supplies were beginning to take their toll. Exhausted, cut and bruised, the four men were inching their way along, with Wild and Socks bringing up the rear. For the unshod pony the glass-like surface was far worse than the deep snow of the Ice Barrier. And then, on 7 December 1908, disaster struck. The scream from Wild echoed between the valley walls. Shackleton whipped round to see only Wild's head and shoulders showing from the edge of a gaping hole. His diary entry, written later that night, tells the tale, 'We stopped at once and rushed to his [Wild's] assistance, and saw the pony sledge with the forward end down a crevasse and Wild reaching out from the side of the gulf grasping the sledge. No sign of the pony . . . poor Socks had gone.' The sledge was miraculously wedged at an angle into the crevasse, still intact. They rushed to haul Wild from the ink-black hole and to retrieve their equipment, balanced perilously close to the edge. Wild was ashen white, and devastated that his loyal friend had plunged to his death. They all lay on their stomachs peering into the hole but not a sound was heard. Hopefully, they all thought, it had been a quick end.

Frank Wild's brush with death – later a lead story in a French magazine.

2008

On 19 December, we were camped right opposite the Socks glacier, as it was later named by Shackleton in the pony's honour. Just before I drifted off to sleep I remembered the impact that this tragic episode had had on many of the schoolchildren that I had lectured to prior to our departure. Once news of our expedition had filtered out through the media, we had received a number of requests to lecture in schools about our forthcoming journey. The demise of Socks always caused sighs of pity and sadness among the children. I was often asked whether we might find him, but to this day Socks is probably still somewhere out there, trapped in his tomb of ice, slowly moving towards the Ross Sea, where he will finally come to rest.

The following day, our thirty-seventh, we had covered four hundred and thirty-five nautical miles but it was obvious to me that we were about to have a testing week. We had been spoilt on the Ice Shelf. The weather had been perfect, the snow firm and we had covered the first four hundred miles eight days faster than I had planned. But now we were being challenged to think, and required to solve problems. The one issue that I could see needing firm leadership and a clear decision was over which route we should follow. Swan had stayed along the western edge of the glacier and had moved fast, covering in excess of fifteen miles each day. And over to the eastern side I could also see a flatter surface. Henry was all for cross-graining to the west, but I could see the world of hurt that we would have to go through to get there, and even then there were no guarantees that the surface would be any easier. It didn't take long after we had set off – aiming to find a course through the middle – before the doubts began to surface.

'I fundamentally disagree with the route we are taking. I think we should be over there,' Henry said, pointing to the west with his ski stick. 'It may take us a day to get through the crap but I think it is worth it.'

Will disagreed and wanted to carry on with the potential middle route, as did I. I could see these diverging views would be damaging if a firm decision was not made immediately, for we were all becoming frustrated with the situation. I had to step in and make a decision quickly.

'Look, mate,' I said – knowing I had to be firm – 'we need to keep heading southwards and upwards. While that side looks OK from here, it may not be when we get there and I simply don't think we are equipped to cut across the grain of the glacier – it looks horrendous; far worse than here. We are coping at the moment and are not far from the middle where it will be least disturbed, as we saw yesterday. So, although I understand why you feel so strongly about it, we will continue on this route.' Henry said nothing, but I sensed he was thankful that a quick and firm decision had been made. I turned and set off, clinging to the hope I was right. This had been the first direct challenge to a decision I had taken. I had sensed it had been brewing, as ever since the crampons started to break the three of us had grown more and more frustrated each day.

I felt that the Beardmore had us in its grip and was playing with us as an angler plays a fish and now we were being made to think and problem solve. But that was good, for it drew us together and forced us to focus on our vulnerability. The contrast in our progress was marked. Now we were slow and cautious and fed up with the numerous falls – at any time someone could be badly hurt. Swept together, these circumstances formed a pile of disappointment and aggravation that had to be watched like a hawk.

Our progress over the rest of the day was slow and very ungainly. On two occasions I was pulled over by my sledge because of the pathetic grip my boots had on the surface. It was agony as I broke the fall with my elbows, forearms and my back. I felt every ridge of ice as I was dragged over its vicious surface to the low ground where the sledge finally came to rest. But towards late afternoon we finally emerged on to the obstacle-free centre of the glacier, where at last we could move more quickly. I was now having to stop every hundred yards or so to tighten the collection of metal attached to my boots. The mounting frustration with our situation was obvious. Stopping late in the day to tighten my straps yet again, I signalled to the others, who had moved ahead of me, the sign that I was fine so they continued on. But soon they were out of sight. That was the last I saw of them for more than an hour, for they were in low ground and gone from view because of the gently undulating surface. As many minutes passed, I began to get furious. The three golden rules of polar travel, drummed into us by Matty McNair, had been broken – 'stay together, stay together, don't separate' had been the mantra.

Slowly and awkwardly I moved to every piece of high ground I could find and looked in the direction we were heading but still I could not see them. Then, finally, I caught a glimpse of a black dot highlighted against the backdrop of the blue ice. Henry was retracing his steps to find me. I sensed he knew what I was about to say when we finally met. I let rip.

'That was completely out of order. We have been out of visual contact for over an hour. Anything could have happened. My crampons are in a shit state. You know the golden rule. And why the hell didn't you move to some high ground to look for me? I have spent the last hour doing just that. It's your lack of common sense and awareness that really pisses me off.' I was fuming.

Henry knew that he and Will had been very careless. I unleashed the same rocket to Will when I arrived at the campsite and he was similarly contrite. Once I had taken off my boots and gathered my stuff together for the evening I had calmed down and they had apologised. It was a stupid mistake, but enough had been said. It had been a trying day, we were all tired and infuriated and tempers were worn through.

Reading Shackleton's diary that evening it was perhaps unsurprising to note that he was having similar difficulties, both with the surface and with subsequent damage to his equipment. But it was the matter-of-fact way it was written that I so admired, in such sharp contrast to my outburst, 'We have the satisfaction of feeling that we are getting South, and perhaps tomorrow may see the end of all our difficulties. Difficulties are just things to overcome after all.' As I closed the book I could only smile and agree that his was the approach required, and the way to behave.

Progress up the glacier over the following three days slowed to an alarming rate. Every step had to be taken with care and unhurried. We were all nursing painful bruises and scraped shins having been pulled off balance by our sledges on countless occasions as they slid freely behind us, searching for the fall-line. Those moments were no longer funny. And despite our best efforts each evening, our re-made crampons were only just able to provide the grip that we required. The surface of the glacier was becoming increasingly broken and bent into an icy maze which resembled very rough sea, suddenly frozen. Rounded hillocks and small valleys of fifteen to twenty foot channelled us in directions we did not want to go. 'Once again went up hill and down dale, over crevasses and blue, ribbed ice . . .' wrote Shackleton on 13 December 1908. But there was no alternative. Our patience was being tested, just as his had been, as we stumbled down cul-de-sacs and then retraced our feeble steps to try another route. '*By Endurance We Conquer*' – Shackleton's family motto could not have been more apt.

Each night, while we waited for the snow-filled kettle to melt and then boil, and as we groped around for yet another absurd design of crampon, we talked through a number of 'what if' scenarios. What if one of us is seriously injured? What if we lose a sledge down a crevasse? What if we lose the satellite telephone, the cooker or the tent? What if we have to carry a casualty in a sledge? What if two people are injured? If anything was going to go wrong and threaten our safety and the journey, it would be here, on the glacier.

Dealing with a serious casualty was foremost in our minds. We agreed that he would have to be pulled in a sledge and his kit be repacked into another. But where would we go? I knew that there was an ice runway capable of taking a Twin Otter at Plunkett Point, at the head of the glacier and that behind us we had passed suitable landing strips near Mount Hope. But in each case they were a good four or five days' walk away, especially if the accident occurred in the midst of the rubble and pressure ridges we were currently in. It would be a dreadfully slow journey and fraught with further dangers because of the lack of suitable crampons. Moving on skis on the ice was still out of the question. It could also take a number of days for the aircraft to reach us, because of the distances involved and the vagaries of the weather. Patriot Hills was well over six hundred miles away, so extra fuel would have to be carried to complete the journey to reach us. Any rescue attempt would be a major undertaking.

It was good to talk all of this through because it served as a stark reality check and I found it reined me back from taking any unnecessary risks during the day – such as gambling with the strength of a snow bridge rather than spending extra time to find a safer place to cross. I remained confident that we had trained hard and that there was a very strong bond of trust between us, but none of us would risk the welfare of the others by being cavalier and sloppy, especially when the stakes were so high in terms of failure and rescue.

It was quite apparent that Will was finding the glacier a mental as well as a physical challenge. When we travelled roped up he was always in the middle. That was how we had trained. It's an unenviable position, as you can be pulled both forwards and back-wards by the other team members as well as having to grapple with any slack in the rope if the speed of the group is inconsistent – which it always was. Travelling roped up is hard enough to contend with when simply walking on a flat and firm surface. But on uneven ice, at an irregular pace, with no grip and pulling a sledge across threatening crevasses, it is easily understandable why Will occasion-ally displayed some anxiety. I found being roped up instilled in me a huge level of confidence. I reckoned that at worst case I could fall into a crevasse, but I felt protected knowing that Will and Henry were behind me and, despite the state of our crampons, the two of them would hold my fall – helped by the uneven surface and likelihood of a sledge becoming jammed in a crevasse. Will did not seem to share my optimism; not surprising as, being middle man, he had to frequently untangle himself from the coils of slack rope that inevitably formed as we negotiated endless obstacles by pulling our sledges up and over ice walls.

Rather unfairly, Henry and I had devised a secret signal to alert the other that we were watching Will thrash about, shouting filthy profanities as he fought to untangle himself while keeping a safe distance from crevasse edges. We would lean forward and rest on our ski sticks, heads bent down and laugh as quietly as possible, which was not easy but at least we could hide our mischief behind our goggles and face mask. I don't think he ever knew just how much entertainment he gave us.

After seven days on the Beardmore we had dropped some way short of our required daily mileage if we were to make the 9 January rendezvous on time. Our calculations in the tent each night told us that it was still possible, but we would have to work exceptionally hard and cover at least fifteen nautical miles per day from now on. We simply could not do that on the glacier. We had only managed eight miles per day over the last three days. But in the course of each day, this rarely entered my mind. On the Ross Ice Shelf there had been plenty of time to think about those things. Here, our minds were occupied with getting through the day as safely as possible, and that required total concentration. Each footstep was studied with care. Roped up, we were three working parts of an engine and we had to work in time with each other to function efficiently. Your mind wandered at your peril, and furthest from our minds was letting each other down.

1908

Following the loss of Socks, and nearly Wild too, Shackleton displayed extraordinary leadership by holding his team together and keeping them focussed on the ultimate goal. The expedition was falling apart around them and they still had the return journey to face, yet for a further seven desperate days they battled on. The ground disturbance eventually gave way to a smoother surface, but by now it was clear they were climbing. At first it had been barely discernible, but the daily gain was now in the region of two hundred feet. Then quite suddenly in the afternoon of 16 December 1908, they saw ahead of them the tips of three peaks jutting above the furthest ridgeline. As they climbed, the peaks grew into small mountains and by the end of the day there appeared to be an island, surrounded on all sides by the glacier. Surely this must be the end.

They passed the island on its eastern side, to be faced with the steepest gradient that they had encountered, but it was clear that they were leaving the glacier and heading for the plateau that would lead them to the Pole. In later years, Shackleton hinted at who he was thinking about as he passed that point, for he named the collection of peaks after his generous friend from New Zealand, Buckley Island.

Buckley Island marked the end of Beardmore Glacier.

2008

In the evening of our seventh day on the glacier, we crested a ridgeline and saw ahead of us a flat plain leading all the way to our exit point, marked by the same three low mountains that had punched their way through the ice to form an island. A hundred years on, we were treated to that same view of Buckley Island. Later that evening, reading Shackleton's description of the moment that we now shared, I was transported back and was literally standing beside him, 'Ahead of us lie three sharp peaks, connected up and forming an island in what is apparently inland ice or the head of the glacier. The peaks lie due South of us. To the Eastward and Westward of this island the ice bears down from the inland ice sheet, and joins the head of the glacier proper.'

Despite being more than eighteen miles away, it was a fantastic sight and the perfect end to another hard slog. The southerly wind was beginning to gather, and the temperature was dropping to -30°C, but the sun still shone and we were through the hardest bit. At last, the Beardmore's grip was starting to weaken. That day, 22 December, had been my most enjoyable day so far on the whole journey. It had been a day covering the full range of emotions – angst, disappointment, trepidation, amusement and then finally elation. As I lay in my sleeping bag that night, warm and well fed, Will read out Shackleton's diary entry written from the same location. Although typically understated, I could not have expressed better than he did the feeling of overcoming the worst of the Beardmore. 'After last week's trial and anxiety the change is delightful.'

Shackleton's route ran to the east of the island and up through a heavily disturbed area of ice later to be named the Shackleton Ice Falls. We were alerted to the difficulties he had encountered by studying his diary, so our intention was to swing out in a south-westerly direction to avoid the worst of the obstacles, while staying as close to it as we dared. The weather was still perfect – little wind and the enthralling sight of passing clouds. They seemed to undulate through the sky, swooping and soaring over the mountain peaks, changing form to resemble dragons and spirits. If spirits had a shape then surely this was what they looked like; mysterious and ethereal.

Adjacent to us now and off to the western side of the glacier lay the Marshall and Adams mountains. Henry was the first member of his family to have set eyes upon them, and even his great-grand-father would not have known that they would be named after him as he struggled past them in December 1908. Will and I took unfair delight in commenting that Henry's range was visually far inferior to the Marshall range. His was characterised by rather stumpy and rounded peaks whereas Marshall's were towering, steep and looked like mountains should look. He reluctantly agreed but, quite rightly, it failed to dent the thrill of seeing 'his' range for the first time. Shackleton's description of the peaks on the opposite side of the glacier captured the view and his deeper thoughts perfectly, 'These mountains are not beautiful in the ordinary acceptance of the term, but they are magnificent in their stern and rugged grandeur. No foot has ever trod on their sides, and until we reached this frozen land no human eyes had seen their forms.'

Doubling the distance covered the day before, we managed 15.4 miles that day, because the surface was now flat and once more had some snow covering. Now we seemed to be racing along on our ridiculous footwear, chatting, listening to music and bending down every so often to pick up small stones as mementos of the glacier before we started our climb up to the plateau. We camped that night under the shadow of Mount Bowers, one of the Buckley Island peaks and the point where Frank Wild collected a sample of coal. We were thrilled with our progress but in front of us we could see the ominous gradient we would have to ascend. Without doubt, we would have to use our crampons for the climb but for this they would have to hold the combined weight of us and our sledges – not an exciting prospect. Still, we had no alternative. We would just have to find a way.

Over a supper of Thai Chicken Rice I kept looking at the state of my crampons. They were now in a terrible state and barely offering any grip at all. Faced with the climb ahead, I had to find an alternative as I simply could not see myself getting enough grip with the dead weight of the sledge hanging off my hips. We had long since run out of loose pieces of metal and odd screws, so I had to find something new that we hadn't used yet. I rummaged around in the small bag that held some of our spare items. First out was a spare basket for the ski sticks – no good. Then I pushed my hand to the bottom of the bag, like a child hoping to find the last present at the bottom of a Christmas stocking, and pulled out one of three spare bindings for our skis. I was looking for something that would offer substantial grip, so when I turned it over and saw three screws already set into the plate of the binding so it could be screwed straight on the ski, I clenched it in my fist and punched the air. I had found something that might give me the grip I needed to get me up the icy slope and, eventually, on to the snow. Half an hour later I had added some straps and found a way of fastening it to the underside of my right boot. It was too risky to use a second one, as we would then only have one spare. Still, I went to sleep satisfied that I might just cope with the trials of the next day.

The following morning, we passed Mount Bowers and started to climb towards an endless series of false ridgelines. I found it very tricky and slow. Despite my new invention, each step was placed with extreme care. I aimed to place the ball of my foot into one of the ice cups, using it like a small step but with the two new screws providing the grip. The sledge, now an 85 kg deadweight, was anchored from my hips and would have dragged me – at great speed – to the bottom of the incline the moment I stumbled, slipped or fell.

Will made the best speed and at an appropriate moment secured his sledge and returned to help me. He clipped himself into the loop at the front of my sledge and helped to pull. Unfortunately, it was of no help. Neither of us could climb in unison to share the load which threatened to tug one of us over whenever any slack in the rope appeared.

'Better if I push from the back of the sledge,' said Will sensibly.

That made all the difference and within an hour all three of us had crested the steepest part and were taking our last look at the Beardmore as we nibbled salami and chocolate. From this height it all looked so welcoming. Looking back from our vantage point we could see the Cloudmaker, which we had passed five days before. The surface to it looked so smooth and safe. There was no sign of the chaos and menace in the ice that we had just battled over. But we had learned to our cost that that was the glacier's character – like a skilful chess player, she lured you in on a safe passage and then blocked your every move.

By the end of the day we had climbed fifteen hundred exhausting feet. For the final two hours we had travelled on skis, roped up as there were a number of crevasses still lurking under deceptive snow bridges. The gradient was too steep for me to attack head-on so I led the way, zigzagging my way up, ten minutes in one direction then ten minutes in another, pausing at each turn to look down to the floor of the glacier more than a thousand feet below us. As we climbed each foot, the glacier slipped slowly from view.

It was 24 December 2008 and as we had decided to take the following day off, I pressed on as fast as I could manage to find a suitable campsite on flat ground. We had agreed to stop at eight o'clock but it would be satisfying to get as high as possible. We moved our first campsite because of the intimidating hollow echo we heard from under the surface of the ice as we hammered in the metal tent pegs. Without doubt we were sitting above some vast empty spaces. Our final choice was not much better, but despite a huge hole just a few yards from our tent, we were satisfied that we were safely sited on firm ice.

Late in the day a blanket of low cloud gathered, which made it difficult to make out our final view of the glacier through the flat light. I lay in my sleeping bag mulling over what to write in my diary. This was an important day. We had just successfully completed the one phase of the journey that I had been nervous about. And we were also leaving behind a very special place. A place of utter beauty, rarely witnessed by man; of mountains, valleys and glaciers still untouched by the footfall of a human being. And a place where no advanced life form survives. My pencil raced across the page as I attempted to capture my thoughts on Christmas Eve, 2008.

'I was genuinely sad to be leaving the Beardmore. I felt that through all we had experienced we had begun to know her character. I'm sure we might have been able to have found an easier route but that, in a masochistic way, would have been a shame. We had struggled with the surface and found ourselves trapped down cul-de-sacs of rubble, rises and deep gullies. We had had glimpses into the azure and black-bottomed lift shafts to the underworld. And we had taken advantage of the smoother surfaces when we found them. And it had been at times a very slow struggle. Travelling roped up is a slow business; constantly checking behind, coiling in slack rope and waiting for each other to cross obstacles. We had worked hard to gain each mile and that is why I found it so rewarding. I shall also miss the company of the peaks, glaciers and icefalls. The views had been awesome – mountain tops piercing the clear blue sky – rarely any clouds, save those hugging the highest sides. Twenty-four hours of cloudless skies for eight days was too spoiling.

'I also will miss getting closer to EHS's team as they struggled along facing adversity with every step but meeting it head on with unwavering optimism. My respect for them increases day on day as I realise just what they went through, not knowing what lay over the next ridge.

'In sum it had been a wonderful day and a totally absorbing week. Only Robert Swan and Captain Scott had ascended the Beardmore and exited via the Shackleton Falls since Shackleton had. I can't believe we now join that list. Of that I am proud.'

The last nine days had been both mentally and physically gruelling. I felt the isolation particularly acutely, as I was so aware of the high likelihood of this being the one place we could be injured. The ordeal that would have faced us in getting a casualty to a point where a plane could land would have been phenomenal, and because of the crampon failure we were ill-equipped to move at anything more than a crawl. But we had trained hard for this phase of the journey and built up a tremendous level of trust between us, so I was always confident that we could have carried out a complex rescue if required. But the Ice Shelf and the Beardmore were now almost behind us. We had covered four hundred and eighty-nine nautical miles so far but the Pole was still a further three hundred ahead of us. To hit the 9 January rendezvous we would now have to cover more than thirteen nautical miles per day. Any delay would mean that we would not make it on time. With the dangers now behind us, all that lay in our path was the polar plateau.

About to lock horns with our nemesis. Onto the Beardmore Glacier between Mount Kyffin (left) and Cape Allen (right).

Roped up on the Beardmore Glacier, we kept well apart to avoid all plunging through a weakened snow bridge into the mouth of a crevasse.

Looks can be deceptive – there were few crevasses big enough to swallow you whole but plenty waiting to snap a leg.

Due to the glacier's icy surface, food bags and a sledge replaced aluminium pegs to hold down the tent. Shackleton's diary confirmed he did the same.

About to lock horns with our nemesis. Onto the Beardmore Glacier between Mount Kyffin (left) and Cape Allen (right).

Roped up on the Beardmore Glacier, we kept well apart to avoid all plunging through a weakened snow bridge into the mouth of a crevasse.

Looks can be deceptive – there were few crevasses big enough to swallow you whole but plenty waiting to snap a leg.

Due to the glacier's icy surface, food bags and a sledge replaced aluminium pegs to hold down the tent. Shackleton's diary confirmed he did the same.

Shackleton described the Beardmore Glacier better than I could: 'Falls, bruises, cut shins, crevasses, razor-edged ice and a heavy upwards pull have made up the sum of the day's trials, but there has been a measure of compensation in the wonderful scenery.'

Time to test our resourcefulness. Broken crampons at the end of day two on the Beardmore Glacier.

Shackleton had the answer: 'If we had only known that we were going to get such cold weather as we were at this time experiencing, we would have kept a pair of scissors to trim our beards.'

Left to right: Will, Henry and me on Christmas Day. Cigars, a teaspoon of crème de menthe and a Christmas pudding to replicate part of Shackleton's celebration a hundred years earlier.

'Ahead of us lie three sharp peaks, connected up and forming an island in what is apparently inland ice or the head of the glacier. The peaks lie due south of us. To the eastward and westward of this island the ice bears down from the inland ice sheet, and joins the head of the glacier proper.' EHS, 16 December 1908, describing Buckley Island (below).

Will on the polar plateau, alone with his thoughts and Jimi Hendrix on his iPod.

Shackleton's compass, which he carried with him on the original journey, became an astonishingly powerful talisman. His initials can be seen scratched on the underside of the lid.

To be standing at the place that Shackleton, Wild, Marshall and Adams had stood exactly one hundred years earlier was the fulfilment of a dream that at times had seemed out of reach.

The complete team of descendants at the 97-mile point. Left to right: Henry Adams, Tim Fright, Me, Andrew Ledger, Dave Cornell, Ronnie Gray, Will Gow (Matty MacNair took the photo).

The day before we reached the South Pole, we were treated to the sight of a perfect parhelion. Or was it a sign from those who had gone before that they had been keeping watch over us throughout our journey?

920 miles, 66 days unsupported. We were pretty happy!

CHAPTER 6

Masters of Our Fate

'We hope all the time that each ridge we come to will be the last, but each time another rises ahead, split by pressure, and we begin the same toil again.'

EHS, 20 December 1908

With Buckley Island behind them, Shackleton and his team exited the Beardmore Glacier and gradually entered the world of the polar plateau. Three hundred miles ahead of them lay their prize but the journey was now taking a heavy toll. Day after day they climbed, praying to God that the endless ridgelines would come to an end and that the plateau would flatten out. For every foot climbed the wind seemed to gather in intensity, as it raced straight through them on its journey to the sea. Hunger was ever-present in their minds but the thought of spoiling themselves on Christmas Day lifted their spirits. Images of Christmas pudding were fleeting however, for there still lurked the menace of crevasses to concentrate the mind – formed this time by the head of the glacier tumbling off the high ground and down the steep slope to the valley floor. Linked together by the heavy hemp rope, by now stretched and fraying, they were still having to move their sledge loads in relays. On a return journey to pick up a load, Adams shot through the surface up to his waist, jerking Wild backwards.

'Have you found it?' asked Wild. His question had become a standing joke whenever someone fell into a crevasse, but it helped to dilute the dangerous predicament they were in. When Christmas Day finally arrived the dishevelled and weary team were camped at nine thousand feet. The evening meal they had spent so long dreaming about was now laid out before them. A stew of pony meat, ground maize, pemmican, Oxo and biscuits steamed away over the Primus stove. Then, in the water used to boil the cocoa, Wild placed a plum pudding, given to him by a friend. When the pots had been cleaned and stowed, Shackleton produced some cigars and a small bottle of crème de menthe from which they allowed themselves a spoonful each. After such a fine dinner, Shackleton was loathe to dampen spirits, but he had to discuss the situation they faced.

Christmas Day camp 1908

'From here to the Pole and back to this point is about five hundred miles,' he said. 'We only have enough food for a month and are low on biscuits. So we are going to have to make a week's worth of food last us for ten days. And, to lighten the load, I must ask you to dump everything except the absolute necessities. We will even have to leave behind the spare sledge runners. But, spirits up, men; it is a fine open air life and we are getting South.' Wild thought Shackleton's optimism extraordinary, but cutting the rations at this stage proved just how desperate was the predicament they faced.

2008

We had been looking forward to Christmas Day, for during our preparations we had agreed that we would celebrate by taking a short rest and spoil ourselves, as Shackleton had done, with a few welcome treats. Unfortunately, we were three days' walk from the spot that he had reached, but nevertheless we intended to mark the day in similar fashion. As always, a lie-in was most welcome, for the fifteen hundred feet that we had ascended the previous day had drained us. I knew that leaving the Beardmore was always going to be a steep climb and because we were still travelling roped up due to the relentless threat of crevasses, it had been a slow and exhausting business as we zigzagged our way up the same ice-cupped slope parallel to the Shackleton Falls, before we finally reached enough snow to enable us to put our skis back on.

We awoke at midday on 25 December feeling ravenous. Breakfast was our first Christmas treat, a 'boil in the bag' meal consisting of sausages, bacon and beans in a tomato sauce which, still frozen solid, we stuffed into the boiling water in the kettle to thaw out and heat up. Thirty minutes later, the change from the monotonous taste of porridge was glorious. With my eyes closed and sighing with intense satisfaction, I savoured each mouthful, forcing my spoon deep into the corners and seams of the packet as I neared the end.

I even scooped up tomato sauce that had dripped onto my trousers, such was the pleasure of eating something different. It was some time before any of us had finally finished licking the entire length of our spoons, delighting in the taste to the very end.

With a hot breakfast inside us we climbed back inside our sleeping bags to escape the cold. Outside, there was little wind but the air temperature was touching -25°C. Low cloud was racing across from the west and slowly concealing our final views of the Beardmore and the towering peaks of the Dominion range. Late in the afternoon we each took it in turns to venture outside for a degree of privacy to speak to our families via the satellite phone, and wish them a Happy Christmas.

I had spent a few Christmases away from Joanna and the children but adjusting to the separation at that time of year never really gets any easier. All was well at home but, to my surprise, I learned that Max had asked to go to church with other family members. Joanna rightly gave no explanation during my call but on my return to England I found out that he had chosen not to speak to me despite the pre-arranged time we had agreed. Joanna told me that he was understandably very angry with me for being away at a time when families should be together. Having been placed on the sidelines for five years, my absence on that day epitomised my selfishness and was the last resort. There was little I could say to defend myself. Looking back, I had been completely consumed by the project, trying to fit everything in to the end of each day while holding down a busy job. Nevertheless, I should have found much more time for Joanna, Max and Alicia, for I owed them so much in return for their unwavering support over the course of the project.

Following my call I spent some time reminding myself of the 'Christmas Day' we had spent at home in October by scrolling through some photographs especially stored on my camera from that day. Then, later in the evening, after one of our routine, mundane meals, we treated ourselves to a small plum pudding that

Will very generously provided, and had stoically carried in his sledge for forty-two days. Our final act of the day required us to wrap up warm. We all stepped outside, lit up a cigar and each swallowed a teaspoon of crème de menthe. It was a small gesture to replicate Christmas Day 1908, but nevertheless it was a poignant moment as we contemplated what Shackleton had written in his diary that evening, when he decided to make a week's worth of food last ten days. The contrast seemed too cruel.

It was hard to imagine what those men must have been thinking, in the personal space of their freezing reindeer-skin sleeping bags, as they considered the unquestionable difficulties that lay ahead and just how each of them would cope. 'We are very far away from all the world and home thoughts have been much with us today, thoughts interrupted by pitching forward into a hidden crevasse more than once. Ah well, we shall see all our own people when the work here is done,' Shackleton had written. But no better example exists of his indestructible optimism than in the last sentence of his Christmas Day entry. Despite the gravity of the situation, he still felt able to write that extraordinary line, 'It is a fine open air life and we are getting South.' I thought that remarkable.

After breakfast the following morning, I laid the map out on the floor of the tent and we discussed the route we would take to get us safely and quickly on to the polar plateau. From the Beardmore, Shackleton and his team had taken a direct bearing due south, which had drawn them towards an area of yet more broken ice, still festooned with crevasses, created by the ice flowing off the high ground and down into the glacial valley. This was later named the Shackleton Falls. Frank Wild was dead against this route, as he recorded on 22 December 1908, 'I advised keeping further W. today to get out of the pressure but was overruled three to one in favour of going S.'

In order to avoid similar difficulties, we decided to continue in a south-westerly direction for at least a day or two in order to bypass the ominous-looking obstacles that Wild had tried to warn about. Still roped up and heading into a gathering southerly wind, I set off in the lead. I paused and glanced back as often as I could, trying not to disturb the rhythmic, uphill pace and thus annoy the others – but I was saying goodbye to friends. I wanted to catch as many last glimpses as I could of the Beardmore Glacier and surrounding peaks, for the Transantarctic Mountains had been our constant companions so far. Ahead of us the familiar horizon would soon be interrupted with infernal false crests as we inched our way up the remaining three thousand feet to the summit of the plateau. Very soon, and for the first time on the journey, we would have nothing at all to look at. No background scenery, only the next ridgeline and a headwind for company.

By the end of Boxing Day we were one hundred and ninety-one miles from the 97-mile point and had calculated that we would have to cover 15.4 nautical miles per day to reach that point on 9 January. If we were to arrive on time for the rendezvous, we would have only one day in hand for delays. Achieving that kind of daily mileage on the Ross Ice Shelf had been relatively easy, because of the favourable weather and firm surface, but here the conditions were totally different. Every day we would be climbing hundreds of feet and the relentless wind chill would push the temperatures to the lowest we had experienced.

At this early stage of the final phase of the journey I began to have doubts about my ability to sustain that daily mileage over the remaining two hundred miles, and it made me nervous. We were already losing weight rapidly due to the daily exertion, and this would affect our future performance. It was a daunting prospect, best described by a quote I remembered that I kept mulling over in my mind, trying to stay positive, 'when a devil smiles at a man, all a man can do is smile back'.

The hands of each hour passed slowly as I willed my mind to focus on something positive, but I found it increasingly difficult to overcome the mounting fatigue and feeling of hollowness that began to dominate each uphill mile. Despite my best efforts, I found my head start to drop and my stride to shorten. Thankfully, only a day later, I felt the grip of the Beardmore around us weaken, the threat of crevasses wane and for the final time we stowed the rope and tackle in our sledges, and travelled free again. It was a marvellous feeling to enter the final phase of the journey, yet I knew that there would still be long and exhausting days ahead. I was desperate not to have to ski a single yard more than I had to, so our detour out to the south-west, despite its advantage in avoiding the larger obstacles, was hugely irritating. It was an enormous relief when after two days we altered the bearing on the compass to take us once again due south to follow the 160°E line of longitude to a point where all of the lines converge at 90°S. I was not blind to the signs that this last stage would require me to dig very deep into my reserves of physical and mental strength. The endless repetition of ridge after ridge bullied me mercilessly as we fought against the driving wind and a constant -40°C of wind chill. 'Every time we reached the top of a ridge we say to ourselves perhaps this is the last, but it never is the last, always there appears way ahead of us another ridge,' Shackleton wrote, and I shared his sentiments exactly as I became increasingly anxious about the days to come.

Soon I was finding each hour a worrying struggle, and was starting to become very conscious of my weakening condition. I was in no doubt that Will and Henry were also feeling the same demands being asked of them, but they appeared to be much stronger than me and were consistently edging away in their tracks as we slid slowly over the endless uphill miles. Whenever it was my turn to lead, I had to dig as deep as I could and draw heavily on my bank account of willpower. I dreaded the spectre of becoming overdrawn. Having led a leg, I felt I could not hand over a deficit of even one-tenth of a mile to the next man, so I found myself going on beyond the allotted one hour by a few minutes, just to make sure I was certain of covering the distance. We all congratulated each other for keeping the pace at the required speed, despite the effort it was taking but I was very troubled that over so few days I had begun to fade so quickly. No single factor seemed to be the cause of my difficulty; it was a combination of several. The freezing southerly wind, the lowest temperatures we had experienced, the rising altitude and the 'wet sand' consistency of the snow. These factors when combined made each slide of the skis, each plant of the ski pole and each drag of the sledge a massive effort.

Our average ascent was now two hundred and fifty feet a day and each night as we studied the map we could see from the contour lines what the next day held in store for us. It was still uphill. Our route to the South Pole would take us across an area ten thousand feet above sea level known as the Titan Dome and only over the final couple of days would we finally descend to finish the journey at 9,700 feet. The increasing altitude was already having a marked effect. Telling changes to our simple daily routine were becoming noticeable now. The mornings had become much quieter. We were chatting less and the level of banter had dropped off markedly. We took longer to get organised, were reluctant to pack away our scratchers, slow to slide our tender feet into frozen boots, still wearing the same dirty socks for yet another day.

We were staving off the inevitability of having to set off, for we knew what an ordeal the day would be; we simply took longer to do everything. The tent was always the last item to be stowed away, but never before we had scraped the rime from the inside walls. It was a foul task, as a dusting of fine frost rained down from the fabric to settle all over your head, face and then down the back of your neck. But no matter how lethargic we felt, it had to be done. For in the evening, with the cooker on and the heat generated from the refracted sunlight, any frost remaining would melt and drip through the tent lining on to sleeping bags and dry clothes. The sight of a single droplet would often cause one of us to utter one of Matty

McNair's golden rules, drummed into us three years before, 'You get wet, you die.'

Because of the biting temperature and force of the wind, each of us now routinely wore our windproof smock with its fur-lined hood pulled forward to protect our face. Additionally, we were protected by goggles, balaclavas and an assortment of face masks designed to specifically protect the nose, cheeks and lips. But no matter how shielded you were, the build-up of ice produced by the freezing of our exhaled warm breath was instantaneous. Within minutes our thick beards would be matted with icicles which soon stuck to the fabric of the balaclava. In extremis, the only way to prevent too much ice building up and threatening us with the first stages of frostbite was to attack the bristles with a pair of scissors. Things were no different for Shackleton either, 'If we had only known that we were going to get such cold weather as we were at this time experiencing, we would have kept a pair of scissors to trim our beards. The moisture from the condensation of one's breath accumulated on the beard and trickled down on to the Burberry blouse. Then it froze into a sheet of ice inside, and it became very painful to pull the Burberry off in camp.'

Everything we now did was an ordeal, as the weather became increasingly unpredictable. The wind was always vicious, freezing any exposed skin that had carelessly been left uncovered. It gathered speed and raced downhill like an unseen breaking surf, northwards from the Pole to the Ice Shelf. Described as a katabatic wind, it varied in intensity but gusted from thirty-five to forty knots with ease. The white darkness had also returned; no different to the conditions recorded by Frank Wild in his diary, 'The weather has been the same all day, light snow, bad light, and nothing to be seen . . . For six days now we have been tramping along into nothing, so it seems.'

Through goggles you could periodically make out the horizon, but often you would be fooled by a mirage caused when the similarly-coloured surface and sky, caught in the flat light, merged into one. And then there were the infernal, and seemingly endless, ridgelines. 'When, oh when, are we going to stop rising?' wrote Wild. To make matters worse, on some mornings we would wake to a light dusting of snow that had fallen in the night, but which, once wind-blown, created vast patches of drift that were hellish to haul our sledges through.

I found each day was now following a familiar pattern. The first two or three hours were relatively straightforward. It was hard work, this consistently uphill movement but, with an evening meal, a good night's rest and breakfast to provide the fuel for the day, we would set off in reasonable spirits. But all that would change around midday, when I had to fight hard not to drop back. Sometimes I was only ten or fifteen minutes behind, but it was significant enough to develop quite a gap between the other two and myself. My days were fast turning into a raw, bare-knuckle fight against fatigue and, as I entered the final rounds of each day, I was seldom the victor. Energy just poured from my body, to be snatched away and dissipated by the wind. My legs would not work any faster. Each stride of the ski seemed locked at a precise distance. I could go no faster, just slower and slower. Because of the altitude, now close to eight thousand feet, I was also frequently short of breath. Every ten minutes or so I would have to stop, suck in the freezing air to repay the oxygen debt in my bloodstream and then continue. I could feel my lungs burning with every gasp followed by a rasping, dry, hacking cough. But to stop for more than just a few seconds was hopeless, for you were instantaneously freezing. I simply had to keep moving.

At the hourly breaks, between sips of the warm lemon-flavoured energy drink, I sought refuge from the hardship by complaining to the others about the gradient. It was a pointless exercise but somehow I felt a touch better by blaming the unforgiving slope for my performance rather than admit my own physical failings. It was very noticeable, to me at least, that we were still travelling uphill. My guide was to align the head and shoulders of the man in front in relation to the horizon line. When they remained below the horizon I sensed we were going uphill and the weight of the sledge would reinforce that as it hung off my hips, sliding across the 'wet sand' snow.

My thoughts when I wasn't leading were now dominated by the physical turmoil in which I found myself. It was becoming hard to motivate myself through the seven legs that we had to cover each day if we were to meet the 97-mile point on 9 January, as I could not project my thoughts beyond the physical arena of each hour. I required everything I had inside me, both the physical and the mental, to will me along. Beyond this, there was barely any space in my mind where my thoughts had the freedom to roam. But at rare moments, especially during the mornings, I gained a burst of strength simply by imagining Shackleton and his team persevering alongside us. I had admired his style of leadership for many years but now that I was beginning to scratch the surface of how he must have felt I marvelled at his ability to convince his team to keep going, when also faced with a return journey of hundreds of miles back down the same route to the waiting *Nimrod*. That seemed to me to be a shining example of strong and true leadership – persuading others to continue when they felt it was time to stop.

When we read the diary entries each night we would now search between the lines for even some disguised suggestion that it was dawning on Shackleton that perhaps he wasn't going to make his goal after all. But even with the odds stacked firmly against him, it was still hard to find any doubt. The optimism that had dominated his approach so far was plain to read on every page of his diary in December 1908. But the observations of Frank Wild were perhaps more discerning. On 30 December 1908, Wild wrote, 'S is getting a bit down, but I think we will do alright.' But the next day the first chink appears, 'I am now beginning to be doubtful of success, as I don't think we can make our food supply last long enough.'

Although it was bordering on masochism, our uphill battle was the only way to experience what they went through over those final hundred miles. For it was only under these conditions that we could come anywhere close to understanding and really respecting the decisions that Shackleton was about to have to make. To gain even further strength, I simply had to consider that they were only just reaching the halfway stage of their journey. How could I begin to complain about my weakening condition? It was a shameful thought. We did not have to walk all the way back again.

It wasn't all an ordeal. One aspect of the day that consistently lifted my spirits was the palette of polar colours that would one moment drift across the snowfields to our front and then intermingle with the immense scale of the cloud cover above us, as if mixed by wind-borne brushes. Shades of grey interspersed with curious bands of white light would race across the snow in parallel lines as the clouds were pushed on their way by the southerly winds. Then they were gone, replaced by more low grey cloud that, moments later, would be shot with shafts of the palest yellow through which fleeting glimpses of the distant horizon were revealed. It was mesmerising, and did much to lift my spirits.

1908

Over the final days of the year Shackleton's team covered on average twelve miles a day. The weather remained harsh and the wind never abated. Because of the altitude, headaches and nosebleeds were commonplace. Alone with their thoughts as they angled themselves forwards and strained on their harnesses, doubts of reaching the Pole began to take root. New Year's Day was no cause for celebration, despite the warmer weather. The silence in the tent after a paltry meal a day later was broken by Shackleton.

'I cannot think of failure yet,' he started, 'I must be sensible, and don't think for one moment that I place your welfare behind glory and attainment of the Pole. We can only do our best but we are facing the strongest forces of nature.' There was no reply, just the sound of spoons scraping the corners of the tin plates in search of any minute morsel of food.

2008

A century later we were far from contemplating failure, but we were having to work hard for our reward. The mornings were still silent and our preparation still slow. Once under way, I found it so important to think positively about the day ahead. Despite being well practised by now, it still required a huge effort to focus beyond the exhausting prospect of the day's mileage. But we remained on schedule and 13.5 nautical miles per day was now required to reach our 9 January goal. A delay of just one day would, however, snatch that prize from us. Because of our slower pace, we now needed to travel for eight hours each day to remain on track for that deadline; that extra hour, while essential, was a killer. Invariably, at the end of the day, I was the last to arrive. Will and Henry were usually sitting on their sledges, hunched forward, head down and munching on the remains of their lunch bags or sipping the last, now tepid, cupful from their flasks. Each day's march now ended as it had begun, in a moment of thoughtful silence which spoke volumes about the way we felt. My immediate task on arrival was always to power up the GPS and announce the day's mileage. It was always an anxious moment, but we could now judge the distance pretty accurately so were rarely surprised; but it was an important ritual that drew a line under each long day.

New Year's Day gave us an excuse to treat ourselves to a two-hour lie-in, even though we had learned by now that a lie-in was a false friend, for despite longing for more rest, it made the following day a real trial. It just seemed to take so long to get going and we never felt the additional sleep had made any difference, so we decided that this would be our last. The day started off well, as at last we seemed to have reached the plateau. For a few hours it certainly seemed dead flat, with no sastrugi or any disturbance to slow us up. It was very noticeable to me that at last we were on an even surface, for I felt the sledge moving with a touch less resistance and my guideline suggested that as the lead man's head and shoulders were just above the horizon line, we were not in for an uphill climb. Despite the level surface though, the wind seemed delighted to resist us head-on. The light patterns continued to entrance me and their absorbing display helped pass the time. New Year's Day was one of the more lovely. Bands of grey and bright, intense yellow passed by in familiar parallel lines across the snowfield to our front and contrasted with blue patches behind transparent swirls of the thinnest cloud above. It will be one of my abiding memories of the entire journey. As a very amateur painter I became engrossed in trying to imagine how I would capture such a scene in oils. I spent hours squeezing out make-believe tubes of paint, infuriating myself by failing to match the natural colours. It was fun and, just like painting on a canvas, I found it incredibly energising to be lost in thought.

But by the final hour of the day I was finding the going very hard and yet again I seemed to be running out of fuel. I felt so weak and physically drained, it was utterly demoralising. Even the power of positive thinking could not lift me over the wall of those last few miles. I had spent some of the afternoon trying to work out ways in which I could simply keep up with the others. I considered setting off early each morning to try and give myself a head start, but I knew they would easily catch me up no matter what time I set off, and it wouldn't be safe either. Then they would overtake me anyway. It was too ghastly to contemplate any further. Pausing for a short break before the final, draining mile of the day, Henry suggested an alternative.

'General, let me carry some of your load. Some fuel, some food, the camera kit. Come on, give me something.'

Before replying, I reminded myself of a conversation we'd had over supper one evening in Punta Arenas. We all agreed that there would be no egos, no pride and if someone was feeling unwell or travelling slowly, then he should have no difficulty in accepting the offer from one of the others to carry some of his weight. I was now faced with that very situation.

'Fuck off,' I snapped, leaning heavily on the handles of my ski sticks, but not really meaning it. I was exhausted and on the defensive.

'I won't have it. We are all completely done-in, so why should you? It's a very kind offer but I cannot accept it. I'll find a way. It's my problem to sort out and the answer lies here,' I said, tapping my temple with my gloved hand.

But how could I say that after having discussed it so honestly in Punta? I was simply being stubborn; I'd be admitting to weakness if I had agreed to Henry's offer. We had come so far now and I was damned if I was going to let anyone help me. If I had been putting our goal at risk, then I would have had no alternative, but that was not yet the case. The matter was dropped, but I did need to find some way to lighten my load. Pouring away fuel was unthinkable. The answer lay in burying my emergency rations.

Usually the final mile of the day was hell but this time I had much to think about. I calculated how many days it would take us to get from our current location to the 97-mile point and then beyond, to the Pole. Barring any serious emergency or being tent-bound because of bad weather, I worked out with relative confidence that, based on our current speed, I could afford to get rid of eight days' worth of food. It was perhaps a risky call, but not an extreme one. I would go hungry though, if we arrived at the Pole after 18 January.

When we stopped, I explained my decision to Henry and Will and they were fully supportive, even offering some of their own emergency rations should I need them later on in the journey. It was a hugely generous gesture from both of them and it enabled me to offload eight kilos, which I did that evening. It was simply a matter of slitting open the food bags and pouring the contents into a deep hole, covering it up and then stowing the empty sachets in my sledge. I felt a touch guilty, but it was so necessary. I was having a dreadful time. I hated dropping back, and it was beginning to matter more and more to me that we finished the day together. On reflection, throwing away food might have seemed a drastic measure but I just had to find a way to lighten my load. I was convinced that every gram lost would make a difference and I was feeling really desperate. I was leading this expedition and this was no time to lead from the back. I didn't think that the risks were too high, I needed to act and over the coming days I just knew we would manage.

As well as the mornings, the evenings in the tent were now also silent affairs as we lay resting, longing for the water to boil in order to have our meal and then climb straight into our sleeping bags. If you weren't cooking you would take this opportunity to doze off and grab a few minutes of sleep. This had never happened at any previous stage of the journey, and was a stark indication of our general fatigue and weakened condition. We were nearing the end of our seventh week.

The morning after I had buried my food I was eager to discover what a difference a lighter sledge was going to make to my day. The spare room in our sledges was now noticeable. Seven blue bags that had once each carried a week's worth of food were now rolled up and stowed neatly away. Empty fuel containers, rubbish bags, ropes and climbing harnesses slid around the bottom of the sledge. No longer could everything be packed tightly. Yet the remaining seventeen days' worth of food still seemed to weigh a ton. I got off to a good start, immediately noticing a huge difference. I was thrilled and did the first three hours comfortably. But it was short-lived; I crumpled over the remaining four hours.

Henry and Will were extremely good about it and they took the lead instead of me, as I really didn't think I could keep up the average. This was a significant change from the norm, but I had to accept their offer. It was at the end of this day, on 2 January, when I had set off in such good spirits with a lighter sledge that I ended the day forty-five minutes behind the others – the furthest behind I had ever been. When I eventually reached the spot where the ski tracks ceased for the day, the tent was up and the stove was on. Utterly distraught, I inched myself closer to the campsite. I was close to tears when I arrived. I don't think I can remember at any stage in my life feeling so empty, so feeble and so beaten as I did that evening. Will was inside the tent, supervising the melting of the snow and Henry was outside seeing to items in his sledge. With about a hundred yards to go, my head slightly bent, shuffling one ski slowly in front of the other, I saw Henry look up, stretch out his right arm, clench his right fist and tap his heart twice. This had been our sign throughout the journey to silently urge each other on. It simply meant 'I'm feeling strong; I know this is hard, just keep going because I know you can.' No words were needed. It was a simple sign to dig deep, but it was Henry's silent support that took me close to the tears that I felt welling up behind my ice-encrusted goggles.

Two hours later, fed and warm, I lay in my sleeping bag and listened to Will reading Shackleton's diary from 2 January 1909. 'I cannot think of failure yet, I must look at the matter sensibly and consider the lives of those who are with me. I feel that if we go on too far it will be impossible to get back over this surface and then all the results will be lost to the world. Man can only do his best and we have arrayed against us the strongest forces of nature.' While I was never in any doubt that we wouldn't make it, I found it so ironic that exactly one hundred years ago Shackleton was beginning to contemplate failure. I hadn't reached that stage at all but I was beginning to get a sense of the desperate times that he and his team were facing.

The following morning we woke to a calm wind and wonderfully bright sky. It was perfect, and with the likelihood of a level surface to ski over, we got off to a prompt start and made very good progress all day. I found it much better, largely because the ground had flattened out. Although I was still ten minutes behind the others at the end, it didn't really seem to matter quite so much. We were blessed with a rare day on the plateau and took advantage of very little wind and bright sun. As we lay in our tent that evening we worked out that we had covered 16.3 miles, which was an astonishing distance and one not achieved since we had been on the Ross Ice Shelf more than a month earlier. We were now well on course to reach our goal comfortably. But as I lay in my sleeping bag, pleased with our progress, I was conscious that the fabric of the tent was beginning to flap. The wind was on the move, which did not bode well.

My prognosis was right, for the following morning the wind was gusting thirty to thirty-five knots and it had made for a very disturbed night. We knew by now that the high winds and the lower temperatures always meant a slower start in the morning. There was drift to be cleared, and it was noticeably colder. Just before setting off Henry measured the wind chill temperature. It was -47°C. Another day in the freezing wind tunnel lay ahead. My performance over the day was no different than before, but the added factor to cope with now was the temperature and the wind – deadly when they hunted as a pair. It was bitter. For the first time on the journey I noticed that my left hand seemed to be frozen to the core, numbing up and shutting down within minutes, caused mainly because it was battered on the windward side as we skied along. To help the circulation I wore a mitten on my left hand all day, massaging my hand as best I could and placing it under my arm when we stopped in an attempt to coax the blood back into the collapsed capillaries in my fingers.

The messages and colourful designs that my children and Joanna had painted on the length of my skis were now proving to be a powerful motivating force. It was at this stage in the journey that I needed contact with their smiling faces the most. Despite being so close to the end, the days were getting harder and I would be forced to occasionally stop to catch my breath, thus dropping back even further. Shattered, I would slump forward on to the handles of my ski sticks and stare down at the messages from Max, Alicia and Joanna. I drew enormous energy from those simple comments and bright, patterned drawings. I remembered so vividly watching them being painted. The memory of their faces and the look of concentration as they carefully placed each brush stroke was so clear to me. They most definitely carried me through those dark hours and painful miles. Today the skis are propped up beside my desk, scratched and battered from the nine hundred and twenty-mile journey but still a vivid reminder of what physically and spiritually carried me to the Pole.

As the day's journey drew to a close, and willing my imagination to transport me beyond the wall of wind we were battling against, I had the feeling that we were being sent a clear message from this extraordinary continent, and I tried to capture this idea in my own diary that evening, 'You had an easy time on the Ice Shelf. I gave you good weather; a flat, firm surface and mountains to gauge your progress by. You took advantage of the conditions and made good distance. On the Beardmore Glacier I tested you and you were found wanting. But you were resourceful and persistent. I rewarded you again with fine weather. But now on this high plateau I want to know how much you want to claim your prize. You will have to earn every inch you claim off me. For I shall resist your every step of the way with the wind and the cold. As you weaken; I will strengthen.' I was finding the plateau beguiling. It was resisting us every inch of the way. Yet, in exchange for extreme physical and mental effort it allowed us to progress – just. I could slide my skis, but only so much. My sledge skimmed over the snow, but not quite enough to maintain a rhythm. And the gradient seemed endless, but not enough to slow us right down. Everything we were doing seemed opposed in some way but there always seemed room for progress if one is prepared to make that extra effort and go 'Always a Little Further' – a line from James Elroy Flecker's *Hassan,* which I had written at the front of my sledge to remind me to put in an extra bit each day.

1909

At about the same point on the plateau, events in early January 1909 were becoming increasingly desperate. Shackleton and his team were dangerously weak, there was not enough food and they were now openly contemplating the return journey. But while they could still place one foot in front of the other, Shackleton wanted to drive on and at least finish at a point inside the elusive circle, one hundred miles from the Pole.

On 6 January he decided to leave the sledge and camp equipment and push as far south as possible in the day and then plant the flag. But the polar plateau was a merciless opponent and she put Shackleton's iron determination to the test. For two whole days she bludgeoned their threadbare tent with wind and blizzard of such ferocity that sleep was hardly possible. Spindrift penetrated the tent fabric and settled on the sleeping bags. Valuable food was being eaten, but no miles gained. There was nothing to do but to lie still, shiver and pray not to be attacked by cramp. Diary entries over those days describe their feelings. On 3 January Wild had written, 'The same old drag today. We have now come to the conclusion that we cannot get to the Pole. S is very disappointed.' And the following day, 'We are therefore going only 3 more days, which should put us within 100 miles of the Pole. It seems hard we cannot do the remainder, but as it is absolutely certain we should all die if we did, it would not do us or the world much good, as we have anyhow made a splendid record.' Shackleton agreed, 'The end is in sight. We can only go for three more days at the most, for we are weakening rapidly.' It is hard to imagine the utter distress of the four men as they huddled around the pan of their steaming hoosh, their bearded, wretched faces etched with hunger and fatigue as they faced defeat and dared to contemplate the return journey.

2009

On the morning of 5 January 2009, the three of us, on our hands and knees, rolled up the tent very untidily in the face of a fierce, freezing southerly wind. We knew then that, even in the closing stages, we were in for a real test. We set off this time straight into the face of forty-five-knot winds. The drifting snow snaked past us, filling and covering our tracks in seconds. Only my feet harboured some sort of warmth; the fingers suffered as blood shunted to their tips in an attempt to keep them from becoming deep frozen. The wind was unyielding; we had to stand right beside each other and shout to make ourselves heard. The horizon, normally a clear flat line, was a greyish-blue blur of drifting snow and airborne ice crystals. Our hourly stops were now just hurried pauses. It was too cold to hang around for a natter and the iPods lay lifeless in our sledges. Movement created a degree of warmth, so we had to keep going; but the temptation to pitch the tent and call it a day was ever-present. But that could only be a fleeting thought, for the moment we stopped, our dream would be crushed and irretrievable. Whatever the ordeal required to get there, get there we must. I took great comfort from re-reading a number of the quotations, jokes, lines of poetry and quotes from the scriptures that Joanna had gathered from close friends for me to read when I needed them most on the journey. I had first opened the envelope she had given to me when we were stuck in the storm on the Ross Ice Shelf, but now the notes were proving their worth. That night, I picked a special one out and read it to the others, for it summed up our situation perfectly.

'Sure I am this day we are masters of our fate, that the task which has been set before us is not above our strength, that its pangs and toils are not beyond our endurance. As long as we have faith in our own cause and an unconquerable will to win, victory will not be denied us.'

It was a quotation from Winston Churchill, and one that I am sure inspired millions of people during the Second World War. At this stage of the journey it was exactly the motivation that I needed to ensure we reached our goal, now only four days away.

'Read it again, General,' asked Henry.

When I had finished, not one word was spoken. We just turned on our sides to sleep.

Shackleton's compass, which I had been carrying in my right-hand trouser pocket, was now becoming an immensely powerful talisman. During those dark moments of the day when I was dropping back, I wouldn't need to take it from my pocket, but simply just tap my right thigh and feel the shape of it pressing down on the top of my leg as I skied along. It was an extraordinarily strong link to Shackleton and his team and I drew enormous comfort knowing that it had passed so close to where we were now and that, at this stage, it had guided those four men across this desolate and unforgiving plateau.

The wind did not abate, it worsened. We set off into the same formidable, forty-five to fifty-knot gusts. Combined with an air temperature of -30°C, we were now enveloped in -52°C of wind chill; our coldest day to date. Since leaving the Beardmore Glacier there had lurked within the wind an added, ominous, foe. And the conditions were now in its favour for it to become a real threat. Frostbite.

I have always been very respectful of frostbite but I regard it in the same way that sunstroke is classified in the army – as a self-inflicted wound. Both are avoidable but require the highest standards of meticulous personal administration, a determination not to cut corners and no delay in taking immediate, preventative action. Frostbite also requires close teamwork and regular checks to look for the early signs of it in each other. We were finding the vulnerable areas were our noses and cheeks and then the tips of our fingers. While our feet and toes became bitterly cold, they never came close to any form of cold injury. But because of the extreme temperatures, the build-up of ice on the underside of our face masks and balaclavas was instantaneous from the moment we set off. The danger lay in the coating of ice resting for long periods on our skin. Henry seemed fine; I was developing a small frozen patch on my left cheek but Will was showing signs of blisters and swelling. Uncharacteristically, and despite the cold and the wind, I felt strong throughout that day, much stronger than before. The leaden feeling had gone from my legs and I felt upbeat.

Our progress was still slow but steady; however, Will was feeling unwell and had lost his appetite. Then, very suddenly in mid-morning, Henry dropped back and on rejoining us at the next break announced that he had just been sick. There was no explanation for this and its suddenness was a shock. With Will also not feeling well it fell to me to take up the lead. The only other alternative was to stop. On any other day I suspect we would have pitched our tent and allowed Henry and Will to recover, but to stop now meant shattering our dream to meet the rendezvous target. It was as simple as that.

'We have to keep going,' I said, my voice raised to compete with the wind. 'We can stop if you feel really rough. But if we do, then it's all over. We'll never get there on time.'

Suddenly, I was no longer the slowest in the convoy. In fact, quite the opposite. I felt in good shape and, under such circumstances, I was required to be decisive and lead from the front. Henry and Will looked to me for a decision.

'Right, Henry. I will take your sledge and you can take mine,' I said. Henry's sledge was always accepted as being the heaviest because he was carrying slightly more food to feed his voracious appetite; not much of the fuel he was carrying had been used, either. And I guessed that my sledge was probably the lightest.

'And Will and I can take it in turns to pull it,' I added. There were no arguments or disagreements. Slumped forward on his ski sticks, Henry spat on the snow to get rid of the taste of sick and looked relieved to swap. So I clipped myself into his trace and handed him mine. I would lead, allowing Henry and Will to travel at a speed which was comfortable.

So on we went, into the freezing wind, towards a blurred line of blue and grey; no clear, flat line that day. I enjoyed the following few hours. I was out in front and no longer the invalid. Sudden responsibility had energised me and given me a second wind. At last I was a help, not a hindrance. Henry's sledge was nowhere near as heavy as I had imagined and he said he was grateful to be pulling mine. I remained strong enough for Will and I not to have to swap sledges, or the lead. I started feeling very tired over the last few hours but was determined to keep as close as I could to the required mileage. Despite the predicament we found ourselves in, and it being the coldest day that we had yet experienced, we still managed 12.3 nautical miles which, given the conditions, we agreed was a very creditable performance. Most importantly, we remained on track.

Towards the end of the day Henry and Will regained their strength and, once inside our tent, fed and in the warmth of our sleeping bags, the situation we had found ourselves in that morning had all disappeared. Before I went to sleep I reflected, with a degree of contentment, on my performance. It had been a very emotional and intense day. We all agreed that it had been our hardest yet. It had been very demanding and the wind chill had been brutal; but as a team we had kept focussed on achieving our dream in the face of mounting hardship. The suddenness of Henry's sickness was alarming and we had been forced to contemplate stopping for the day. Our dreams had hung on a simple 'Yes' or 'No'. Thankfully, the ailments were not serious; Henry had put his nausea down to motion sickness brought on by the flat light but they had exposed just what a tightrope we were feeling our way along.

The following morning we awoke to a raging storm. The wind had not let up through the night. But if we were to make 88° 23´ on 9 January, we simply had to keep going. At eight o'clock we decided to delay a decision for two more hours. By ten o'clock the conditions had not improved. We were running out of time, but chose to make a final choice two hours later. At midday and with no let-up in the storm, the time had come to resolve the situation once and for all.

'The choice is simple, guys. Either we sit this out or we leave as late as we can in the hope that it calms down, which will have to be this afternoon. It will mean walking into the night hours and buggering up our body clocks. But if we stay here for twenty-four hours then that's it.' I paused, but not long enough for the merest hint of doubt to seed itself. 'It has to be a unanimous decision. I want to go on. We have to.'

'No question,' replied Will.

'C'mmmmooon,' yelled Henry, his wide, toothy grin splitting his ginger beard as he raised his fist in the air.

By late afternoon the wind began to ease slightly and at four o'clock we had no option but to leave. We repeated the endless routine of breaking camp but this time it seemed strange, getting underway at the time of day when we would normally be close to stopping. Ahead lay seven and a half hours of pain and fatigue. My body felt horribly confused and reluctant to set off, so I offered to lead the first leg in the hope of squashing those feelings.

'General, are you sure we're on the right bearing?' questioned Henry after a few minutes. 'The wind is cutting across us. Normally we are walking straight into it.'

He was right. The wind had, uncharacteristically, switched to the east for the first time on the journey. A change to the normal routine and familiar conditions seemed so out of place. He thought our navigation must be at fault.

'Trust the compass,' I replied. 'The wind is coming from the east, that's all. I checked the bearing just before we set off,' I carried on, not sure that Henry was convinced.

The easterly wind proved far more favourable than a headwind. Like a small boat being constantly rammed by a fierce cross-wind, perpendicular to its direction of travel, our sledges drifted way out to our right-hand side and off the line of their normal travelling position, which was always directly behind us. Bearing the brunt of the wind, the left side of our bodies became very cold very quickly. The fingers on my left hand wasted no time in shutting down, despite the extra gloves and mittens I wore. I was forever tucking them into my armpit or windmilling my left arm around while shuffling along on my skis, using only one arm for balance. There was no time to keep stopping. We just had to keep sliding one ski in front of the other. In simple terms, that was all this journey required. How difficult could that be?

The delayed start turned our body rhythms inside out. We didn't finish our day's ski until one o'clock in the morning, which meant that we would have to sleep through to the following midday, not starting off until early afternoon, if we wanted a full quota of sleep – which we badly needed. Because of the constant presence of the sun, there was no familiar dusk to mark the ending of the day. All I had as an indication of when to stop was my watch and a feeble signal from my body that it was tiring.

On 8 January we camped at 10,146 feet, the highest point yet. The surface was now pretty flat, although we were still gaining fifty feet a day in altitude. We had only twenty-six miles to go – just two days of travelling. Chatter in the tent was on the increase again as we begun to comprehend the achievement of reaching that lonely spot on 9 January – for, barring accidents, it was plainly clear to us now that we really were going to do it.

My thoughts turned to our rendezvous with the 97-Mile Team. Before settling down to sleep I phoned through our position to Patriot Hills, hoping also to get an update on the team's progress.

MASTERS OF OUR FATE

'Hi, Victoria. Shackleton Expedition here. Our position is South 87° 56.990′, East 161° 47.919′. Distance covered today is 13.7 nautical miles. We travelled for seven and a half hours. Altitude is 10,146 feet. Over.'

Victoria then correctly repeated our position.

'Due to poor weather we are having to travel much later in the day, so we will have to slip these updates to around midnight. When we can, we will resume some form of normality but we have to get to the 97-mile point in two days' time. Any news of the others?' I asked.

'That's fine,' she replied. 'Dave, Matty and the others have been delayed in Punta but are on their way here. It will be a close-run thing for them to reach you on time, provided you all make it. Over.'

'Oh, we'll make it all right. Speak to you tomorrow. Out.' I said, with a tone of certainty. I removed the battery from the phone and placed it back into the warmth of a chest pocket before turning over to sleep, with the significance of those final words still ringing in my ears. Often in the night I would be woken up by the batteries digging into my chest as I lay on them, but on this occasion it was the familiar sound of Henry peeing into his bottle. The noise never failed to interrupt my sleep – it was the sweet, sickly smell of warm urine that hung in the air and my nostrils. No matter how far I burrowed down inside my sleeping bag I couldn't seem to escape the odour.

We awoke at lunchtime to a perfect day. The ferocious wind had dropped off, the sun was strong and full and there were no clouds. Despite nearing the end, we still seemed to have a huge distance to travel when marked on my map. But we were buoyed knowing that the goal was so close. Because of the fine weather and little wind we packed up the tent with no delay and for the fifty-sixth time got under way. I felt so good. I kept pace with the others, despite the still gradual incline. But once again, at the midday point I was enveloped in the familiar cloak of lead and I became the stick-man in the distance. Even at this eleventh hour I was going to have to work for every inch of the remaining miles. At midnight, after 14.6 miles, we stopped and camped. But despite the ever-present hardship it had been a great day. I had stopped a few times just to stand, utterly still, within the extraordinary silence. The plateau was so tranquil and at ease without the wind.

We were so well set up for the following day. Just 11.6 miles to go, which meant that we should get to the 88° 23′ point at around seven in the evening. We lay in our sleeping bags that night discussing the enormity of the moment we were about to experience. Like three microscopic arrows we were closing in on the bullseye.

Once the chat had died down my thoughts turned once again to those indomitable men plodding on, so desperately, over the same last miles that we were covering, knowing by now that the Pole was out of reach. Foremost in my mind was the important thought that this journey was about them, not us. Now was not the time to feel the glow of pride for what we were about to complete. These final few miles belonged to them.

Cocooned in my sleeping bag, with my blood running fast and warm and my stomach full, I read the entry that Shackleton had written on 6 January 1909. 'I would fail to explain my feelings if I tried to write them down now that the end has come. There is only one thing that lightens the disappointment and that is the feeling that we have done all we could, it is the forces of nature that have prevented us from going right through. I cannot write more.' Because of my deep-seated fatigue I edged a little way closer to empathise with Shackleton's tragic feelings of disappointment. I went to sleep so happy that our odyssey was all but over. But that feeling of accomplishment became a distant runner-up to the image that filled my mind – that of the four indomitable men battling on and so valiantly coping with the rapidly unfolding disappointment.

1909

At one o'clock in the morning of 9 January 1909, the two-day storm eased and Shackleton's party prepared to face their last day heading south. After a pathetically inadequate breakfast the four men set off from their campsite – regardless of the delay, the plan remained the same, simply to get as far as they could. Under his arm Shackleton clutched Queen Alexandra's Union Flag, and in his trouser pocket he carried his compass. Wild carried a small brass container in which were some stamps that had been specially issued for the expedition and Marshall held a camera. After five hours of half-walking and half-running Shackleton came to a stop at 88° 23′ South, 162° East; a lonely, featureless spot just ninety-seven miles from the South Pole.

'I take possession of this plateau in the name of His Majesty King Edward the Seventh,' coughed Shackleton as he thrust the Pole into the snow with all the strength he could muster. The outward journey was over.

They each took it in turns to look through the glasses, but all they saw was the endless white snow plain ahead of them. Marshall took out the camera and captured the historic moment with a photograph of his three companions facing him straight on, beside the royal gift fluttering in the wind. Shackleton removed his hands from his mittens and clasped them behind his back. It was to become one of the iconic polar images of the twentieth century, marking man's 'Furthest South'. When Marshall had finished, Wild hurriedly buried the brass container where he had been standing. It was a rushed ending. A few minutes was quite long enough at that barren and freezing location so, removing the flag, they turned and followed their tracks back to the campsite, which they reached by mid-afternoon. Time was too scarce to lie in the tent and celebrate their achievement, so they pushed on for a couple more hours before camping again. But this time, they were following the needle pointing north on the compass.

Marshall's photograph of (left) Adams, Wild and Shackleton at the furthest point south reached by man on 9 January 1909.

2009

We awoke on 9 January jubilant about the day ahead. There was nothing now to stop us reaching that elusive spot. In order to savour that moment, we had woken ourselves earlier than planned and were under way by 10.30 in the morning. The wind had dropped to a gentle five knots. It was sunny, clear and the air temperature was approaching -35°C. Yet again, I felt weak and feeble as we set off, my legs were still heavy and the sledge seemed no lighter. But it didn't seem to matter what I felt like, today was different. I was lifted by the thought that just over eleven miles away lay the desolate spot that we had striven for beyond all else. Thankfully, we faced only a gentle breeze but the air temperature remained bitter. For the first time that I could remember, my goggles iced up on the inside and my damned beard kept freezing to the inside of my balaclava. Using the warmth from my bare fingers I painfully prised away the bristles from where they re-rooted themselves in the ice.

Over the final hours of this seemingly endless journey, I had hoped to reflect on all the thoughts and decisions that must have been churning away in Shackleton's mind; what made him turn back, would I have made the same decision when glory was so close? Instead I was preoccupied with staving off frostbite, keeping up with the others and just getting through the day. That was the focus of my thoughts. Even over these final miles, there was no space to savour the intensity of the moment. The plateau continued to resist us right to the end.

We didn't hurry. There was simply no way that we could. After seven hours or so we were getting close enough for me to switch on the GPS, which would lead us to that final point. It acquired the satellites very quickly as it lay cupped in my right hand and, with my right ski stick dangling free, I took up the lead. I shuffled along like an old man carefully carrying a cup of tea. An invisible line leading us to the exact spot. I watched the digital display of the distance still to travel reduce with each untidy slide. I glanced over my shoulder to see Will and Henry eagerly waiting for me to stop. We were down to the final few yards and last couple of strides and then suddenly, those historic numbers appeared on the screen, S88.23 E162. I stopped and lifted my left ski stick and drove it as hard as I could into the wind-packed snow to claim that spot again.

'That's it. We've made it,' I announced, with a huge grin. We had struck the bullseye; not a day before, nor a day late. Exactly one hundred years on, to the day, we had reached Shackleton's 'Furthest South'.

We seemed unsure how to react. It felt awkward. The significance of the moment had yet to sink in. Of course there was nothing there to mark the spot, so we were simply left alone to contemplate our success. Getting colder by the second, the more I thought of what I had achieved, the more emotional I became. My poor physical state accentuated my vulnerability, but for the first time since I was ten years old, behind my goggles, I cried small tears of relief and joy. We shook hands in a very British way and then I leaned forward and rather clumsily hugged the others, first Will, then Henry. We didn't say much except to congratulate each other. The cold prevented us from standing around to chat – we could do that in the tent. We had to keep moving, but I was desperate to take a photo of us beside our Union Flag to copy the iconic image of Shackleton, Wild and Adams at the same spot. I gathered the tripod from my sledge, whipped off my mittens and clumsily screwed the camera on to it. Exposing my bare hands to the air was stupid. Every second left to the mercy of the cold was madness, so I had to be quick. I had carried a copy of the original photograph with me which we had studied during the journey so we knew exactly where to stand. I was Shackleton, Will was Frank Wild and Henry was his great-grandfather, Jameson Adams.

'Shacks was right not to go on. Another ninety-seven miles still seems a huge distance to go and then he had the return journey to make. We are nowhere near the state that they were in, so God knows what they must have been feeling like. It was such a great call not to go on, but I simply cannot contemplate them just turning round and heading back the way they had just come,' I said as I composed the photograph.

It was too cold to stand around mulling over the staggering and incomprehensible fact that Shackleton had only reached the halfway stage of his journey. My fingers were getting numb and the others were stamping around and reaching for their down jackets. We pitched the tent, gathered our stuff together and clambered inside. Any more record of the moment would have to wait. With the faithful cooker heating the kettle, the gathering warmth of the tent began to take its effect. For a moment we just sat and stared at each other, smirking at the realisation of what we had just achieved. I lay back into the welcoming softness of my rolled-up sleeping bag, stared upwards and fought back more tears as the relief of having finally made it took hold. We had phone calls to make, to let those at home know we had succeeded, so it wasn't long before I had the satellite telephone assembled and was talking to Joanna. Will and Henry called home shortly after and then we each left a message to be put on the website in which we attempted to describe our feelings. Supper followed and, having finished the routine end-of-day administration, we wasted no time in getting into our sleeping bags to write up our diaries and then sleep. The euphoria was still there, but we were holding it back.

'What a day this has been,' I said. 'Who would have thought, five years ago, that not only would we make it to this point, but do so on the actual day. It is remarkable.' Will and Henry agreed, but we were all too tired to enter into a long discussion; instead we needed some time to ourselves and our thoughts. I certainly did.

Feeling practically dead, I lay on my back like a corpse; arms by my side with the sleeping bag zipped right up to my chin. Inches from my face, my socks and gloves hung from the washing line but with no hope of drying out – it was far too cold. I always made sure that it was my socks that dangled above me, as I could tolerate the smell of my own but not the others. With my eyes open I stared upwards, thinking that this must be close to what it feels like to win an Olympic gold medal. Dedicated years of preparation and money worries; endless days of driving towards a single goal, forcing and teaching the body and mind to endure; a gruelling race against time and distance; and then, only for the best, a prize for the first to cross that fine line that separates victory and defeat.

My mind was awash with emotions. The feeling of utter relief was the most intense. A huge burden had been lifted from my shoulders, the burden of possible failure and letting others down. We had delivered on what we had promised our huge group of supporters. There would be no need to have to cope with disappointment for the rest of my life. Quite the opposite, we had pulled off something really quite special. But it tasted so sweet because we could not have worked any harder in order to have achieved it. We had been in a race from the moment we set off and had crossed the line with just a few hours to spare. That is what would make this expedition so special in years to come.

Then my thoughts returned to the century before. Ever since I read about the decision taken by Ernest Shackleton at the point we had just reached, I had often wondered how it would feel to stand there, having travelled more than eight hundred and twenty miles, and to contemplate his dilemma for myself. For I was puzzled why he didn't ignore the risks and push on. Surely the lure of the prize and then glory were overwhelming? He would have gone down in history as the man who planted Queen Alexandra's Union Flag on the last place on earth where Victoria's Empire had yet to reach. Fame and fortune, which Shackleton was not averse to, were certain. How, then, had he taken the decision to turn back?

His diary over the final few days of the outward journey is typically understated and frustratingly fails to paint the entire picture. He writes about the lack of food, of fatigue and the return journey that they faced. But, most of all, there is no reference to the most important feature of Shackleton's leadership – that of the love he had for his men. Even at the moment when his name could have been lit in eternal flames, he would not play poker with the lives of his fellow travellers. Perhaps they might have reached the Pole, but they would never have got back. The risk was too great to take.

Only a couple of hours earlier I had been standing at the point where he made that decision, just yards from our tent. It was impossible, of course, to replicate what his physical condition had been. Fifty-seven days at the mercy of the Antarctic had taken its toll on me, but we had had enough food and clothing to see us through. Shackleton and his men had neither. But, unbelievably, they also had the prospect of a return journey over the same eight hundred-odd miles. As I stood at that spot in the late evening of 9 January, I really could understand why he had taken the decision, and I think it was probably quite an easy one for him, despite losing the prize.

I felt utterly drained at that moment, quite physically empty. I was mentally strong and I had been driven on to reach that point by sheer willpower and the burning importance, to me, of not letting down the original team. How could we possibly fail when that date and location were well within our grasp and all that was required was great physical effort? But under the conditions that Shackleton faced, I do think that the prospect of a two-hundred mile round trip back to this same spot, then back all the way to the start line, was out of reach. He only had to consider the lives of the men who were with him for that decision to be taken with huge regret but, actually, with some ease.

There was no other way to end the day than by reading Shackleton's diary entry for 9 January 1909. 'Our last day outwards. We have shot our bolt, and the tale is latitude 88° 23 South, longitude 162° East. The wind eased down at 1 a.m. and at 2 a.m. we were up and had breakfast. At 4 a.m. started South, with the Queen's Union Jack, a brass cylinder containing stamps and documents to place at the "Furthest South" point, camera, glasses, and compass. At 9 a.m. we were in 88° 23 South, half running and half walking over a surface much hardened by the recent blizzard. It was strange for us to go along without the nightmare of a sledge dragging behind us. We hoisted Her Majesty's flag and the other Union Jack afterwards, and took possession of the plateau in the name of His Majesty. While the Union Jack blew stiffly in the icy gale that cut us to the bone, we looked south with our powerful glasses, but could see nothing but the dead white snow plain. There was no break in the plateau as it extended toward the Pole, and we feel sure that the goal we have failed to reach lies on this plain. We stayed only a few minutes, and then, taking the Queen's flag and eating our scanty meal as we went, we hurried back and reached our camp about 3 p.m. We were so dead tired that we only did two hours' march in the afternoon and camped at 5:30 p.m. The temperature was minus 19°F. Fortunately for us, our tracks were not obliterated by the blizzard; indeed, they stood up, making a trail easily followed. Homeward bound at last. Whatever regrets may be, we have done our best.'

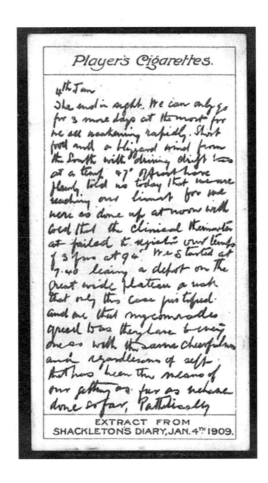

CHAPTER 7

Rendezvous with History

'Given average luck and weather, we ought to get to Hut Point by the 27th of February, which would be in time for the Nimrod.'

Frank Wild, 10 January 1909

For Shackleton, Wild, Adams and Marshall their journey was over – or at least, the first half was. That night they celebrated their record achievement with an extra portion of pemmican and a tot of sloe gin. Wild puffed on an Upmann cigar which he had been keeping for the day they reached the Pole, while Shackleton captured his thoughts in his diary. Looking up, he read aloud what he had just written.

'We have shot our bolt . . . Homeward bound . . . we have done our best.' Their feelings must have been in turmoil. They were proud, disappointed, relieved, empty and shattered. But, foremost in their minds, each knew that the return journey they were about to face would be a race against death.

Before the *Nimrod* had departed from McMurdo Sound, Shackleton had left clear instructions with Rupert England that if he had not returned from his southern journey by 15 February 1909, then the *Nimrod* was to leave for New Zealand with the expedition members and return again in the spring of the following year – but with a new captain, if Shackleton's request to replace England had been carried out. Based on that time frame the four men, huddled together in a tent more than eight hundred miles from the coast, had the race of their life ahead of them. Failure to complete the journey on time would mean another winter marooned in the hut at Cape Royds. The task facing Shackleton was huge, and there were a number of significant obstacles in his path. He had thirty-seven days to retrace his steps. Food had been running dangerously low for some time, so it was vital that they found all the depots they had previously laid on the journey – some of which contained the meat from the dead ponies. The end of the summer was approaching, the weather would become more and more changeable, and their physical condition was deteriorating. After three months in the open air of the Antarctic they were all terribly weak and suffering from frostbite, snow-blindness and advanced malnutrition. But, scratching for the positive, it would be downhill so their daily mileage should be greater and Marshall, the doctor, had yet to detect signs of scurvy.

2009

In the brutal week leading up to 9 January, my mind had been totally focussed on just getting through the day and completing the required miles. The sheer scale of the daily trial blocked out any space into which I could crawl to think and dream. To allow my mind to wander in a positive direction required it to be clear of any immediate demands. I needed to feel good about the day and be in a strong state to deal with all that the plateau was throwing at me.

On the rare moments that I found my mind could focus on anything but the present ordeal, I had started to think about the meeting with Dave and his team, just a few days away. And it troubled me that the overriding feeling was not one of looking forward to seeing them. Quite the reverse; it was one of resentment.

Way back on the Ice Barrier when, because of our speed, it was looking just possible we might reach the 97-mile point by 9 January, Will, Henry and I spent an evening discussing how long we would wait for the others to arrive and whether we would all travel on to the Pole together. I recalled the snippy manner in which we each expressed our views. While the three of us respected the right of Dave and the others to share in the exhilaration of standing at the point that their forebears' tracks had stopped, we didn't want our space intruded; we wanted to savour our achievement by ourselves. The bond that had formed between the three of us was now very tight. It had grown and matured from the initial years of training, but it had also hardened through the collective sharing of real endeavour, bloody-minded graft and many happy – and miserable – moments together along the journey. Although I never admitted to it, inwardly I felt the point that we had just reached should belong only to the three of us. With time to think this over, I was disappointed with myself for being so selfish. To the charitable, my feelings could be explained as being a natural reaction given the circumstances but I was surprised, and even shocked, . Both Dave and Tim had every right to play their part, in fact much more so than I, because of their direct lineage to Jameson Adams and Frank Wild. And without Dave's fund-raising efforts, none of us would have got anywhere near the Antarctic.

But with every passing hour after our arrival at the 97-mile point, the realisation of our achievement began to sink in and I became far less bitter about being joined by the others. Henry, Will and I had time to ourselves, which was what we had really wanted. In fact, the more the hours passed by, the more I looked forward to seeing the 97-Mile Team. We knew that our meeting would only last for a short time and after years of preparation it was quite right that we were all able to drink deep from the same cup of success. Nevertheless, I was still annoyed that I had allowed vanity and selfishness to get the better of me over the previous week. These were character traits that, in others, had always offended me.

The following morning I called in our position to Patriot Hills.

'The Shackleton Expedition reporting in from a very special place. Our position is South 88° 23.000′, East 162° 00.017′. Distance travelled yesterday was 11.6 nautical miles. Current altitude is 10,244 feet, which was a gain of 71 feet. The wind was calm and the temperature was -35°C.'

It was a great moment to report those simple string of numbers as I read out the details of the previous day from my diary. They matched the same latitude and longitude co-ordinates that Shackleton had written in pencil in his diary exactly one hundred years earlier. As usual, our position and distance travelled was repeated back and then I listened to warm comments of congratulation. For the past fifty-six days Victoria had stuck the pin marking our current location into her map, seeing it move closer to our goal each day. I could tell by the excited tone of her voice how thrilled she was for us.

'What news of the others?' I asked.

'Well, they are still on track to meet up with you. They arrived from Punta a few hours ago and have just left with Terry to join you. They will take about four hours, so should be with you about midday, your time.'

Will and Henry had listened to my phone conversation from the warmth of their sleeping bags and were equally thrilled to hear that Dave and the team would be with us soon. An added bonus was that we could carry on sleeping until the Otter arrived. I dismantled the satellite phone, faithfully stowed the battery back into the warmth of a chest pocket and turned on my side for another four hours of sleep.

We snapped sharply upright in response to the alien sound of an approaching aircraft. It had been almost two months since we had heard the noise of a machine, so it was unsurprising that it jolted our senses so acutely. We were up and booted faster than on any day of the expedition so far. As Henry unzipped the entrance to the tent we saw the Otter flying towards us at no more than thirty feet and about to buzz our campsite. I caught a glimpse of Dave's grinning face framed by a port-side window, as Terry did one last pass before landing and taxiing towards the Union Flag that we had planted the day before. I could see a lot of movement inside the plane as thick jackets, gloves and hats were being put on. Once the propellers had ceased turning the co-pilot jumped down from the cockpit and placed a small step ladder below the rear door and opened it. Dave was first into the doorway and came down the steps with arms outstretched. He fell into Will's arms and hugged him tightly. Then it was Henry's turn to be molested. Amid the excitement I caught snippets of Dave saying 'What you have done is amazing', 'unbelievable', 'so many people are following you'. I tried to capture the moment on the video camera until it was my turn to greet him. Dave was in ecstatic mood. All my selfish thoughts of resentment at their arrival had gone. Having bear hugged me too, Dave placed his gloved hands on my shoulders and almost shouted, he was so excited.

'And what is so incredible is that today is still 9 January, based on GMT. We have made it with just one hour to spare.' From the outset, meeting up at this point had been very important to us all, but for them to arrive at the right time as well as ourselves was the second bull's-eye of the expedition, especially after their earlier delays due to weather had looked likely to scupper the plan. Dave and the others had every right to be over the moon. Next to be greeted was Tim, and then Matty. We had not seen Matty since our training in Norway so seeing her again at a place we only dreamed about years before was very special. It was largely due to her initial guidance and tuition that we were so well prepared. It was also a wonderful moment to see Terry again. He had flown us from Patriot Hills to Shackleton's Hut and, I learned later, had organised his own flying schedule around supporting our journey. He wanted to be there at the beginning, at the end and every moment in between, such was his admiration for what we were doing, so it was fitting that he should share in our historic day. Competition winner Andy Ledger and Ronnie Gray were the last to step down from the plane. Andy was in his usual positive form, full of banter from the moment he saw us and for the first time I met former soldier, and friend of Dave's, Ronnie, who had very generously risen to the challenge at short notice to become the final member of the 97-Mile Team.

'Bloody hell, Will, you look like you have been dug up from over a hundred years ago,' Tim remarked. Will did look quite a sight. The early stages of frostbite on his nose and cheeks had scabbed up nicely, his lower lip was bloody and blistered, his eyes were puffy and all this was framed by a straggly beard and an unusually blonde moustache. Matted and filthy hair sprouted out from the sides of his hat. In short, he resembled a Mongol warlord. In fact, the three of us must have looked quite a spectacle and in such contrast to the clean-shaven others in their shiny, unsoiled and new-looking clothing.

As we stood and chatted it was apparent that the cold was tracking down the new arrivals. It was easy to forget that only four hours earlier they had been enjoying the comfort of Patriot Hills where the temperature was about -10°C and the altitude is around twelve hundred feet. Now they were standing still and chatting in a mild wind at just over ten thousand feet and the air temperature was around -40°C of wind chill. No wonder that I could see the end of Tim's nose turning porcelain-white as I talked to him, while the others stamped around, clapping their gloves together in the hope of warming their blood. They had quite an acclimatisation task ahead of them; the cold was getting the better of them very quickly. Matty goaded them into action to put up the tents. Will, Henry and

I retreated to our tent to eat brunch and to start stowing things away ready for our planned departure later in the afternoon. Terry put his head into the tent to bid us farewell, with a promise that he would pick us up from the Pole. Moments later he started the engines of the Otter, taxied a short distance and within seconds was airborne, heading back to Patriot Hills, but buzzing us just one more time for good measure.

Over the next couple of hours, we all crammed into one tent and caught up on each other's news. Up until now, Britain had seemed like a distant planet, but listening to stories of the world beset by dire financial gloom brought it starkly closer. As I listened I tried hard to bring into sharper focus quite what was being described, but it was of no real interest to me. We would be immersed back into all that turmoil on our return, but our home for the time being was the Antarctic and, despite her being at times a demanding hostess, I was loath to leave her – physically or mentally. In contrast, our tales were full of descriptions of the Cape Royds hut, of the Ice Barrier, the Beardmore and the crampon drama and the struggle to reach the rendezvous on time. I watched as Matty dispensed tea to everyone, but Will, Henry and I declined her offer as we were keen for our journey to be 'unassisted and unsupported', which meant we could receive no outside support at all – not even a cup of tea or piece of chocolate. By mid-afternoon it was time for the three of us to be getting on our way.

'Before you guys leave we must take some photos,' said Dave. So we left the warmth of the tent to assemble in varied groups for a series of shots around the Union Flag. It was bitterly cold so it was a hurried but nevertheless important task, especially for those linked to the team in the original photo. Once complete, we walked over to our sledges and started to put on our skis and harness up. The others followed and looked on with interest as very soon it would be their turn. For them it would be the first steps of their journey and I sensed within them the same feeling of trepidation that we'd had on the sea ice outside Shackleton's Hut fifty-eight days before.

Before the expedition had started, we had all decided that it would be highly unlikely that both teams would travel on to the Pole together. We would be desperate to finish and Dave's team would need to acclimatise, so we had agreed to travel separately.

'We'll chart your progress when we give our daily updates,' I said to Dave as I stowed my down jacket. 'Have a great journey and good luck. See you at the South Pole. I bet you never thought I'd be saying that to you, five years ago.' Dave smiled. I looked down at the compass, adjusted my position to align the needle on to the bearing, nodded to the others, then we were off. It was too cold for a prolonged farewell, and soon they were out of earshot as we headed into the southerly wind once again.

Focussing on the positive, my mind turned immediately to the events of the past twenty-four hours. Our achievement was beginning to sink in, and it had been a fantastic bonus that Dave and his team had managed to meet up with us. But it wasn't long before their campsite was reduced to a dark speck on the horizon behind us and then, finally, disappeared from view. As was always the case, starting the journey after a prolonged break never came easy. I felt sluggish and lethargic and I was heartened to hear Henry say at our first stop that he felt in a similar way. Our intention had been to get a fair distance from the others before we camped for the night. Although it had been great to see them, we really wanted to be back on our own again and have the plateau to ourselves. For me, the feeling of being totally isolated on such a vast expanse had now gone but over the final ninety-seven miles I was determined to recapture the feeling of solitude through which we had journeyed so far. After an hour we stopped for a break.

'I know that Matty's plan, not surprisingly, is to take it easy for their first few days,' I said. 'My guess is that they will do about five miles tomorrow. So I suggest we go for about four hours, aim to do eight miles and then camp.' Henry and Will nodded in weary agreement while each gnawed unenthusiastically on a frozen flap-jack, now strongly flavoured with salami after nearly two months side by side in the same bag.

The following three hours passed by very slowly, despite there now being a definite feeling of turning into the home straight. I was back to disciplining my mind to focus on thoughts that would carry me away from the endless, repetitive slide of the skis and plant of the ski poles. I turned to thinking about events on this plateau exactly one hundred years earlier. No matter how hard I tried, I still seemed unable to comprehend how Shackleton and his men could contemplate setting off on their return journey. Naturally, it was a question of survival and they had no other option, but the enormity of the task that lay ahead of them was quite simply unimaginable. And the more I thought about it the sadder I became, because we were no longer in their footsteps and there was no diary to read each night. We were closing in on a place that Shackleton had dedicated his short life of forty-seven years to reach, but had never managed to do so. But in my trouser pocket was his compass; a direct link to him and his dream, and nothing would stop me now from delivering it to 90°S, where it rightfully belonged.

Despite travelling for three and a half hours we managed only 7.1 miles. But we had put some distance between ourselves and the others. Once again, we set up camp in fatigue-induced silence. Our duties were so familiar by now that within minutes we were able to clamber inside and relax. Chat after supper centred on the others and we amused ourselves by unkindly discussing the likely difficulties that lay ahead for them. Because of the delay in Punta they had had no time to acclimatise at Patriot Hills – something which Matty and Dave had planned to do – so the effect of the altitude and the temperature would undoubtedly take its toll during the early stage of their journey. Our rather cocky mischief-making fizzled out as the warmth of our sleeping bags slowly increased. With our diaries written and eye masks pulled down, we slipped into sleep. But not before I read Shackleton's entry for the first day of their return journey on 10 January 1909. I needed to be reminded of their ordeal.

'We started at 7.30 a.m. with a fair wind, and marched all day, with a stop of one hour for lunch, doing over 18½ geographical miles to the north. It has, indeed, been fortunate for us that we have been able to follow our outward track for the force of the gale had torn the flags from the staffs. We will be all right when we pick up our depot. It has been a big risk leaving our sledge tracks to guide us back. Tonight we are all tired out, but we have put a good march behind us. The temperature is minus 9°F.' As I closed the book I reflected for a moment that this was the first entry in his diary which Shackleton had had to write that he was heading north – away from the Pole. From now on, this would be a miserable daily reminder for him that his dream had ended.

1909

It took Shackleton nine days to reach the head of the Beardmore Glacier, marked by the familiar shape of Buckley Island and the steep descent to the valley floor. With every sinew straining over their bony frames, the sledge was lowered down the icy wall to prevent it from racing ahead and being dashed to pieces. Once on the flat they retraced their route to find the depot they had placed on the western edge of the valley.

Shackleton was leading by supreme example but it was taking its toll. He was bruised all over, he had been suffering from a thudding headache for weeks and both his heels were split wide open due to frostbite. It surprised no one when he collapsed at the depot camp.

Due to the pursuing wind and a makeshift sail for the sledge, the men maintained their good progress. Twenty miles a day were being achieved but it was the minimum required if the food they had was to last them to the next depot. The sledge was now moving on a broken runner, but at least they had the luxury of pony meat, ground maize and the odd item of clothing waiting for them at weekly intervals once they spied the telltale black flag on its bamboo pole that marked each dump. On 28 January they exited the glacier by passing back down The Gateway under the eye of Mount Hope again. Repacking the sledge with food and equipment from the depot they had laid there, Shackleton turned to Wild, repeating what he had written in his diary a few days before.

'Those were the hardest and most trying days that we have ever spent in our lives, and which will ever stand in our memories.' Wild agreed. The hell that they had been through, for the second time, was now over. All that stood between life and certain death was the flat plain of the Great Ice Barrier and, hopefully, a waiting ship. Compared to the mental and physical challenges of the blue ice and crevasses, there were no significant dangers lurking on the Ice Barrier except being imprisoned in their tent due to the weather – which would spell certain disaster.

2009

On 10 January we awoke to a band of fine low cloud drifting past us, carried by a gentle southerly wind. Will was first outside, a shovel in one hand and a packet of tissues in the other, intent on his morning ablutions. Unusually for him so early in the day, he spoke. What he said caused Henry and I to stare at each other in disbelief.

'We've got visitors,' he announced from outside the tent. Initially I was astonished but seconds later it all made sense. While we had slept, Matty had guided her group over the first leg of their journey and knocked off seven miles, which was highly creditable. But I was hugely irritated. I really wanted to be alone. I was finding it very difficult to adjust to being among other people, to see their tents and, God forbid, see their tracks. Would we be playing a daily game of catch-up with them over the final miles? If so, then we might as well all join up and travel as one team. If I needed anything to motivate me from now on, it would be to get going and finish as a team of three. But the last thing I needed at this final stage was a race.

I scrambled outside and saw the collection of tents about half a mile away. I watched a figure walk to a sledge, bend forward as if to retrieve something and then return. I could make out one of the Union Flags flying stiff in the gathering wind as the low cloud begun to dissipate.

'I am thankful that they had the good grace to camp some distance away from us,' I said. 'I guess that they can't have been there long and, because they are on Chilean time, they will always travel when we sleep.' I sounded like a spoilt, petulant child but I sensed that the others were equally irked at this intrusion.

'Best we get underway as soon as possible and get a good mileage in today to stop that happening again,' I continued unfairly. So after breakfast and having filled two flasks each, we continued on our way with renewed urgency. The conditions were ideal and as we were descending slightly I found each hour a touch less demanding, allowing my mind to wander. During the afternoon I tried to fire myself up with the fact that I would soon be standing at the South Pole – a place I had only ever dreamed about when following the progress of Fiennes and Stroud. How extraordinary would that be? But not wanting to be churlish, I just couldn't summon the same enthusiasm and excitement that everyone else who has ever laboured to get there must have felt. Our 'South Pole' had been reached in a unique way two days earlier. Perhaps if we had missed our rendezvous then arrival at the Pole would have carried far greater meaning. But I was so proud that we had yielded to nothing and honoured Shackleton's historic achievement on the day that mattered. I reminded myself that one of the options discussed five years ago had been for us to be picked up and flown out from 88° 23′ and not go on to the Pole. Writing with total honesty now, and strange as it may seem, I probably could have lived with that decision.

Over the course of the following three days we kept up a consistent pace and were covering fourteen miles each day. We were desperate to finish now, so we needed no encouragement. The very gradual descent was barely discernible but was helpful nevertheless.

But despite the advantage it gave us, I was regularly arriving ten to fifteen minutes behind the others at the end of the day. It wasn't much, but still it weighed on my mind. Each of us, I was shortly to learn, had lost close to two stone in weight by now and it was starting to have an effect. But I seemed to be feeling it the most, and had done so ever since we reached the plateau. And then, I suppose because my body had had quite enough and was totally run down, for the first time in my life I developed piles. I had craved for very little on the journey, but had recently begun to yearn for fresh fruit and vegetables. It was the lack of fibre in our food that was one of the obvious causes of my extreme discomfort. I counted myself lucky that they had not struck me during the tribulations of the Beardmore Glacier, when we had quite enough to think about; but they were not welcome. Much to the amusement of Henry and Will I grimaced each time I slid one leg past the other. The days seemed even longer and certainly more uncomfortable but we carried suitable ointments in the medical kit for such an eventuality, so at least I was able to treat them and hasten some sort of recovery. Then at a snack break, to add to my discomfort I split a tooth on a piece of frozen chocolate. My body seemed to be telling me something.

I learned from my daily call to Patriot Hills that the other team were averaging about eight miles each day, so a gap was opening between us – and so it should have, but I was wrong to be smug. However, I was pleased that any chance of them arriving at the Pole directly behind us was now highly unlikely. A day or two later would be fine.

1909

On 15 February, slowly gaining ground over the Ice Barrier, Shackleton tried hard to celebrate his thirty-fifth birthday. Wild handed him a cigarette made from pipe tobacco rolled into some coarse paper but, under the circumstances, it was quite the best present he could have wished for. They were now past the date until which the *Nimrod* was expected to remain, but they would surely perish if they slowed up now – they had to keep going, just in case the ship's crew was still looking for them along the coastline of McMurdo Sound. Three days later, they spied the outline of Mount Discovery in the distant hazy mirage of the Barrier. Such a familiar sight lifted their spirits, for they knew it could also be seen from Hut Point by the waiting party. The next day the sky was clear enough to recognise Mount Erebus. Surely they would make it now. But even so close to the finish, each man's physical condition was becoming life-threatening.

Ever since Wild had feasted on Grisi's meat where the pony's body had been depoted, he had suffered from acute dysentery. In fact, all were suffering from the same stomach cramps and debilitating discomfort due, they imagined, to the build-up of toxins in the muscles and flesh of the poor distressed pony prior to his death. But onwards they pressed, shadowed by death every yard of the way. They were now into the early stages of the autumn. The evenings were definitely getting darker as the sun departed below the horizon. On 22 February Shackleton stopped suddenly to examine some unusual tracks in the snow. He counted a party of four men and some dogs. Before setting off, Shackleton had instructed Joyce, a reliable expedition member, to depot some food near Minna Bluff for their return journey: surely these were his tracks. Making the assumption that the supplies were ahead of them, why had Joyce ventured further?

The following morning, the eagle-eyed Wild saw the telltale black flags that marked the Bluff depot dancing in the wind on top of a cairn of snow. Before they even celebrated the sighting, such was the acute level of their hunger the four men immediately devoured the biscuits that they carried in their pockets for there was no longer a need to save them to last out the day. In mid-afternoon, guided by the beckoning flash of sunlight on the edge of a biscuit tin, they reached this snowy oasis. Shackleton climbed to the top of the considerable mound that Joyce had built and started to dig into the snow to reveal the treasure. There were tins of biscuits, eggs, cakes, plum puddings, crystallised fruit and fresh boiled mutton. There was also a letter dated 20 January 1909 from Evans, the new captain of the *Nimrod*, which informed them he had arrived on 5 January. That night they made the most of the fresh food store, but remained anxious as it was now more than a month since the letter had been written and the likelihood that the ship had stayed for so long was slim. The following morning they breakfasted on porridge, eggs, pemmican and biscuits, but in reasonable quantities, for they knew the dangers of overindulging on weak stomachs – a painful lesson that Shackleton had learned on Scott's journey in 1903.

Bluff depot.

2009

Like Shackleton, our journey was also nearing its end. During the endless hours of each remaining day I continued to ponder the significance of arriving at the Pole. As each step took us closer, a fire deep within me began to take hold and glow, faintly at first but with increasing intensity as we ticked off the minutes of latitude and eventually entered the eighty-ninth degree. Nothing could better what had happened on 9 January, but my enthusiasm for reaching the South Pole was definitely building. We would normally have celebrated crossing the final degree but the whisky had long since been finished and what happened instead, after two months on the Antarctic and with just five days of the journey left, was rather telling and revealed in a small way just how finished and emotionally brittle we had become.

It had been a particularly cold day. The wind had been gusting five to ten knots per hour, driving the temperature down to -42°C and we were all done in. After supper all I wanted to do was get into my scratcher and sleep, but Henry was still boiling water and to have bodies lying prostate across the tent would not have been helpful. We had to do things together in such a cramped space, so scratcher heaven would simply have to wait.

'Move over, could you, General,' Will asked, as he unfurled his sleeping bag. I was not in a good mood. Very tired and irritated that he couldn't see the knock-on effect to Henry and I, I snapped back.

'Hold on, Will. Can't you see that we are not ready? You have a habit of doing this and I've let it pass until now, but it really pisses me off.'

'Well it really pisses me off that you keep arriving late,' was his quick reply. I could see that he was angry with what I had said, but I was in no mood for a slanging match so late in the day – I sensed that we had both already said things we didn't really mean. Anyway, I just didn't have the energy to argue. However, I was taken aback with what he had said. Once in the warmth of his sleeping bag and wired into his iPod, Will turned on his side without saying a word, leaving me to stew in my own juice. Wisely, Henry had said nothing at all.

Eventually he turned off the stove and the tent was reduced to a heavy silence, save for the wind sweeping past outside. I couldn't sleep before I had worked out how to resolve this petty disagreement. Clearly the air between Will and I had to be cleared as soon as possible otherwise the rest of the journey, and in particular the confines of the tent, would have been very awkward. So I resolved to be the first to apologise in the morning. What I had said was fair I thought, but it was not delivered in a clever way. I could have got my point across just as effectively by making light of the effect of his actions but fatigue had got the better of me and, I suspected, of Will as well. However, the more I turned his comment over in my mind the more irked I became. I was confident he would apologise as well, but I decided to tell him just how out of order I thought his remarks were.

I slept fitfully that night and woke in good time to make the daily morning call to Patriot Hills. The time had now come to find out about Sean Smith's plans. The plan had always been that we would film the journey ourselves, but that we would meet him a few miles out from the Pole so that he could do some filming. I had barely given the rendezvous any thought until now, but the time had come for an update.

Having passed on our position and the distance travelled, we were updated on Sean's intentions. 'Sean is currently at the Pole with Shaun Norman and they intend to ski out to meet you so they can film your final few miles. I will give you their satphone number and they would like you to call them this time tomorrow morning. They are on the same time zone as you. You are well inside the final degree now. Not far to go.' As I was stowing away the battery and phone I noticed Will stirring to wake. I waited no more than a minute before speaking.

'Will, I want to apologise for last night. I was wrong to speak to you like that. I was completely knackered and in a scratchy mood. It was unnecessary and I am sorry.'

'Me too. I didn't mean what I said. I am sorry as well,' he replied. But I wanted to say my point, which I had rehearsed the previous night.

'Thanks. But I just want to say a couple of things about your comment. From the moment I started to drop back and arrive late, I have apologised to you and Henry on almost every occasion. I have always kept up the required mileage when leading and never caused us to stop early. I can tell you it is no fun at all being so far back and don't forget I am working like buggery for up to an hour longer than you on most days.' My point was made, and that was the end of it.

In my research for the expedition I had read extensively about the experiences of those who had travelled in a team, rather than solo, because the dynamics of their interaction – especially under stress – interested me. Reinhold Messner and Arved Fuchs, who had travelled in the opposite direction to us, fell out; Ranulph Fiennes and Mike Stroud, while remaining close friends after their record-breaking 1992–93 journey, wrote honest accounts of the clashes that had occurred between them. Robert Swan described the relationship with his fellow 1985 team members to me as 'terrible'. Even Frank Wild's words about Eric Marshall highlight ill feeling, 'I sincerely wish he would fall down a crevasse a hundred feet deep . . .' But, apart from the issue over safety on the Beardmore, this was our first disagreement – in fact, I couldn't even remember one occurring since Baffin Island in 2006. So our brief exchange the night before was of very little significance and it faded from my mind immediately.

With the air now cleared and each of us ready to depart, there was one small matter to see to. I had to apply cream to my piles which were by now very painful. But I needed some help to do it accurately. So, once alone in the tent, I pulled down my trousers and pants (which I hadn't changed for over two months), rocked back on to my shoulders and tucked my arms under both legs as if about to give birth. Then I turned to face the tent opening, to achieve the greatest effect for what I had planned next.

'Henry,' I shouted.

'Yes, mate,' came the reply.

'Could you come in here and give me a hand with something?'

'Sure thing.' The zip was pulled down and Henry's head came straight through the opening, face to face with my ailment.

'Jesus . . .' he exclaimed, unable to say any more as a rasping mix of scream and laughter took over. I was most grateful that, once composed, he turned out to be a gentle and accurate marksman with the tube of cream. Henry chuckled to himself for the rest of the morning, clearly amused by the awful vision he had been faced with on entering the tent. It was good that we were all laughing again. We had a tiring day, deciding in the late afternoon to stop after six hours of travel. We had completed 12.6 miles and another couple would make no real difference. It was a pity that the last few days were turning into such an endurance test but I was determined that they were not going to spoil the end of the journey, so an early end to the day was welcome.

1909

For Shackleton, on the other side of the continent, time was fast running out, but he refused to believe that Evans and the *Nimrod* had abandoned them. Just this once, Shackleton prayed that his orders had been broken.

The four men rose at 4 a.m. on 25 February, but by now Marshall was in a bad way. His dysentery was acute and he was fading fast. Outside the tent, as they were eating breakfast and preparing to leave, the wind suddenly increased and within a few minutes they found themselves in the eye of a blizzard. Marshall was in no state to battle against it, so they were faced with no option but to sit it out. It was a dangerous strategy and Shackleton knew he could not pursue it for long. Raising his voice to be heard above the persistent beating of the wind on the wall of the tent, Shackleton looked first at Marshall.

'If you have not improved by tonight, then I have no choice but to leave you here with Adams. Wild and I will go for help. I gave instructions to Joyce to stay at the depot we have just passed until 10 February and then to make his way back to *Nimrod*. We have four days to get to Hut Point, otherwise they will leave without us.' It was a stark picture that he painted, and the remaining journey to Hut Point would take the timings right to the edge.

Joyce had done exactly as he had been ordered. He had set out with a dog team and dropped off the food, fuel and clothing where he had been told. But, nervous that he had not seen the southern party, he headed further south with the dogs for two days in the hope of meeting the team coming the other way – hence the tracks. But Joyce had found nothing and returned to the coast fearing the worst. The blizzard kept Shackleton and his team trapped the entire day; crucial hours were lost. But luckily, the wind died at midnight. Having rested all day and with Marshall in slightly better spirits, they needed no encouragement to set off and managed to cover twenty-four miles in as many hours. Marshall barely coped, but was uncomplaining. However, the following day it was no good. Strong leadership was called for, and Shackleton decided to leave Marshall and Adams, as he had warned, and continue with Wild in the hope of stopping the ship. Taking two days' food and the barest minimum of gear, they set off with a sledge so light that they hardly noticed it behind them. It was the last day of February 1909.

Pausing briefly throughout to scan the high ground ahead of them for dots of life on the skyline, they saw nothing and pushed on. Periodically they also stopped to use the heliograph but nothing responded to their sign. Then the open sea of McMurdo Sound came into view. Scott's *Discovery* hut was nearly in sight. Wasting no time, they abandoned the sledge and hobbled on as fast as their swollen and bleeding feet allowed.

2009

I had called Sean, as arranged, and he had given me the coordinates of his campsite, which was where we agreed to meet to do the filming. Thankfully, it was on our approach route, but the thought of hours of standing around in the severe cold, putting up and taking down the tent and giving more interviews was not, in truth, something we were looking forward to. But Sean had to make his film and we owed it to him to be professional and support him. He knew exactly how we felt, but had been understandably persuasive on the phone, promising to make the delay as short as possible.

Our days on the Antarctic were fast running out. Very soon we would be back in the world we had left so far behind us in mid-November; now every uninterrupted moment left together was important to me. We were travelling at a steady speed now, covering thirteen miles each day. Sometimes we would draw up together and walk abreast for short moments until we naturally fell back into single file; but they were good moments to chat and I certainly felt the bond between us as we seemed to move as a single unit. When we stopped every hour, the breaks often lasted longer than usual as, subconsciously, we realised that time was running out and these were moments to savour and remember, rather than hurry. Often I would just stand in silence and, with slow movements of my feet, turn a full circle, focussing intently on the horizon and contemplating yet again the overwhelming scale of the place. I must have thought about it hundreds of times over the course of the journey, but I never tired of it. Our presence on a landscape of such immensity seemed an out and out irrelevance and something I knew I would, most probably, never experience again in my life. At other times we chatted aimlessly but I recognised the looks we gave each other as those of a team that has been through demanding days. I had experienced that look in the eyes of soldiers. The sharing of tough times and prevailing against all odds creates a special bond, and the more precarious the experience, the stronger the bond.

No words are needed. It's simply a look and a nod and to know 'I was there'.

Our last evening together was special. After supper, when we could now eat double helpings as we no longer needed the food set aside for the emergency reserve, we went outside together to spend a few moments under the eye of the brilliant sun. The wind had dropped slightly and the cold was snapping at us in seconds, but we managed a few brief moments to savour the feeling of achievement before it was all over and we were joined by others. The memory of 9 January was still foremost in our minds. We could have done that journey a hundred times and not once arrived on the specified date. It had been the 'stunning' effort required to achieve it, first mentioned by David Rootes, that made the taste so sweet.

The following morning, after our sixty-fifth breakfast of the journey and still enjoying double rations, we set off to meet Sean. By my calculations, we still had ten miles to travel to the Pole but there was no sign of it – not that we really knew what to look for, except something that punctured the horizon and was quite obviously out of place. It was apparent that we were getting close because the occasional C-130 aircraft was now passing low overhead on the planes final approach to a runway. We strained our eyes to try and see them land but still they went just out of sight. Locating and meeting Sean was forefront in our minds that morning, for the sooner we found him the sooner we would be on our way. I had programmed his location into the GPS and we did as it told us and followed the bearing. After an hour, Will saw something.

'There he is,' he shouted, pointing to a black dot on the landscape. But it was off to one side of our direction of travel.

'It could be their tent,' I agreed, 'but it's not on the bearing.' I continued, 'There's a bright, white speck where we are heading, but I admit it doesn't look like a tent. It's far too bright. Let's make for your dot, Will.' I should have known better and trusted the compass.

It was a foolish error to be making at this late stage, and I had fallen into a common trap of navigation by convincing myself to alter course on to something that I thought to be right – when the compass was telling me something different. So we altered course, but I still kept one eye on the white speck on the horizon.

'There is another black dot,' Henry shouted, pointing with his ski stick. We drew up together and tried to work out what we should be aiming for.

'I think all these dots are part of the science stuff out here,' I said. 'Best we stick to the bearing. Their tent may not be the white speck, but let's just keep going along that line.' We kept going and moments later we made out two figures. They seemed to be heading out to our flank, then suddenly they stopped and began to set up something.

'It's definitely them,' Henry cried. He was right. Sean was setting up his camera to film our final approach. We had found them.

Without anyone suggesting it, we pulled level with each other and headed straight towards him. He was less than a mile away and we were closing in on him fast, lengthening our strides beyond what we were used to. We were so focussed on Sean that we failed to notice the shape of the South Pole Station emerging just above the horizon, off to our left about five miles away. An inky, oblong structure, like a dark smudge backed with blue on a pure white canvas, shimmered at the limit of our view. The black dots we had seen earlier had become small huts. The occasional snowmobile was just visible in the distance and the white speck on the bearing, reflecting the sun, was a snow wall that had been built to protect Sean's tent. So the compass had been right – in fact, it is always right. In the short time it takes to cover less than a mile on skis we had been thrust back into the world we had left behind for two months. Aircraft, people, machines and man-made structures were all around us now. We needed no further reminding; our journey was fast coming to an end.

1909

Inside the *Discovery* hut, Shackleton and Wild slumped, devastated, on to the softest thing they could find. Unlike February 1903 when Shackleton had returned with Scott and Wilson to the same place, there were no cheering crowds, no hot meal, no tobacco and no ship. In fact, no sign of life at all. In the gloom of a Primus lamp he had managed to light, Shackleton found a letter. Unfolding it gently with numb and swollen fingers he held it to the light. At last, this was a sign of life. In a rasping and faint voice he read it out to Wild.

'It says that the northern party made it to the magnetic pole and that everyone has been picked up except us. The ship will be at anchor under the glacier tongue until 26 February.' Shackleton looked up and stared at Wild, who hadn't stirred. Placing the letter into his jacket pocket, he continued.

'I think it is now 28 February and the glacier tongue is another day's march away.' He dared not say more, for he feared that they had been left behind. Instead, he set about preparing an evening meal from the abundant provisions strewn around them; some from the *Discovery* expedition stores and more recent items left by the *Nimrod* team. Wrapped in a tarpaulin, stiffened by frost, they huddled together dreaming of their rotten and fetid sleeping bags out on the abandoned sledge. To keep the blood moving inside their hollow bodies and to attract attention they went outside and tried to set fire to the small weather station behind the hut, but it was no use. They also tried to fly Queen Alexandra's Union Flag from Vince's memorial cross, but their fingers were so bloated and weak that even the knots defeated them.

A fire was their only hope, so at dawn they tried again, this time with greater success. With the weather station ablaze and the smoke lifting into the sky they looked out across the sound and prayed. Hopeless minutes passed as they scanned the waters towards the glacier tongue. Neither man spoke. Shackleton's mind flitted between the image of Marshall and Adams huddled together and close to death still out on the Ice Barrier and the thought of another winter in the hut at Cape Royds. Then something moved and caught his eye. The tip of the tallest mast on the *Nimrod* broke the distant cliff line that marked the coast. Their prayers had been answered. The smoke had been seen. They were safe.

On board the *Nimrod*, among friends, the emotion of the rescue engulfed everybody, for the southern team had been given up for dead. Each had questions to ask and the first one was expected, though like the southerly wind, it cut Shackleton to the bone. He looked them all in the eye and answered in a proud but faltering voice.

'No. We had ninety-seven miles more to travel. And if I had had fifty pounds of food then we would have made it. But we are all safe and must thank Providence for having delivered us home.'

2009

Among those who had been so intimately involved in our expedition, and apart from my immediate family, there was no person I would

A boat from the Nimrod *meets Shackleton and Wild at the Discovery Hut. Adams and Marshall remain out on the Ice Barrier.*

have chosen above Sean Smith to meet us during the closing stage of our journey. Not only had he been with us in Greenland and filmed the final stages of our departure from Britain, but he had been with us in the *Nimrod* hut and seen us off from Cape Royds. I didn't need to see his face, as I could tell from his voice and body language that, like us, the emotion of meeting up again was too hard to contain. I was the last to be greeted by him. With outstretched arms he hugged me tight and long, as a parent might greet their child. I will never, ever, forget the depth of that embrace. His quietly understated praise was very special to hear. He knew what it was like to step into the arena to be counted, so applause from him was a treasured moment.

A few miles from the South Pole is no place to stand around chatting, whatever the circumstances, so we made our way over to their tent to set up our camp. There was a short delay as Sean sorted out his camera because now he needed to capture everything we did. Once he was ready, the tent went up in minutes and we dived inside to get the cooker on for some hot drinks. Sean followed us, but very soon was having difficulties with his camera lens misting up because of the sudden change in temperature. With cups of hot chocolate in hand we set about making a plan.

Getting to the Pole, which we could clearly see five miles away, was now our primary aim, so we wanted to get this stage over as quickly as we could and get going. The rest of the day was spent filming the various shots that Sean wanted which, naturally, took ages. The cold was sapping the energy from the batteries of his camera and we were reluctant actors, putting up and taking down a tent when all we wanted to do was stow it away for the last time. But the day finally came to an end and we zipped up the entrance to prepare for our last night of the journey. There were no celebrations. Sean joined us for a chat but it was all very low-key and soon we were ready to sleep. Tomorrow really would be the end.

Then, that evening, something happened that could be explained away by simple physics or meteorology. But, just like my sighting of the snow petrels on the Ross Ice Shelf, I chose a more powerful explanation. I exited the tent in the late evening when all was quiet for my final, solitary walkabout. I had done this religiously every night from when we set off, before I finally turned in. I still longed for that moment each day as it brought closure to whatever I had endured. I always turned away from the tent and sledges, so that any sign of life was out of view and behind me. On some days I had faced a never-ending expanse of nothingness, on others it was just mountains and glaciers and me. I just adored being alone, especially at that time of the day.

But on this, my last evening of an incredible journey, I was faced with something so unbelievably stunning that I stopped dead in my tracks and just gazed in awe. What I was looking at was a parhelion. It is a relatively common sight during the Antarctic summer and is created by the sun's rays passing through wind-borne ice crystals that, when refracted, create a perfect circle of intense light, lit from the centre by the sun. And when the conditions are just right, cups of light, or 'sun dogs', mark each quadrant of the circle. We had seen a couple of blurred examples on the journey but nothing as precise and magisterial as this one. Resting on the horizon, it looked like a vast hoop, burning white hot. And suspended within was a sun, not round, but diamond-shaped, hanging against a backdrop of grey. It was the scale and perfect symmetry that seemed to place me in another world. Why had it appeared on our last day of the journey with such intensity? My guard was down again, as I was done in, physically finished and my emotions had been unlocked. I needed an explanation, and physics was not the answer I was looking for. Surely this was a sign from the Antarctic that it was finally releasing its grip? Or was it Shackleton, Adams, Wild and Marshall letting me know that all along they had walked beside us, but that now their task was over? I didn't care really. To me, on that last evening, I captured a spiritual moment when some other force seemed at work and I was left free to interpret it as I wished.

Breakfast the following morning carried none of the importance of the previous sixty-five. We had barely five miles to go to complete the journey when we could at last stop and eat as much as we wanted. Sean filmed us packing up the tent, putting on boots, adjusting our traces, packing our sledges and putting on our skis for the final time. We set off, with Sean still filming from the flanks, dead ahead and behind us; a slow process but we were in no real hurry now. We knew it would only take about three hours to reach our final destination, so we were content to wait for him to get his shot.

Finally, just after midday, he had finished and we were let off the leash to cover the last couple of miles uninterrupted. There was too little time to soak up the realisation that the end was upon us and very soon we started to pick up the edge of the runway, compacted hard by the planes as they landed on skis. I looked down and realised that I was now skiing in the tracks made by a snowmobile. On either side of us, cardboard boxes were piled high, some marked 'Mattresses and Pillows', others 'Broken washing machines'. And, looking very forlorn, an artificial Christmas tree caught my eye as its tinselled branches shimmered in the wind. This was not quite how I had imagined the South Pole Station.

Just as I was getting accustomed to new sights, new smells took over. The wind became scented with a confusing mix of aviation fuel and frying food, as we skied closer and closer to the main building. It was clear that we were coming in through the back yard, as there was not a flag or ceremonial marker anywhere. What I had seen so far had not really surprised me, but somehow I was not prepared for what came next. As we made our way slowly down the corridor of cardboard boxes we were halted in our tracks by a car. We stopped and peered in, somewhat in disbelief.

'Hi, guys. Where have you come from?' the driver asked in an American accent.

'Cape Royds. We set off in November,' I replied with huge satisfaction and a big grin.

'Ah, you must be the Shackleton lot. Good to see you. We heard you might be arriving about now. Well, you are nearly there. The South Pole marker is round the building in front of you. Just follow the track round to the right, past the ceremonial flags and you will see it beside the sign. Can't miss it. You will also see where to pitch your tent. When you are ready we will send someone over to show you round the station and give you a cup of coffee and a biscuit. That's all we can do, I am afraid. Catch you later.' And with that, he drove off. The situation seemed so bizarre and comical that we just chuckled to ourselves as we continued our final approach.

1909

Shackleton, summoning renewed strength from the relief of the rescue, formed a party of four to head back on to the Ice Barrier to bring in Marshall and Adams, leaving a weak and beaten Wild on board the *Nimrod*. Midway through the following day the rescue party reached the solitary tent to find Marshall and Adams alive and in reasonable spirits. Marshall, still suffering, had improved

Marshall waits patiently for Shackleton to return.

229

enough to face the final miles. Early on 3 March they arrived back at Hut Point, but could hardly believe their eyes. The *Nimrod* had gone, obviously forced away from the water's edge by the ice forming in the sound. Facing another night in the *Discovery* hut, they tried one more time to attract the ship's attention, wherever she was. Breaking open a tin of carbide used for the acetylene lighting system, they took it in turns to urinate on the crystals. It was enough to generate the smoke and flames for the signal to be seen. Although she was nine miles away, the *Nimrod* steamed in to pick them up and at last the entire crew were safe and alive on board. Shackleton checked on his loyal friend Wild, who was eager to know how his fellow travellers had fared.

'All is well. We can head home,' replied Shackleton.

2009

At the front of the building of the Amundsen-Scott South Pole Station is a collection of flags belonging to the original signatories of the Antarctic Treaty. They are arranged in a semi-circle around the iconic glass ball that serves as the ceremonial marker and is the place where most photographs are taken. But this is not the South Pole. The point that the earth spins on was located, this year, about a hundred yards further on and marked by a modest brass ball on top of a slender pole. With just a few yards to go until we reached it, we slowed up and then skied to a halt. In turn we placed our palm on the top of the ball and then punched the air. We had done it. It was 4.32 p.m. on Sunday, 18 January 2009. The dream had been fulfilled. We hugged and slapped each other. There was not a soul around, not even a face at a window. Fittingly, I thought, we had the moment to ourselves.

Once our very brief celebration had died down, unnoticed, I removed the glove from my right hand and thrust my hand immediately into my trouser pocket. The warmth of the metal was noticeable as I curled my fingers around the worn, smooth rim of the compass and drew it into my palm. For a few seconds I squeezed it tight before bringing it out into the open. I wanted to prolong the final moment it still remained part of me, for once it was on display it somehow became the property of others and my umbilical link to it would be severed. It had been a talisman of such influence and inspiration that even now I can pinpoint the moments when it gave me an inner lift which literally carried me through those final, dark days, as I teetered on the absolute edge of my soul, in order to reach that lonely spot on time.

'Hold on, before we head for the tent we must get out the compass,' I said in a very matter-of-fact way. 'This moment, after all, is what the journey has in part been about.' As I uttered the last words I took the compass from my pocket and prised open the lid to reveal the card, excitedly spinning. It seemed to know exactly where it had reached, such was its feverish movement. As it began to settle I stroked my thumb over the three letters that Shackleton had crudely scratched on the underside of the lid to claim it as his own – EHS. Irrevocably, a part of him had finally reached 90° South.

CHAPTER 8

Reflections in the Ice

'. . . but in memories we were rich. We had pierced the veneer of outside things. We had suffered, starved and triumphed, grovelled down yet grasped at glory, grown bigger in the bigness of the whole. We had seen God in his splendours, heard the text that nature renders. We had reached the naked soul of man.'

EHS, *South*, 1919

In the gathering light of 4 March 1909, *Nimrod* set a course north and headed out towards the open sea bound for New Zealand. The shoreline of Ross Island passed by on the starboard side. Adélie penguins porpoised through the dark water and Weddell seals, resting on the dark rocks, raised their heads with a look of puzzlement as the ship moved past. Shackleton stood alongside Evans on the bridge, describing how they had set off across the same frozen sea with the ponies five months before. In a moment of quiet his eye was drawn towards Mount Erebus, the great sentinel that had watched over them as they departed on their journey and then guided them in at the end. On the shore, Shackleton fleetingly noticed a sheltered spot that he thought would be a perfect site for another hut. It was a random thought, and he had no idea that in just two years' time Captain Scott would return and build his *Terra Nova* hut there and follow Shackleton's route to the Pole in his race against Roald Amundsen.

As they passed Cape Royds the crew began to assemble on the deck. Shackleton gathered together his three indomitable companions for a photograph to mark the end of their expedition. With tails wagging, some of the dogs wandered into the shot, pleased to see familiar faces once more. Adams thrust his hands into his pockets but Shackleton's were too frostbitten and swollen to do the same. Marshall stood at the back and Wild waited patiently, puffing away on a fresh cigarette and appearing immune to the cold, leaving his jacket unfastened. No matter how hard they tried to convey pride in their achievement it was hard to disguise the look of utter exhaustion, despondency and the marks of their recent race against death.

L–R: Wild, Shackleton, Marshall and Adams on the deck of the Nimrod – *homeward bound.*

Once the photograph had been taken they returned to join the rest of the crew. As they rounded the familiar sight of the penguin colony, their little hut came into view. Some men cheered while others stood in silence. Shackleton looked on with regret that he was not able to visit it just once more. It had been a happy home, still alive with great memories. A place of laughter, of silence, of friendship, of prayer – but most of all, of hope.

The memory of that moment stayed with him over the coming months and resurfaced with great clarity when he sat down to write an account of his historic journey in *The Heart of the Antarctic*.

'We all turned out to give three cheers and to take a last look at the place where we had spent so many happy days. The hut was not exactly a palatial residence, and during our period of residence in it we had suffered many discomforts, not to say hardships, but, on the other hand it had been our home for a year that would always live in our memories. We had been a very happy little party within its walls, and often when we were far away from even its measure of civilisation it had been the Mecca of all our hopes and dreams. We watched the little hut fade away in the distance with feelings almost of sadness, and there were few men aboard who did not cherish a hope that some day they would once more live strenuous days under the shadow of mighty Erebus.'

2009

Within a few hours of reaching the South Pole, Will, Henry and I were prised from the warm hospitality at the Scott-Amundsen base – the promised 'biscuit' had soon been replaced by somewhat more substantial fare – by the sound of the ALE Twin Otter that had come in to pick us up. Terry greeted us each with a congratulatory bear hug but wasted no time in getting airborne again for our flight back to Patriot Hills. Before leaving the Pole behind us, Terry circled the plane over the site for one last look. I could easily make out our route over the last few miles, past the junk yard of cardboard boxes and surface-laid pipes. The runway stood out and I could see a C-130 Hercules waiting to fly three hours back to McMurdo Sound, a journey that had just taken us sixty-six days.

During our flight back to Patriot Hills I passed the time just gazing out of the window, imagining myself somewhere back on the frozen surface below us. I unfolded the map on my lap and slowly followed the line of the course we had taken, reminding myself of the more poignant moments of the journey. How alive the hut had seemed, the frustration of the storm, the view from Mount Hope, the anguish but beauty of the Beardmore and then the sweet taste of success on 9 January 2009 after the long, brutal uphill struggle against the polar plateau. The complete journey was captured on that map by a simple series of dots and numbers but, as I carefully folded it away, it was hard to believe that it was all over.

On our arrival at Patriot Hills we were given a big-hearted welcome by David Rootes, Steve Jones and the rest of the ALE staff. Even Børge Ousland, the legendary Norwegian polar explorer who had been guiding a group to the Pole, praised our achievement.

'Congratulations. Great journey,' he said, as he signed my map.

The invitation to Shackleton's homecoming reception in June 1909.

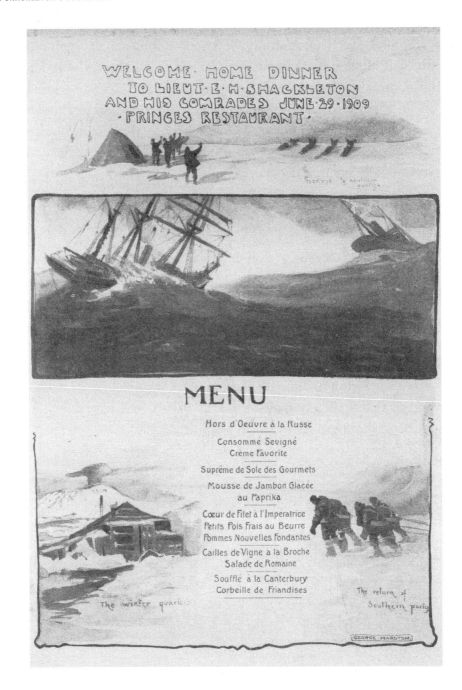

It took Dave, Tim, Andrew, Matty and Ronnie ten days to reach the South Pole from the point we had left them. Their journey had been straightforward enough but, not surprisingly, some found acclimatising to the altitude and low temperatures a not inconsiderable effort. It was not until their final arrival at Patriot Hills on 19 January, when we all stood together again, that we could finally say that the expedition was really over.

1909

On 14 June 1909, Shackleton and his crew reached England to a welcome befitting a returning polar hero. Almost immediately he was made a Companion of the Victorian Order and then, seven months later, was knighted by King Edward VII. Roald Amundsen and Fridtjof Nansen heaped praise on his achievement and, in particular, the selfless decision to turn back even when faced with the glorious prize. Shackleton became the darling of London society; every one wanted a piece of him. But, still heavily in debt, he embarked on an extensive European lecture tour, being wined and dined by anyone who was prepared to pay to share his captivating company.

2009

We returned to England in late January and fell into the outstretched arms of our loving families and messages of warm congratulation from our many followers. It didn't take long for the normality of life to return and it was vital that I got into step with it immediately. I'd had my break, now my time belonged to others. But what of the experience now?

2010

Over the last year, time has allowed me to step back and reflect on memories of what was undoubtedly a significant period of my life and that of the team. Foremost in my mind is the feeling of pride in what we accomplished. There were many before us who had thought about retracing Shackleton's journey but, apart from Rob Swan leaving Scott's hut in 1985, no one had stepped out from the *Nimrod* hut and travelled unsupported in his footsteps to the point he stopped on 9 January 1909; however, I do also remind myself that no one has yet managed to retrace the entire journey, for we only went halfway. But it was much more than the accomplishment of the journey. It was overcoming the enormity of the five-year project that stemmed from Will Gow's initial idea. It was the painstaking research, the weeks of training, the nail-biting rounds of fund-raising and the constant drive required from all of us to prevail over the frictions that lay in our path. It was mastering those areas and much more, all strikingly similar to what Shackleton experienced, that created the feeling of achievement.

There is also a feeling of utter relief at having delivered on something for which we'd had so much support from others. I well remember being awash with this emotion when, on 9 January 2009, we stood in silence and contemplated just what we had achieved. I hate letting people down and although this endeavour carried a high risk of failure, I treated it no differently to other challenges much less hard. But to be unburdened from the weight of people's expectations and hopes felt sublime.

The friendships that we forged over the life of the project have all remained strong. I think it is remarkable that a group of complete strangers came together and collectively pulled towards a common goal – no doubt helped by the polar genes. But of course there were also differences. During many of our meetings, big personalities clashed. Some were challenged for not having pulled their weight in the fund-raising and I was griped at as the leader for not offering praise to the team for their uncomplaining efforts. Despite all of that, the friendships endure among all of us. But, not surprisingly, it is my lasting bond with Will and Henry that I prize the most. In an earlier chapter I mention examples of polar journeys where friendships have been placed under great strain and even some where friendships have not recovered, so I count us lucky that we escaped that misfortune. In our favour, our characters shared common ground: we were driven, we were grafters, we were optimistic, we were often childish, we could take the mickey and have it taken in equal measure but, most important of all, we each had fire in our bellies to honour and celebrate the achievement of those who went before us, at all costs. The training sessions in Canada, Norway and Greenland were crucial to forging our friendship, but we were never able to replicate spending two months in a tent together. The time in training did allow us to understand one another's strengths, weaknesses, likes, dislikes and many others character traits that emerge when faced with boredom or pressure. But most important to me was that we learned to trust each other – if necessary, with our lives. We trusted each other to be open and honest, to make a decision for the greater good of the team and to know which knot to tie during a crevasse rescue. However, what really binds the friendship is that we shared an intensely physical journey that pushed us to our limits and we came out the other side triumphant. It is the sharing of the highs and lows of an experience such as we went through that will forever tie us together. When we are old and grey we'll be able to look each other in the eye and say 'we did it'. Shackleton summed it up best, 'There are good things in the world, but I am not sure that comradeship is not the best of them all.'

As I did many times during the expedition, I stand in far greater awe of just what Shackleton and his team endured and achieved on their journey south in their attempt to claim the Pole. We never even scratched the surface of their hardship, but I do think Henry, Will and I can now understand far better than most just what they put up with. Although we never went hungry, our clothing and equipment worked perfectly (apart from the crampons), we suffered no serious ailments and, over all, we had better weather, reading Shackleton's diary every night from the same place he had written it, gazing out from our tent at the same views he was describing. As our journey progressed and we faced our own problems, we began to scrape beneath the surface of their suffering.

On the Ross Ice Shelf we had an easy time, but for many days I envisaged those wretched ponies stumbling along beside us in the deep snow, weakening by the day. On the blue ice of the Beardmore Glacier we shared many of the same daily trials that Shackleton had faced; our shins, elbows and knees were bashed and bruised from countless falls, our crampon failure overlapped with similar equipment problems he faced. But it was the long haul up the gradual incline of the polar plateau where I really felt closer to comprehending quite what Shackleton, Wild, Adams and Marshall achieved. I have attempted to capture the brutal struggle I faced as I tried to carry out the simple movement of sliding one ski in front of the other. It sounds straightforward enough but by that stage each of us had lost two stone in weight and were utterly exhausted, battling daily against a driving wind and severe wind chill. The same mental determination that drove us on drove Shackleton on too. We had to reach the ninety-seven mile point on time because not to have done so would simply have meant that we had given up. Shackleton had been driven on to be the first to the Pole, to claim it for Great Britain. Yet he stopped. It was over this final stage of our journey that Henry, Will and I began to understand just what an achievement the original party had accomplished; then they turned around and headed back down the route they had come. Now that I have done that first half of their journey and stood at the point at which Shackleton made that decision, it is clearer to me just what was going through his mind. Until we got there I had thought that surely, when faced with such a prize, Shackleton should have just said 'Let's go for it'. But we know that rather than satisfying his ego and guaranteeing fame and fortune, he chose not to in order to protect the lives of his men. Faced with the return journey and almost a two-hundred mile round trip to the Pole and back to the same spot, it was a simple decision. Given the state they were in, it was simply too far.

This account of our journey would, for me, be incomplete without any reference to the invisible presence of others. I do not consider myself a particularly spiritual person but, looking back, I still feel that when I saw the snow petrels on the Ross Ice Shelf and the parhelion the day before we finished the journey, these were signs that something had been keeping an eye on us. Of course, my interpretation of those two events could be put down to extreme exhaustion and heightened emotions but at the time I thought very differently, and still do. The presence of some higher being is not unknown in times of utmost danger. Shackleton wrote about the Fourth Man when he crossed South Georgia in May 1916 and others have written about a similar feeling of 'not being alone' in times of danger, such as trying to escape from the Twin Towers on 11 September 2001. So I feel privileged that, perhaps, I shared the same experience.

One aspect of Shackleton's leadership that intrigues me still is how he managed to keep his team going forwards after Socks had died on the Beardmore Glacier. At that stage, with all the ponies dead, the days must have been looking desperate for them. But still Shackleton managed to lead them forward through the most unimaginable hardship. For the Edwardians, the lure of the big prize must have beckoned them onwards, but still it would have needed an extraordinary force to also push them from behind. Somehow Shackleton managed to do that. He placed 'optimism' at the top of the qualities he looked for in a fellow polar explorer and this sings out from his diary entries that cover even the darkest days; maintaining that 'cup half-full' approach throughout the journey was astonishing, and it is not surprising that the team followed.

I have left until last what I learned on the journey and, not unsurprisingly, the lessons are all interwoven. First, I was reminded just what is possible when you are having fun. Even the most demanding circumstances can be overcome with a positive and optimistic attitude and a healthy dose of humour. Shackleton was right to place optimism at the top of his list. I was constantly reminded, both during our training and on the more challenging days of the expedition, of the powerful effect that enjoying oneself can have. We felt we could take on anything despite the difficulties that lay in our way. I see it time and again in the army. Largely through black humour and leg-pulling, the British squaddie can endure all that is thrown at him by adopting the same approach.

The importance of having a positive mindset became so apparent during the latter stages of our journey. I always hoped that what I might have been lacking in physical strength I would make up for with an iron will to succeed. I had prepared carefully for this eventuality. I had a database of past experiences that had demanded everything from me tucked away in my brain, so that I could remind myself just what I was capable of – the Yukon race was a recent addition. But it was also the unimaginable experiences of others that I had read about that reminded me just what a picnic we were on by comparison. How can you feel unable to face the day when you have read *An Evil Cradling* – Brian Keenan's account of being chained to a radiator in Lebanon for five years? How can you feel unable to face a physical challenge when you have read *Touching the Void* – Joe Simpson's account of crawling, on broken bones, across the snowfields of the Andes? And, of course, I include Shackleton's account of his journey in my database too. Mental preparation is key to a grand undertaking and, in your time of need and as long as your database is full, it will quietly say to you, 'others have had it far worse and made it through – so pull yourself together'.

My final thought concerns two areas that are inextricably linked – when passion becomes obsession, and the cost of that obsession to those who stand and wait. There is no doubt that over the five years of this project my passion to fulfil my dream became obsessive. Every waking moment when I wasn't at work, I became embroiled in something to do with that quest. But to complete an undertaking as bold as ours required total immersion. Therein lies the danger. Something has to stand aside for it to succeed and, in my case, it was my family. I was incapable of satisfying both and I truly believe that when driven by such obsession it is impossible to do so. No man could have been given greater support to fulfil his consuming passion than I got from Joanna, Max and Alicia. And of one thing I am certain, it was only because of those invisible hands pushing me on from behind, that I was able to achieve my dream. Until the day I die I will never forget that.

In 1911, just two years after Shackleton's return from the *Nimrod* expedition, Captain Scott and Roald Amundsen raced each other to the South Pole. Scott set out from a new hut that he built at Cape Evans and Amundsen picked a point further west, at the Bay of Whales. The result is well known. Amundsen, using dogs and skis, was the victor. Scott arrived at the Pole three weeks later and his party of five heartbroken men all perished on the return journey. So, with the South Pole finally claimed there remained only one more crowning achievement – the crossing of the Antarctic from coast to coast via the Pole. In 1914, under Shackleton's leadership, the Imperial Trans-Antarctic Expedition set sail from Britain on the first day of the Great War intent on claiming that prize. The ship they were travelling in was called the *Endurance* and the story of disaster and rescue that unfolded over the following two years confirmed Shackleton as a giant in the field of inspiring leadership. Many accounts of the expedition, accompanied by Frank Hurley's awe-inspiring photographs, have been written but it is quite clear to me that if Shackleton had not been faced with situations that tested his judgement, his risk-taking, his ability to make men do things against all odds, as we have seen throughout this story, then the outcome of the *Endurance* expedition might well have been very different. After the Great War, which so cruelly claimed the lives of some of the *Endurance* crew members, Shackleton continued to be drawn by the siren's call of the South. On 22 January 1922, on board the *Quest* and about to set sail from Grytviken, the whaling station on South Georgia, he suffered a heart attack and died. He was forty-seven. Shackleton's extraordinary journeys had ended and it was there, by his grave, that my own long journey to follow in his footsteps began.

'We are the Pilgrims, master; we shall go
Always a little further: it may be
Beyond the last blue mountain barred with snow,
Across that angry or that glimmering sea'

From Hassan *by James Flecker*

The Shackleton Foundation

'The Shackleton Foundation supports individuals of all ages, nationalities and backgrounds who exemplify the spirit of Sir Ernest Shackleton: inspirational leaders wishing to "make a difference", in particular to the less advantaged.'

www.shackletonfoundation.org

From the very outset of this project there were two aims that we set out to accomplish. We wanted to complete 'unfinished family business' in the centenary year of Ernest Shackleton's original expedition, but we also wanted to leave behind a legacy to the great man and his exemplary leadership. The former we accomplished through the journey to the South Pole and the second lives on in the form of the charity we set up - The Shackleton Foundation. What we are trying to achieve is explained in the charity's vision statement:

'Whilst Shackleton never achieved his personal dream of being the first to reach the South Pole, his reputation as a leader of men is based on a still greater success: the survival and safe return of all of his team members, whilst overcoming almost unimaginable odds. Shackleton's name lives on as a synonym for courage, bravery and most of all, leadership.

Shackleton's era of heroic exploration is now long gone. However, The Shackleton Foundation believes innumerable and significant challenges still exist where the rallying power and indomitable spirit of Shackleton is needed, in order to make a tangible contribution to the greater good.

Thomas Pynchon wrote 'Everyone has an Antarctic.' The Foundation exists to support and encourage people who may not otherwise have the opportunity to identify and cross their own Antarctic, particularly where the applicant's chosen project can be shown to directly benefit the less advantaged. Whilst we support projects within and outside the physical arena, it is evidence of Shackleton's spirit that we seek.

We believe that singular people making singular contributions to the public good can act as beacons of inspiration, and we wish to support them in their endeavours.

The Foundation hopes that beneficiaries will develop or possess the personal qualities that define leadership: a fierce personal commitment to succeed, a willingness to take intelligent risks, and the ability to inspire and energise those around them to do their utmost towards worthwhile causes.

Ice Team Travel Log

Date	Day No	Latitude	Longtitude	Windspeed	Wind Direction	Temp Deg C	Altitude (Ft)
14-Nov	1	77 40	166 25	12-15 Knots	NW	-10	0
15-Nov	2	77 50	166 38	0		-5	0
16-Nov	3	77 52	167 11	18	S	-8	0
17-Nov	4	77 53	167 57	0		-10	82
18-Nov	5	78 01	168 28	0		-16	86
19-Nov	6	78 12	168 32	0		-8	118
20-Nov	7	78 23	168 28	16	SE	-12	141
21-Nov	8	78 31	168 20	20	S	-12	168
22-Nov	9	78 45	168 12	0		-10	183
23-Nov	10	78 58	167 48	0		-10	186
24-Nov	11	79 09	167 32	20	S-SW	-25	186
25-Nov	12	79 22	167 27	15	SW	-15	193
26-Nov	13	79 34	167 49	7	SW	-10	202
27-Nov	14	79 48	167 47	15	SW	-30	171
28-Nov	15	79 48	167 47	40	S	-30	171
29-Nov	16	79 48	167 47	40	S	-25	171
30-Nov	17	80 04	167 51	17	S	-21	172
01-Dec	18	80 18	168 04	10	SW	-4	190
02-Dec	19	80 32	167 50	11 to 12	SE	-10	186
03-Dec	20	80 45	167 41	5 to 7	SW	-10	185
04-Dec	21	81 01	167 39	5	NW	-5	194
05-Dec	22	81 13	168 04	0		-2	164
06-Dec	23	81 27	168 40	5	SW	-10	179
07-Dec	24	81 42	169 09	5	SW	-7	171
08-Dec	25	81 57	169 23	0		-5	132
09-Dec	26	82 14	169 36	12	SE	-10	168
10-Dec	27	82 29	169 43	6	SW	-8	199
11-Dec	28	82 46	169 58	5	NW	-5	194
12-Dec	29	82 59	170 05	3		-10	188
13-Dec	30	83 15	170 28	4	SW	-7	94
14-Dec	31	83 30	170 56		NW	-13	307
15-Dec	32	83 31	171 02	7	S	-10	609
16-Dec	33	83 42	170 58	8	NW	-20	1096
17-Dec	34	83 56	170 46			-20	1910
18-Dec	35	84 13	170 21	4	NW	-14	2557

Distance Travelled (nm)	Hours	Total Distance	Weather
7.7	7	7.7	Bright and sunny
11	7	18.7	Extremely hot and uncomfortable
7.2	7	25.9	Headwind
9.8	7	35.7	Good
10.3	7	46	Glorious sunshine
10.4	7	56.4	Glorious sunshine
10.8	7	67.2	Whiteout then clear from midday
8.2	7	75.4	Strong headwinds. Wind chill -22
14.4	7	89.8	Very calm, still. Uncomfortably warm in the evening
13.9	7	103.7	Very calm and sunny. Warm in latter part of day
12	7	115.7	Sun was out, but flat light. Heavy sastrugi
13.1	7	128.8	
12.6	7	141.4	Heavy low cloud. Flat Light
13.4	7	154.8	Low cloud mid-afternoon
0	0	154.8	Very strong (40-50 knots) headwinds
0	0	154.8	Wind still very strong but reducing. Forecast to clear.
16.2	7	171	Sun out, high clouds, strong headwinds. Overcast later
14.3	7	185.3	High cloud and sun
14.1	7	199.4	Low cloud and flat light
14.1	7	213.5	Low cloud, clearing in the afternoon
15.2	7	228.7	Flat light then clear skies
13.5	6	242.2	Uncomfortably warm. Poor visibility, clearing p.m.
15.2	7	257.4	Clear, then fog and light snow, then beautiful sunshine
15.4	7	272.8	Fine day, high cloud
15.3	7	288.1	Total sunshine. Very hot
16.4	7	304.5	Bathed in sunshine this evening
15.6	7	320.1	Incredibly hot today
17.2	7	337.3	Wind increased in the late afternoon
13.5	6	350.8	Very low cloud - currently clagged in
15.6	7	366.4	Very low cloud again, lifting in the late afternoon
15.7	7	382.1	Wind died off by mid-afternoon
1.3	1	383.4	Overcast with low cloud, flat light and poor visibility
10.5	5.5	393.9	Unbelievable blue sky all round, very few clouds
15.1	7	409	Sun all day, not single cloud
16.4	7	425.4	Clear blue sky, 100% visibility

Date	Day No	Latitude	Longtitude	Windspeed	Wind Direction	Temp Deg C	Altitude (Ft)
19-Dec	36	84 23	170 13	22	S	-25	3056
20-Dec	37	84 30	169 18	30	S	-20	3560
headwinds							
21-Dec	38	84 36	168 17	15	SW	-20	4379
22-Dec	39	84 42	167 19	25	SE	-21	4813
23-Dec	40	84 53	165 15	12		-18	5417
24-Dec	41	85 03	163 34	14	SE	-25	6864
25-Dec	42	85 03	163 34		SE	-20	6864
26-Dec	43	85 12	161 12	15	SW	-33	7374
27-Dec	44	85 24	159 45	10	SW	-30	8145
28-Dec	45	85 39	160 19	5	N	-15	8315
29-Dec	46	85 53	161 02	10	SE	-35	8635
30-Dec	47	86 09	160 57	20		-35	8821
31-Dec	48	86 22	160 47	15	S	-35	9140
01-Jan	49	86 34	160 41	10		-20	9244
02-Jan	50	86 48	161 01	25	S	-25	9532
03-Jan	51	87 04	162 30	5	S	-25	9643
04-Jan	52	87 17	162 14	30	SE	-47	9881
05-Jan	53	87 30	162 35	40-45	S	-30	9968
06-Jan	54	87 43	161 48	40	E/SE	-25	10090
07-Jan	55	87 56	161 47	8	SE	-22	10146
08-Jan	56	88 11	161 45	5	SW	-20	10173
09-Jan	57	88 23	162 00	5	S	-35	10244
10-Jan	58	88 30	161 42	5-10 Knts	S	-30	10172
11-Jan	59	88 44	162 12	5		-25	10045
12-Jan	60	88 57	164 34	0		-28	9879
13-Jan	61	89 11	166 55	5		-32	9776
14-Jan	62	89 23	169 54	5	SW	-25	9589
15-Jan	63	89 36	177 08	5	S	-25	9410
16-Jan	64	89 49	174 09	0	W	-31	9307
17-Jan	65	89 55	172 26	5	SW	-25	9325
18-Jan	66	90 S		0		-33	9310

Distance Travelled (nm)	Hours	Total Distance	Weather
10.1	7	435.5	Wind in faces, very clear and sunny, few clouds
8.8	7	444.3	Clear sky, bright sunshine, no clouds, fierce
8.5	7	452.8	Clear sky, very sunny
8.3	7	461.1	Very sunny, no cloud, wind picked up in the last hour
15.4	7	476.5	Clear sky, bright sunshine, no clouds
13.3	8	489.8	Clear sky, very sunny
0	0	489.8	Very overcast, light wind
15.4	7.5	505.2	Very sunny and no clouds
13.7	7	518.9	Very sunny and clear
15.7	7	534.6	Light snow flurries, very low cloud, poor visibility
14.6	7.5	549.2	Low cloud. very poor visibility
15.5	8	564.7	Clear and sunny
13.8	7.5	578.5	Good visibility
11.8	6	590.3	Sunny, periodic clouds
14.6	7.25	604.9	Sunny but strong headwind. Wind chill -43
16.3	8	621.2	Clear sky, high cirrus
13.6	7.5	634.8	Clear sky with high cloud. Whiteout late afternoon.
12.3	7.5	647.1	Sunny, high cloud. Snow drifts. Wind chill -52
13.5	7.5	660.6	Hazy sunshine. Thick cloud, sometimes whiteout. Wind chill -45C
13.7	7.5	674.3	Overcast
14.6	7.5	688.9	Clear. Sunny. Ideal conditions.
11.6	6	700.5	Clear. Very cold
7.1	3.75	707.6	Sunny then overcast. Wind chill -43
14.2	7	721.8	Sunny. Perfect weather. Wind chill -33
14	7	735.8	Sunny, low cloud mid-afternoon
13.9	7	749.7	Wind chill -42
12.6	6	762.3	Hazy sunshine. Wind chill -37
13.6	6.5	775.9	Overcast. Difficult light. Wind chill -33
13.1	7	789	Sunny. Some low cloud.
5.95	3	794.95	Hazy. Generally overcast. Sunny intervals. Wind chill -33.
4.7	3	799.65	Sunny, perfect conditions.

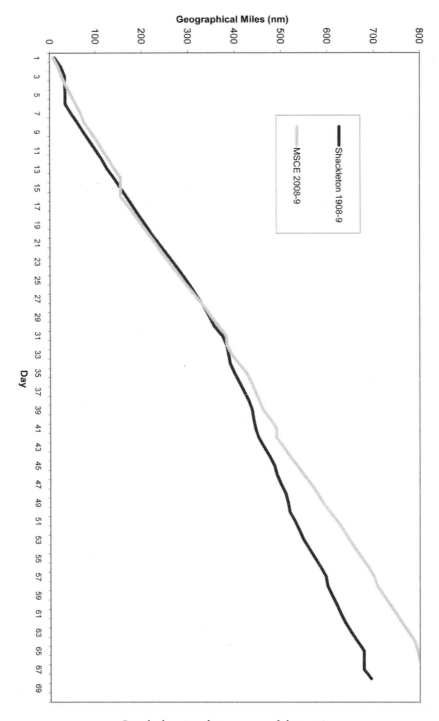

Graph showing the progress of the parties.

Acknowledgements

Expeditions to the Antarctic, whether in Edwardian times or a hundred years on, require huge levels of support if they are to be successful. This modern expedition, to celebrate the centenary of Shackleton's pioneering polar journey in 1908-09, was a huge team effort that lasted five years and there are many people to thank for their commitment, time, advice and sheer hard work. What was remarkable and humbling was that so many people were prepared to do anything they could in order for the seven of us to fulfill a dream.

Matty McNair was the most brilliant teacher who prepared us perfectly for the polar environment. Ross Ashe-Cregan's patience was tested to the limit by our amateurish performance in the early days and Simon Abrahams must be thanked for teaching us simple but effective ways to face the perils of a crevasse rescue. Raising sponsorship depended entirely on the energy, ideas and contacts of the fundraising committee. David Lyon was exceptionally generous with his time and advice. Victoria Mitchell and Mathew Beardmore-Gray were equally supportive and loyal attendees at countless meetings.

In common with Shackleton's expedition, sound financial backing for the modern journey was crucial. Without the support of Matrix

Group, this project would never have happened. David Royds deserves huge thanks for believing in us to deliver on everything we promised in exchange for his truly generous sponsorship, and Natasha Newman and Alice Wingate were utterly reliable and the greatest fun to work with over the life of the project.

And Mark Cooper put up with continual pestering to get us into the public eye, which he did most successfully. Timberland was a great team to work with and we could not have wished for a more unfailing clothing supplier and sponsor - Louise Barnes and Andrew Goodsir deserve special mention.

For straightforward advice and searching questions of our overall plan and expedition route, I owe an incalculable amount to Robert Swan and Charles Swithinbank. Charles equipped me with immense detail of the Beardmore Glacier and described the real world of our forthcoming adventure. Robert taught me how to be utterly respectful of the Antarctic continent and to understand just what a privilege it would be to follow in the footsteps of those who had gone before us. He remains a giant of the polar world and I value his new friendship tremendously.

Nick Jones must be thanked for recognising the potential for our story to be turned into a television programme and Sean Smith deserves huge praise for his skilled camera work in recording our story. Sean was very much a member of the team and we shared many moments together during the training and then down South. His modesty and understated professionalism were notable. David Rootes and his ALE team were positive and enthusiastic about our plan from the outset. He understood the significance and importance of the centenary journey and never once tried to put us off our plans. Steve Jones, himself an experienced polar traveller, ran Patriot Hills with efficiency and optimism and could not have been more encouraging. Terry Welsh, the Twin Otter pilot who dropped us off at the Nimrod Hut and picked us up from the South Pole deserves special mention for his unfailing interest in what we were doing, and for his impressive flying skills. And our visits to the Shackleton and Scott huts would not have been possible without the flexibility and help from Nigel Watson and Al Fastier from the New Zealand Antarctic Heritage Trust.

For the production of this book, I must thank Ed Faulkner for being bold enough to offer me a contract before the expedition had even taken place, and for clear-eyed editorship I am indebted to Clare Wallis. Lucy Martin, from the Scott Polar Research Institute, helped source many of the original photos and Johnny van Haeften allowed me unlimited access to his great uncle's 'Nimrod' albums. Like his great uncle Sir Philip Brocklehurst, he was also an equally generous financial supporter. Katie Leum and Sven Lidstroem, whom I have been unable to trace, will recognise their photos, which I hope they don't mind me using. Zaz Shackleton deserves special thanks for introducing me to her cousin, whose original idea this all was but most significantly, I owe her so much for entrusting me with her grandfather's compass, which I am relieved to say I delivered to the South Pole as promised.

I have left the team to last. Dave Cornell found the sponsors we needed; Tim Fright and Patrick Bergel created the website that entertained and educated so many; Andrew Ledger beat three thousand competitors to win a place on the expedition and Richard Gray very generously came on board in the closing stages. Even the finest prose would not do justice to the thanks I owe Henry Adams and Will Gow for sharing the journey with me. Our memories of that time together will be rich until the day we die.

Finally and simply, of all the people involved in this project I owe the most to Joanna, Max and Alicia.

Bibliography

Fiennes, Ranulph, *Mind Over Matter*, 1993, Sinclair Stevenson, London.

Huntford, Roland, *Shackleton*, 1996, Abacus, London.

Mear, Roger and Swan, Robert, *A Walk to the Pole*, 1987, Crown Publishers, New York.

Messner, Reinhold, *Antarctica: Both Heaven and Hell*, 1991, The Crowood Press, Marlborough, UK.

Mill, Robert, *The Life of Sir Ernest Shackleton*, 1923, William Heinemann, London.

Mills, Leif, *Frank Wild*, 1999, Caedmon of Whitby.

Ousland, Borge, *Alone Across Antarctica*, 1997, Tangen Grafiske, Oslo.

Ralling, Christopher, *Shackleton: His Antarctic Writings*, 1983, BBC, London.

Riffenburgh, Beau, *Nimrod*, 2004, Bloomsbury, London.

Shackleton, Ernest, *The Heart of the Antarctic*, 1909, William Heinemann, London.

Shackleton, Ernest, *Adventure*, 1928, Oxford University Press.

Shackleton, Jonathan and MacKenna, John, *Shackleton: An Irishman in Antarctica*, 2002, The Lilliput Press, Dublin.

Stroud, Mike, *Shadows on the Wasteland*, 1993, Jonathan Cape, London.

Swithinbank, Charles, *An Alien in Antarctica*, 1997, McDonald and Woodward, USA.

Index